Without shying away from any of the p[...] [...]ave communicated how rich a blessing it i[...] [...] may see us old but we feel vital in so many different ways. We have all been told to prepare well in advance for aging. Not to worry. Read *Wise Aging*, and you will be fully prepared.

—Blu Greenberg, author of *How to Run a Traditional Jewish Household*

This is a book I want to give to everyone I love. It's like a series of intimate sessions with two astute and tender guides, who can lead you from confusion and foreboding about aging to opening your arms to possibility.

—Sara Davidson, author of *The December Project,*
a Jewish Book Award Finalist; and *Loose Change*

Wise Aging opens us to the possibility that we may become more as we age: more heartfelt, more connected, more forgiving and more present to the joys of being alive. A fine book to read if you are considering growing old.

—Rachel Naomi Remen, MD, author of *Kitchen Table Wisdom* and *My Grandfather's Blessings*

Read *Wise Aging* and drink in the greatest Jewish wisdom about later life. It hasn't disappeared. The wisdom is more alive than ever in the pages of this book.

—Harry R. Moody, PhD, Vice President of AARP (retired),
author of *The Five Stages of the Soul*

This wonderfully straightforward, intelligent invitation to age wisely is rousing and inspiring at the same time that it is consoling and comforting.

—Sylvia Boorstein, PhD, author of *Happiness Is an Inside Job*

Wise Aging is an essential guide that casts aging not as a "thing" that happens to us but as a developmental process in which we are full participants. The gifts of age are abundant and they are waiting for us. Cowan and Thal distill this great fount of aging knowledge and research into a journey that each one of us can take.

—Marc E. Agronin, MD, author of *How We Age:*
A Doctor's Journey into the Heart of Growing Old

Wise Aging represents a sea change in the way we approach the opportunities for spiritual meaning and growth as we grow older....[A] truly inspiring approach to gaining wisdom as we age.

—Rabbi Angela W. Buchdahl, Senior Rabbi, Central Synagogue, New York City

In *Wise Aging*, Cowan and Thal show us how to do this important "new work" of our later years—weaving threads of experience into something meaningful and whole—and ways to do that work both alone and together!

—Marcy and Rick Jackson, Cofounders and Senior Fellows,
Center for Courage & Renewal

For those of us in need of a serious conversation about aging, this book is a godsend. Cowan and Thal provide a thorough and personal report from the field, covering all aspects of this poignant territory—body, heart, mind, and spirit. This book is the best help so far for taking on aging and dying as a conscious practice.

—Norman Fischer, poet and Zen priest, author of *Training in Compassion*

Once in a while a book comes along that challenges us to understand ourselves in new ways. We are transformed by it, and because of it we are inspired to transform our communities as well. *Wise Aging* is that book.

—Rabbi Laura Geller, Senior Rabbi, Temple Emanuel of Beverly Hills

Wise Aging not only brings wisdom to the challenge and opportunities of aging, but through its exercises opens ways for people to explore where they have been in life and how they still might shape their future.

—Rabbi Michael Strassfeld, author of *A Book of Life*

Wise Aging is a must for anyone who wants to move through the next life stage with a deeper sense of meaning, identity, spirituality, and relationships.

—Helen Dennis, coauthor of *Project Renewment*

With fierce intelligence, the authors of *Wise Aging* help us face up to the reality that we are getting older and yet still celebrate that fact with new challenges and new victories. None of this is easy, but this book is easy reading as we face the hard task of maturing and finding our own spirits.

—Rabbi William Cutter, PhD, Hebrew Union College

Wise Aging

Living with Joy, Resilience, & Spirit

Rabbi Rachel Cowan
&
Dr. Linda Thal

Beth Lieberman, Project Editor

BEHRMAN HOUSE
www.behrmanhouse.com

Development Editors: David Behrman and Ann D. Koffsky
Design: Annemarie Redmond

Published by Behrman House, Inc.
Springfield, New Jersey 07081
www.behrmanhouse.com
ISBN 978-0-87441-921-4

Cover photo: Shutterstock/Dudarev Mikhail

Library of Congress Cataloging-in-Publication Data

Cowan, Rachel, author.
  Wise aging : living with joy, resilience, & spirit / Rabbi Rachel Cowan and
Dr. Linda Thal ; Beth Lieberman, project editor.
     pages cm
  ISBN 978-0-87441-921-4
  1. Aging. 2. Aging—Religious aspects—Judaism. I. Thal, Linda, co-author.
II. Lieberman, Beth, editor. III. Title. IV. Title: Living with joy, resilience, &
spirit. V. Title: Living with joy, resilience, and spirit.
  QP86.C595 2015
  612.6'7—dc23   2015005329

Printed in the United States of America

Visit www.behrmanhouse.com/wise-aging for more resources.

Dedication

We both wish to thank our teachers, Rabbi Jonathan Omer-man, Sylvia Boorstein and Reb Zalman Schacter-Shalomi z"l, whose spiritual wisdom and guidance ground our work to this day.
—Rachel and Linda

In honor of my grandmother Rachel Moore Warren, who taught me that old age can be lived with grace, dignity, and affection for tradition and openness to change. (She went back to finish college in her seventies, and became a Democrat!) And to my grandchildren Jacob, Tessa, Dante and Miles, whose lives will be deeply affected by the legacy our generation leaves to theirs.
—Rachel

In honor of my husband, Lennard Thal, daughters Alona H. Scott and Ariella Thal Simonds, sons-in-law Lacarya Dantuane Scott and Joel Thal Simonds, and grandchildren Mo, Zeke, Noa and Zev, who have been my teachers and endured my efforts to grow into wisdom.
—Linda

Table of Contents

Introduction

Years ago I came to the realization that the most poignant
of all lyrical tensions stems from the awareness that we
are living and dying at once. To embrace such knowledge
and yet to remain compassionate and whole—that is
the consummation of the endeavor of art.

—Stanley Kunitz, "Reflections," from *Collected Poems*

A big birthday comes. Maybe it's fifty or sixty. Perhaps seventy.
We're supposed to be happy—we've made it this far, with blessings we can count. Yet we feel a nagging bit of dread. "It's not
so bad," we tell ourselves. "Sixty is the new forty, after all." Or we say,
"OMG—I *am* getting old. I can see the horizon. Now what? Help!" But
then, we're curious too. What's next? And we realize that we don't actually
feel any different inside. Confusing.

We're happy to receive a discount at the theater, but we're not so sure
we want to join a group or take a tour designated for "seniors." All of us, to
some degree, want to be with the young, not the retirees, codgers, and biddies we imagine will enroll. Even the dignified term *elders* sounds too old.

We come by these attitudes honestly. Our culture promotes a declinist
paradigm of aging. Youth implies future, permanence, and vitality; growing
older is associated with diminishment, disability, and irrelevance. Take a look
at a few of the quips and jokes that circulate among friends and in the media:

> Inside every senior there's an eighteen-year-old wondering,
> "What the hell happened?"

"Grandma, my teacher says little girls can grow up to be anything they choose. Why did you grow up to be an old lady?"

There are three ages of man: youth, middle age, and you look good!

We, Linda and Rachel, have both passed sixty-five and are here to testify that we find it a great time of life. We are learning, growing, and enjoying experiences both new and familiar. Many of our friends and students, who are well into their eighties, even nineties, are fun, vital, and interesting at this time in their lives. But we also experience challenges and losses. We too feel the twin shadows of dementia and death lurking off in the wings somewhere. These concerns are what motivated us to write this book and do the work that we do. We want to know—as we move more deeply into this stage of life—how to remain connected to our own inner vitality, to our loved ones, and to our work. We want to explore what is different about being well seasoned. We want to prepare for the times that will be difficult and to savor the times that are good.

Linda is a Jewish educator, and for the past twenty years her work has focused on adult spiritual development. She was the founding codirector of the Yedidya Center for Jewish Spiritual Direction, an institute that trains rabbis, therapists, and others in providing spiritual guidance to individuals.

Rachel is a rabbi. During her years at the Nathan Cummings Foundation, she worked to revitalize Jewish spiritual practices and integrate contemplative practices from other traditions into Judaism. She also helped secular organizations bring meditation into their work so that they would more directly speak to people living in today's contemporary society. After that, she directed the Institute for Jewish Spirituality, whose mission is to support the continuing spiritual growth of rabbis, educators, and laypeople.

Both of us have spent most of our adult lives in spiritual exploration, teaching and learning with others, individually and in groups. It was while coteaching one such a group, whose members chose to focus on the spiritual journey of aging, that we began to develop the work that would become the subject of this book. We came to call that group our "Wise Aging" group.

The issues in this book are important to huge numbers of individuals and indeed to an entire generation. Ours is the first generation in human history to move into elderhood with twenty years or more of vitality and good health ahead. Once our lives are no longer primarily driven by nurturing family and building careers, we have the chance to make wise choices about how we spend our time, energy, and money. What does retirement mean now when many of us may still be working—by choice or by necessity? What does retirement mean now that there are so many opportunities for learning, for caring, for serving? We can redefine aging.

When we first took up the issues that come with growing older, we knew from our experience as educators that often the most profound learning comes from sharing questions and musings with others, listening to their stories and queries, and immersing ourselves together in the wisdom texts of both traditional and contemporary thinkers.

And so we focused that original spiritual journeying group, which was composed of individuals in their sixties and seventies, on exploring this new stage of life. Each month, for five hours, the group gathered to meditate, study, and share stories and insights.

Over time we began to see substantial changes within our group. One participant, who was hyper-self-critical, began to catch herself in the act and to regard herself with more compassion. Another took on a project that she originally felt she was too old to do, discovering passions and skills that she'd never recognized in herself. Another dared to examine her decision to remain childless and was able to celebrate the impact she had had on the nephews and nieces she had taken into her life. The fact that life was presenting each of us with challenges as well as opportunities— whether it was grandparenthood, cancer, retirement, disappointment with adult children's decisions, the decline of a life partner, a new romance, an encore career—helped us to see that we were all part of a larger story.

Together, our group learned that willingness to face life with an open heart and a curious mind can move each of us toward wisdom and compassion.

We have continued to explore this subject with more groups of men and women. Again and again, we would marvel at each newcomer's excitement in discovering that he or she was not alone in having concerns about growing older, and that there were a multitude of new opportunities to get to know oneself more profoundly and unlock new opportunities for one's life.

In writing *Wise Aging*, we have synthesized our experiences of those early groups with discoveries and insights from teachers and writers of all traditions who had been thinking about aging much longer than we have. We hope the book will guide you to discover the possibilities for living the years ahead with joy, resilience, and spirit. If you have picked out this book, you will be able to do much of the work fruitfully on your own. You may get even more out of this book if you invite a friend to read it with you or share it with a friend in some other way. If the opportunity arises, consider forming your own group of friends and others who are wrestling with these matters, for spiritual work often flourishes best when supported by community.

These years are a gift. Psychoanalyst Erik Erikson, who is best known for extending Freud's theory of human development into mature adulthood, was particularly interested in the developmental challenges and opportunities that life presents to us at different stages of the life cycle. In midlife, he taught, individuals who continue to mature begin to turn their attention outward toward "generativity," the conscious mentoring of the next generation. Most of us have done this with our own adult children and/or with younger colleagues, workers, and friends. And when we do it successfully, we break down barriers between ourselves and others, becoming increasingly embedded in an interdependent, connected web of relatives and friends, associates and colleagues. It is helpful to our sense of self at this age to know that what we are doing is completely age appropriate and fulfills an important social need. It is one way wisdom is passed on.

At yet a later stage, according to Erikson, we will turn inward and gather up the life we have lived, make sense of its ups and downs, wrestle with existential questions, and strive to integrate all that we have learned and experienced. This effort to reach integration and equanimity is what Erikson considers wisdom. Rabbi Zalman Schachter-Shalomi named this *sage-ing*—conscious life harvesting. This process is lifelong, and will intensify as we get older. For now, however, we simply invite you into this journey—an adventure that holds increasing meaning and connectedness with all that is around us.

> ...The[se years] are indeed formative years, rich in possibilities...to deepen understanding and compassion, to widen the horizon of honesty, to refine the sense of fairness....One ought to enter old age the way one enters the senior year at a university, in exciting anticipation of consummation....But the attainment of wisdom is the work of a lifetime.
> —Abraham Joshua Heschel, "To Grow in Wisdom"

About This Book

Although you can read this book straight through, its real benefit will come from working with the materials and spending time thinking about how they resonate with your own experience. Take your time, especially with the reflection questions and the journaling exercises. Similarly, try the meditations and spiritual practices. You may want to read more on meditation, or listen to a recording on the subject, if the practice is new to you.

We approach teaching as a journey to be taken with our students, and we take the same approach with this book. We use some of our own experience when it feels illustrative, and we provide a sampling of approaches and perspectives from which you can fashion your own understandings.

This introduction is followed by nine chapters. If you are using the book in a group, don't assume that you will be able to work through a whole chapter in a single session. You may choose to spend more time on those chapters that are richest for you, or you may narrow your focus to one dimension of a chapter.

If you have picked up this book and note with ambivalence that it contains much "religious wisdom," we still believe this book will be relevant for you. You may have had negative experiences in religious school or over religion in your family of origin; you may be a second- or even third-generation atheist; you may be, as so many Americans claim today, "spiritual but not religious." We welcome you; we sincerely and deeply believe that this book will speak to you as well.

Let's begin by addressing the foundational questions of the work of aging wisely.

What Is a Spiritual Perspective on Aging?

The concept of spirituality can mean different things to different people. For us it represents the notion that there is something greater than the material world we can see with our eyes and understand with our rational minds. What that something is remains mysterious; how we think about it and what we call it will differ from one person to another. Rabbi Arthur Green speaks of an inner life that each person may choose to develop: "This inwardness goes deeper than the usual object of psychological investigation and cannot fairly be explained in Freudian or other psychological terms. Ultimately, it is 'transpersonal,' reaching beyond the individual and linking him/her to all other selves and to the single Spirit or Self of the universe we call God."

If you feel you are spiritual but not religious, you may choose to focus on the "transpersonal" aspect of Green's teaching, for spirituality does not depend on religious practice or belief. For some of us, spiritual practice enhances our connection to other people and to a larger sense of wholeness and relationship with them, or to the natural environment. For others it opens and deepens connection to God.

Building on Erikson's belief that the later stages of life present opportunities for continued growth, Swedish sociologist Dr. Lars Tornstam has proposed a new theory of positive aging that he calls gerotranscendence—breaking through the limited perspectives and awareness that characterized our younger years. In earlier stages of life, we are by necessity focused on a largely individualistic agenda: achieving an education, finding a job, establishing ourselves in a career, raising a family. In later life we begin to understand that our lives are deeply linked to our past and to history that goes back even before our birth. Likewise we are connected to an unknown future that we are in the process of creating. During these years, we learn more about ourselves, appreciating our complexity, accepting our limitations, and developing a new kind of inner confidence and wisdom. We enjoy fewer, but deeper relationships, and find pleasure in solitude. We are less interested in material possessions and freer to be ourselves, even in the face of social conventions.

Why Do We Need Spiritual Practices?

It would be nice to assume that a person becomes wise and compassionate just by gaining years. Unfortunately that isn't so. Sometimes refinement of character happens naturally as we grow older, but for many people that growth is fostered by spiritual practices adopted and followed in a disciplined way. Meditation is one such practice. It is now widely understood that meditation has the potential to restructure the brain, thereby affecting the way we take in the world and act within it. We become open to noticing in a new way life around us and inside us. Meditation can help us to stay focused on what matters, and avoid the useless negative thinking and storytelling that are nothing but the projections of concerns and fears. Meditation can help us to be genuinely and fully present for ourselves and others, focused on the person or event in front of us rather than being caught up in thoughts and feelings that take us away from our actual experience of the moment.

Many of the practices we introduce in *Wise Aging* are meditative spiritual practices. For example, reciting a blessing can, for a brief moment, take us out of the everydayness of life to find the uniqueness and sanctity of what we face: a meal, a tree in blossom, a friend we haven't seen in a long time. In that moment we have the opportunity to develop gratitude and wonder, important components of spiritual life and critical for our growing wisdom.

Other practices that we suggest include writing in a journal, walking in nature, reading poetry, and listening deeply to a friend. The practices help us link our ideas to feelings and to the way we see the world.

To develop and grow spiritually, it is important to practice. And practice takes time and persistence. The more you try and the more you do, the greater the value you will find. We urge you to take your practice seriously: to find moments in your daily life to stop and breathe, to take time by yourself to spend with the practices of your choice.

What Do We Mean by Contemplative?

Contemplation is a mindset of complete openness to that which is around and in front of us. We try to calm and settle our thinking, rather than directing it to a particular focus. We seek to allow ourselves to be absorbed by our surrounding world. Contemplation often involves moving slowly. It is found within a variety of practices, such as meditation, deep listening, reflection, journaling, praying, yoga, or qigong.

As described on the website of the Center for Contemplative Mind in Society:

> Contemplative practices are practical, radical, and transformative, developing capacities for deep concentration and quieting the mind in the midst of the action and distraction that fills everyday life. This state of calm centeredness

is an aid to exploration of meaning, purpose and values. Contemplative practices can help develop greater empathy and communication skills, improve focus and attention, reduce stress and enhance creativity, supporting a loving and compassionate approach to life.

Here are a few examples of how working with this book is a contemplative practice: When you encounter a passage that interests you, stop and take the time to simply linger. Let a word or a phrase catch your attention. Perhaps ask yourself: "Which of these words or phrases speaks to me today?" Focus on whatever it is and let it settle in, like tasting an interesting and subtle flavor. Choose a phrase to focus on and just sit with the phrase and see what associations come up, what images, what insights.

If you are doing this work in a group or with another person, we ask you to listen to one another "contemplatively." That means putting your own thoughts and assessments aside and listening deeply to what is being said, to its tone as well as its content. It means not thinking about how to respond or entertaining thoughts like, "Oh, something like that happened to me too." And it means noticing and releasing any judgments you make or comparisons or opinions that enter your mind. Simply try to listen receptively.

Although many of us—Christian, Jewish, and Muslim—grew up unaware of the contemplative dimension of our own faith traditions, many of us have been reclaiming and renewing this as part of our heritage. Some of us have explored our Jewish contemplative traditions, and have also been enriched by insights from Christian, Sufi, and Buddhist teachers. The process is a mutual one of exchange of ideas and of coevolving consciousness.

Spiritual Texts We Have Drawn Upon

We have studied texts from Buddhists, Christians, Muslims, and Jews, and include passages from some of them for your reflection—verses from the Torah (the Hebrew Bible) and from the New Testament, from Sufi poetry and Buddhist literature. We rely most heavily on Jewish texts because Judaism is the primary spiritual language we speak, but most of the ideas we present can be found in all the great spiritual traditions. We have also included passages from the most traditional Jewish sources, the Talmud and Midrash.

God Talk

A word about God and God language. Neither of us imagines that we know who or what God is. We are personally comfortable using traditional language that sounds as if we have an anthropomorphic view of God because this is the language of discourse in which we were trained. But we are very aware that we stand in the tradition of rabbis and teachers who understood this language as metaphoric, not literal. The God to which or to whom we refer does not control our destiny; does not judge, punish, or reward; does not cure us when disease attacks our bodies; nor allot us a set number of days on Earth. We do sense that there is something—an energy perhaps—mysterious, greater than us, uniting us all, and ultimately benevolent and loving. And that is what God means to us.

If the name "God" is problematic for you, consider a simple word or set of words, or a metaphor with power, grandeur, or significance for you that you can routinely substitute for the word "God" when you encounter it. Words like *Mystery, Energy,* or phrases like *Source of Life* or *the Higher Self* might help. Judaism, for example, does not have one name for God. In Jewish prayer texts the Hebrew letters *yud-hay-vav-hay* are often used to stand in for God's name, and because of God's awesome holiness the name they represent is not pronounced. Some scholars suggest the sound they would make is nothing more than breath. And so God might even be thought of as the breath or pulsation of life.

Whatever you choose, we suggest you focus not on theology, but rather use your intuitions, feelings, and emotions when considering the role of God, or the transpersonal, or the sacred in your life.

Welcome to the club of thoughtful wise agers. We believe the experience will enrich your life and deepen your relationships with those around you. Our society aches from the lack of the voices of wisdom of its elders. Indeed, the nature and quality of our lives on this planet depend as much on the wisdom gleaned from our experiences as it does on the energy and discoveries of younger generations. Our voices, ripened with time and experience, must be heard. We may protest or lobby or speak out. Or we may display our power through the way we are: loving, generous, and wise. We are a blessing.

—1—

Exploring This Stage of Our Lives

Teach us to use all of our days,
that we may attain a heart of wisdom.

—Psalms 90:12

The stage of life we are entering is unprecedented. Many of us will reach our midsixties and early seventies with the possibility of having twenty years of good health and vitality ahead. Yet the extension of human longevity—with increasing numbers of people living into their nineties and even their hundreds—is only part of the story. What is more stunning about this new stage of life that has come into being—active late adulthood—is that it is rich with opportunities for discovery, enthusiasm, and creativity.

If we are to make our days count and attain the psalmist's "heart of wisdom," we face a multitude of choices *right now*. We can use these years to regain at least some of the balance our lives may have lost to the demands of work and family. We can release ourselves from the pressure to achieve, to maximize time, to be networked into an ever-faster flow of information and demand. For many of us, this is the stage where being, creating, feeling, and enjoying *can* take precedence over striving. Where we have time to learn, to reflect, to create, and to cultivate wisdom.

As we pass that milestone birthday, however we define it—it might be fifty, or seventy, or something in between—the first thoughts that hit us are decidedly personal. What? Me aging? What on earth does that word *old* mean to my life? Who am I right now, glimpsing my morning face in the mirror—OMG my mother? Trying to remember a name. Watching a white-haired man or woman stepping animatedly down Broadway and loving the face and the body. And the next minute, turning my face away from an old man hobbling down the street on the arm of his caregiver— too scared to imagine the liveliness that may well animate his mind, asking, "Is that what's next?"

More questions dawn: Is my job taking too much time and energy? Do I love it the way I once did? Am I burned out? Who on earth would I be without this job, this role, this status? If I can't afford to leave my job can I make more time for myself to be with friends and family, or to relax and enjoy another activity, or to join a religious, activist, or social group? Can I begin to move in the direction of greater freedom?

So many more questions! If I could choose, what would I most love to be doing this morning? With whom would I most love to be? What is happening to time, which seems to be disappearing so much faster than it used to? Is the anxiety that wakes me at 3:30 in the morning just normal stress or is it fear of being old, or of dying? My life no longer looks unlimited. What do I want to do with the rest of my years?

How do I want to be?

These are important questions. And we can't simply think our way to the answers, because the knowledge we need is not only found in our rational mind, but also in our hearts and our bodies too. The answers must come from deep inside, and we are likely to need help discerning and articulating them.

We cannot grow older alone. Not if we want to do it well. The good news is that what is true for us is true for others. When we share stories with others, we realize that our personal story is deeply connected to larger narratives. We have a lot to offer to each other and to our communities and our society. We can bring our voices to family circles and to the public square. We can create a wise aging for ourselves and for those around us—an aging that is dignified, supported, and as full of meaning as possible.

As Rabbi Laura Geller, a visionary leader in Los Angeles pioneering the work of community and synagogue transformation around our new longevity, has said, "The norms, rules, and rituals of this stage haven't yet been written; we are writing them together."

Obstacle Ahead: The Declinist View of Aging

One stumbling block we will encounter as we age is the attitude toward aging that pervades our society. It informs both the way we think of ourselves and the way others behave toward us. It is reflected in social policies that leave millions of seniors without the resources they need for their health and well-being. Our culture valorizes youth, strength, and beauty. We older folks no longer manifest these qualities the way we once did. Many of us, both men and women, feel with sinking hearts that we are becoming invisible. Colleagues or family members no longer ask our opinion the way they used to. The feeling of irrelevance can darken the mind and dampen the spirit.

Ageism, a term coined by famed gerontologist Dr. Robert Butler, is "the systematic stereotyping of, and discrimination against, people because they are old, just as racism and sexism discriminate on the basis of skin color and gender." Ageism is a force that we need to learn to recognize— both as it is applied to us by others, and as applied to self and others by us.

Mollie, a woman in her late sixties, successful and experienced in her field, goes on interviews for jobs for which she is eminently qualified by virtue of the jobs she has held. She makes it to the final round and is told over and over that, "This isn't right for you. You are overqualified." She has been unemployed for over a year, seeing the jobs go to younger people, at a lower salary. She has sold her car and the few beloved antiques she had inherited. She now volunteers at her synagogue and in a neighborhood community center. Though she is actively engaged in meaningful projects, she is still hurting and angry at the limits she feels ageism has puts on her life choices.

Harold, a handsome silver-haired man in his early seventies, told a group that being this age was simply not an issue for him. He felt fine about his work, his marriage, and his children. Then his tone of voice changed. "But what I hate is when the maître d' sits me in the back of the restaurant—out of sight."

Anthropology professor Frida Kerner Furman asked approximately fifty college students to come up with prevailing cultural images and assumptions about old age that they held to be true:

> frail, dependent, lacking in judgment, angry, unattractive, conservative, slow drivers, sickly, absentminded, depressive, wise, cantankerous, cheap, nonsexual, forgetful, hard

of hearing, overly traditional, lonely, domestic, inactive, having poor judgment, useless, crabby, whiny, ineffective, more religious, senile, fumbling, deaf, short-tempered, slow, crotchety, nostalgic, needing attention, storytellers, childish, mean, stingy, set in their ways, complaining, alone, stubborn, incapable, decaying, burdensome, experienced, out of touch, humorless, pitiful.

These attitudes, which are widely reflected in cartoons, jokes, and greeting cards, inform and inflame our fears. And these stereotypes exist not only out in the world: most of us have, to some degree, unconsciously adopted many of them. The ideas we internalized in our youth do not go away just because we are the ones who are aging. We too disparage the signs of age and worry that in the future our bodies, our clothes, our way of walking or sitting will be perceived as ugly. When these signs do appear, some of us may panic or obsess about them.

No wonder we want to claim that seventy is the new fifty and that we are still middle-aged. We tell ourselves that we can ward off these undesirable changes—we can diet more faithfully, exercise more vigorously, do crossword puzzles, and alter our appearance with creams and even surgery. Of course it is important to take care of ourselves and feel attractive. We have the opportunity to dress the way we want—with flair and style, or more simply—whatever feels natural to us. The thing to notice is whether we are leaning into the life in front of us, or whether we are just fighting off growing older.

And so we face the basic terror of aging—that we will become invisible, irrelevant, and vulnerable. No wonder we fear that if we give up our habits of doing, achieving, and keeping busy as our primary mode of being, we will be doomed to slide down the slippery slope into feebleness, senility, and death.

Countering the Declinist View: Spiritually, Psychologically, and Scientifically

An evolving counterweight to this paradigm of decline is the paradigm of opportunity. An article in the *Harvard Business Review*, titled "The Existential Necessity of Midlife Change," argues that it is important to shift our focus from what the authors call "deficiency motivations to growth motivations." They quote psychologist Abraham Maslow: "Deficiency motivations are fed by lack....Those who are driven by low self-esteem will be driven to prove their worth. By contrast growth motivations are fed not by a deficiency but by the human need to realize our full potential. Motivated in this way, we may try listening to ourselves in order to discover who we are and what we want."

This paradigm suggests aging as an opportunity for growth, discovery, and new meaning. As an opportunity for us to do some of the most important inner work of our lives. During this stage of adulthood, we can live more deeply and turn away from superficiality. We are able to cultivate a deeper, more spiritual view of life.

For some people these inner changes happen quite naturally; it seems to be an extension of who and how they have always been. Others are jolted into more conscious forms of spiritual work by life's unavoidable ups and downs: a death, marriage or divorce, a grandchild, or sometimes a deep disappointment. Some of us consciously turn to spiritual practice to foster our growth. Those who are not open to change risk missing out on the great opportunity of their stage in life.

Some people feel that doing this work of personal growth is a luxury, available only to those whose lives are fully stable. Faced with the need to keep working, or struggling to make ends meet, or with the pain of illness or the burden of caring for others, they feel they lack resources to pay attention to their inner life. Clearly these conditions make the work more challenging. But they do not make it impossible.

Personal growth need not take much time or any money. People of all incomes and walks of life have changed the way they experience their lives—sometimes drastically. Some have done it alone. Most have found strength in the support of a loved one, a friend, or a teacher, or have sought community.

When we find a community to support us, and practices to open our minds and hearts, we develop confidence, greater equanimity, and balance. We can infuse our lives, even in the midst of sadness or suffering, with transcendent meaning and even joy.

An Open Invitation

We have all successfully made transitions in our lives: when we became teenagers or graduates; when we started families or entered a job or profession. Some transitions were smoother than others. Some of us were supported by mentors, others by therapists, some of us went it alone. Looking back, we can see that no transition happened overnight, that we did not stop being who we had been but rather brought elements of ourselves into each next stage. The opportunity awaiting us today is to make yet another transition in our lives, from adulthood into late adulthood—the period of active aging.

In earlier transitions, we may have been unaware of what we were doing. Today we have the chance to be more thoughtful and deliberate about how we mold our lives. We can reflect, not just for the sake of adjusting to new circumstances but also because our questions offer choices we can make and opportunities for growth. We can be open to choice and change: Where do we want to place our time, our energies, and our hearts? What do we want to let go of, what do we want to keep? The changes may be tiny or large; in either case they can be profound.

Reflection Questions

Before you read further, consider journaling in response to some
or all of these questions:

As you contemplate growing older:

◆ What are you curious about?

◆ What do you want to explore?

◆ What is surprising to you right now?

◆ What is frightening?

◆ What is challenging?

Although we may not be able to change what has been or what is, we can
change the way we think and feel about it, and that may help us change
what will be.

Alice Herz-Sommer, a Holocaust survivor who died at 110, put it this
way: "Every day is a miracle. No matter how bad my circumstances, I have
the freedom to choose my attitude to life, even to find joy. Evil is not new.
It is up to us how we deal with both good and bad. No one can take this
power away from us."

Often change works slowly—we know that from our New Year's resolutions and diets. It comes in small increments. We cautiously experiment,
try out new ideas with trusted partners and friends. We create a plan. And
still, we cling to old habits.

At some point, though, we have to jump in. Whether the change is
big or small, there is something radical about the change that requires dar-
ing. We have to let go of one trapeze before gripping the next one.

In the book of Exodus, Moses is standing at the edge of the Sea of
Reeds while the Egyptian forces bear down on his defenseless people. He
stretches his arm out over the water to part the sea. But here Jewish tradition

teaches that it was not until an Israelite named Nahshon son of Amminadab plunged into that sea that God parted the waters. For change to happen, a leap is required. Faith is required. And it is we who have to jump.

Some mornings as I sit with my cup of tea, the paradox arises. I know I am chronologically older. Closer to the horizon. But it's not just the math; it's the unwelcome changes in my body—especially my upper arms and drooping eyelids. And that inability to find the word or the face I need at the moment when I need it so badly. But do I actually feel older? No. I feel just like me.

Surprisingly, I have developed some equanimity about growing older. Rituals help: every morning I sit up in bed—usually before my alarm clock goes off—and notice early morning light brushing the window shades. I raise my arms as I say the morning prayer—"Gratitude fills me in Your Presence, Source of Life"— only I whisper it in Hebrew. "Thank You"— I am here, a new day, alive, awake, in a room I love, in a bed I once shared with my late husband Paul, now scattered with books, a half-read New Yorker magazine, yesterday's clothes, pillows, my grandson's toy dog.

And yes, darker thoughts come up too. How many mornings will I do this? What if I don't wake up—when will somebody notice? My heart sinks for a minute, but then I take a breath or two, recognize them as just unpleasant passing thoughts, and let them fade. Genuine gratitude fills the void.

I marvel that I can do this. That I am grateful for so very much in my life, despite Paul's death when we were too young. Despite having friends and family members who are struggling with cancer today, and some who've died, younger than I. Yet with practice, I've come to understand that though the impermanence of life can be scary and sad, it also gives value to each moment. The present is what matters, as I can't bring back the past, and the future is basically out of my control. And the present is full of so much that is good. I am really happy.

— Rachel

Life Stages

Sarah is the first biblical character to be described in terms of life stages. We learn in the book of Genesis that she lived "one hundred years, and twenty years, and seven years." Many interpreters saw that division of her lifespan as three phases, each manifesting interrelated spiritual qualities.

Pirkei Avot (*The Teachings of the Sages*), a collection of early rabbinic ethical teachings found in the Mishnah, also explores the stages of life with this description:

> At the age of five—the study of Bible;
> at ten—the study of Mishnah;
> at thirteen—responsibility for the *mitzvot*;
> at fifteen—the study of Talmud;
> at eighteen—marriage;
> at twenty—pursuit of a livelihood;
> at thirty—the peak of one's powers;
> at forty—the age of understanding;
> at fifty—the age of counsel;
> at sixty—old age;

at seventy—the hoary head;
at eighty—the age of "strength";
at ninety—the bent back;
at one hundred—as one dead and out of this world. (*Pirkei Avot* 5:25)

If women's lives had interested the rabbis, they would no doubt have constructed a different model for their life tasks. Since they didn't, women will read this text differently. But the underlying meaning applies to both genders. The rabbis are tracing intellectual, spiritual, and emotional growth from early youth on up into adulthood and into old age. The body begins to change, but mental and spiritual strength remain strong. Toward the end, physical mobility is limited and one prepares spiritually for death.

Reflection Questions

◆ What kind of contemporary meaning can you give this teaching?

◆ Does your life reflect any parts of this pattern of growth?

◆ What ages would you mark and with what life tasks?

Rediscovering the Authentic Self

When Erik Erikson pioneered the concept that life has eight stages and proposed that each stage has a specific psychological task that must be accomplished for healthy development, he identified the eighth stage's task as finding "integrity" in our life's journey. Here we integrate our life history, weaving together stories, finding threads of connections, and discovering the meaning and purpose of our life in the whole.

The work of integrating the pieces of our life story can help us begin one of our most important tasks: the rediscovery and reclamation of that authentic self. What does that phrase mean? Over the years, each one of us has constructed a persona—a public personality—to ensure approval and safety, and to create a functional and satisfactory life. We became adults with particular strengths that enabled us to succeed. Many aspects of our public personality have served us well. But some may have been injurious; others may have been highly adaptive and productive at earlier times, but now no longer suit our needs.

The authentic self lives beneath the surface of that persona. As we grow older, reflecting on accumulated experience may cause us to wonder, "Is this really who I am now? Is this how I want to be now?" We may be completely contented with who we understand ourselves to be and with how we are living our lives. Or we may be hearing the voice of new perspective, calling from the part of us that remains submerged and unfulfilled. It is a deeper voice, perhaps one that wants to say "no" more often, or to say "this is how I *really* feel," or "this is what *I* think." What might it mean to us to learn who we are, free of others' projections, schedules, and expectations? To come home to ourselves and ask: Who is the "me" in me? What do I dare to dream? Who might I be now that I don't have to be who I was?

Psychoanalyst Carl Jung believed that this work of discovering the authentic self was vital and generally only begins at or after midlife, when we start to outgrow the strategies and identities that had served us in our youth. He wrote, "We cannot live the afternoon of life according to the program of life's morning—for what was great in the morning will be little at evening, and what was [true] in the morning will at evening have become a lie."

Coming closer to our inner self may be liberating. It is also risky. To speak and act from our new perspective may disrupt our lives. We may see that we can no longer live with certain arrangements or relationships, but we need patience to allow ourselves to absorb and adjust to the insights that arise as our sensibilities shift. Perhaps the new stories or interpretations we are making are true—or perhaps not. Perhaps it is in our best interest to act on them; perhaps not. It helps to have close friends or advisors with whom to discuss these discoveries, to help us see and feel what is true. Then, perhaps, we can act wisely, rather than rashly. We can let events evolve rather than explode.

There is a wonderful narrative that illustrates the poignant urgency of the task of aligning our inner and outer selves. It is about Rabbi Meshulam Zusya, who lived in the eighteenth century. He was one of the most beloved, learned, humble, and generous rabbis of his day. The story tells us that when Rabbi Zusya lay dying on his bed, his students gathered around. They were astonished and dismayed when they found him weeping. They asked their beloved teacher why he was crying. Could it be that he was afraid of meeting God at the entrance to heaven? Was he worried that God would ask him why he had not been a visionary pioneer like Abraham? Rabbi Zusya answered that he had no such worry, for after all God had not made him like Abraham. Then perhaps God would criticize him for not being like Moses, the most humble of leaders? "Heavens no," the rabbi replied. "If God had wanted me to be like Moses, God would have made me like Moses. No," he told them. "I am weeping because I fear that the Holy One will ask me why I was not Zusya!"

One of our students told us that when she reads this story on the High Holidays each year, she cringes. "What will I answer this year," she said, "when that inner voice wonders, I tried so hard to be the matriarch Sarah. But have I been Ronnie?"

Respond to these questions from your own experience.

◈ How does this legend speak to me personally?

◈ When have I felt most like my true self? What circumstances allow for feeling like I am speaking, acting, thinking from my deepest self? What circumstances tend to cut me off from my true self?

◈ What are the roles I play or masks I wear? To what extent do I over-identify with these roles and/or masks, which may be ideal for my interactions with people but limit the ways I experience my deeper/higher/truer self?

◈ When has my sense of who I am been challenged or changed in a substantial way?

How can we find our own inner voice, which has been in hiding for years? Many women feel that because they have spent so much of their lives pleasing and responding to the needs of others, they do not have a sense of who they are at this deep level. They don't know what they actually want, or they believe it is selfish to privilege their own needs. Many men report that they do not have inner lives and don't know how to find one. They have always felt they needed to look strong and in control, and have shied away from exposing vulnerability and seeming to weaken their masculinity. Some report that they believe that their wives will value them less if they seem unsure of themselves.

Two men in their late sixties shared this fear with their wise aging group: that they had reached the "gray ceiling" in their firms. Each would have to move out of his commanding partner's office to the more obscure space he would occupy in his new, advisory role. Their invisibility and loss of power felt humiliating. E-mail chains dropped their addresses.

Colleagues gathered in the corridors without calling them in to the conversation. They each expressed anxiety about their loss of influence. But worse—who would they be without the titles that had served to define them over so many years? Their question was not only "What will I do?" but the more existential, "Who am I?"

They had never imagined themselves as members of a group that discussed personal issues and found the prospect of appearing vulnerable deeply unsettling. And yet with time, they were able to speak the truth of their experiences. And then to open up to new possibilities. They glimpsed selves that were deeper than they had experienced in years. They found there would be time now for enriching relationships, making new friends, getting involved in new activities, and in serving the community. And they were able to reconnect with the satisfaction they felt in the work they had done and in the particular skills they had contributed to their firms.

Many of us who grew up in western cultures have been encouraged to cultivate a strong sense of self by our parents, schools, and the general culture. The work of finding our authentic inner voice begins with this sense of self. But spiritual growth entails letting go of our own self-importance and surrendering some part of our willfulness and desire to be in control. Our ego needs to take a secondary role to a deeper self that is aligned with a more expansive view of reality. The authentic self extends beyond our usual understanding of our bound self to acknowledge our connections to the people and forces of nature with which we are completely interrelated and interdependent.

Seeking Integrity and the Self

"Where are you?" God calls out to Adam and Eve in the Garden of Eden. *"Ayekah?"* The pair has hidden in the bushes, ashamed after eating from the tree of knowledge of good and evil in defiance of God's one restriction. But God knows where they are located. His question is spiritual, not geographic: "Why are you hiding from me?" It is the first challenge to the human view of self-sufficiency in Western religious tradition.

The story suggests that the authentic self generally feels safer when it stays hidden. In *The Thirteen Petalled Rose,* Rabbi Adin Steinsaltz intimates that the voice of God in the garden—challenging us with the existential question, "Where are you?"—still reverberates "throughout the world, and it is still heard, not always openly, or in full consciousness but nevertheless still heard in one way or another, in a person's soul....Indeed, where am I? The only thing he can say with any degree of certainty is that he has lost his way and is hiding....To anyone, at any time whatever, the question may be flung: Where are you?"

This question takes many forms: Who are you? Where are you going? For what purpose? Why? Steinsaltz explains that these existential questions about our core identity are threatening not only because they stir up so many uncertain possible answers but also because they offer "a glimpse into an abyss of yet further, and unanswerable, questions."

Like Adam, often we would rather hide than face the future. Yet when we stop hiding, when we can face the future, we open ourselves to a broader understanding of our life's meaning and the purpose we have yet to serve.

The realization of the need for this spiritual work may not come to us in the safety of our everyday lives. Something happens, perhaps shattering the illusions of fairness and order that can sustain us day to day. Somebody becomes ill, a loved one dies, or we learn of a terribly sad event or natural disaster like an earthquake or tsunami. We face our own mortality and lack of control. We realize our ordinary skills cannot carry us through this next stage. We can't bear to be alone with it. We need help so that we can begin to search for meaning amidst tragedy.

Or we may open to the challenge of spiritual work when something wonderful happens and we are overwhelmed with joy or gratitude. We want to bless, to celebrate, to give back, to share. One man joined a spirituality group shortly after he turned fifty, for he realized two things. First,

I found an unusual way to learn more about who I authentically was and what I really wanted to be doing. For several months, I had been waking up every night, gripped by an anxiety that was totally out of balance with the normal stress of my job directing a nonprofit organization.

Exhausted and depressed, I consulted a life coach, who suggested that my anxiety might be a result not of poor time management skills, but rather of a suppressed inner need. He set up two chairs facing each other and asked me to have a conversation between two conflicting aspects of myself. I felt extremely uncomfortable with this assignment—it sounded so corny. But I trusted him. In one chair I spoke seriously as the good girl I had been raised to be, the responsible leader driven by the need to succeed, to be recognized, and to please. In the other chair, I spoke powerfully as the rebel girl silenced in childhood, now a spirited woman who longed to be free, to be out in nature, to travel to new places, to try something different.

These two inner voices were locked in a desperate struggle. Each profoundly threatened the other. I had never given full voice to the yearning aspect of myself, even though I often whined to myself that my job was becoming unbearable. Now, witnessing the passion, I knew that spirit needed more space. The coach suggested that I articulate and write down a contract between the two "mes." My CEO self would allow my spirit self more vacation time and let her take weekends off. The inner-wanderer self would promise she would stay in the job for a few more years and continue to be responsible for the well-being of the organization.

Unlikely as it sounds, the agreement worked. I came more lightly into my work and found ways to be in the wilderness more of the time. I delegated more responsibilities and began to formulate a succession plan. The anxiety subsided. The organization thrived without me.

— *Rachel*

that he was extraordinarily blessed—he loved his wife and children and they loved him, his work was lucrative and satisfying, and his volunteer work added a layer of meaning to his life. Second, he felt there must be something more. He hoped to feel closer to God, by which he meant that he wanted to be more aware of gratitude and awe in his daily life. He wanted to transcend the demands of his ego and work more from his heart. He wanted to give more time to his community and enjoy more experiences with his family. He would not have said it, but he was also searching to live in alignment with his deepest, most authentic self.

Reflection Questions

Begin with your journal open, pen in hand. Ask yourself: "Who are you?"

Write spontaneously, saying what comes to mind without worrying if the answer is right or good enough.

When you are finished, sit quietly, and then repeat the question gently.

Then repeat the question two more times.

Sit in silence for a minute.

When you are finished, ask yourself what you have learned that is new, or surprising, and/or important. Write down your answers.

There Is a Time for Everything

The book of Ecclesiastes tells us "there is a time for everything under the sun." This life stage is a time for strengthening our inner spiritual life, so we will be more resilient, more open to possibility, more creative and loving as our journey takes us farther into our years. This is a time to accept and learn to live with insecurity, as we find new balance.

Time to Bring in More Time for Being

We are called human beings, but we define ourselves, most of the time, as human doings. When we meet people, our first question is likely to be, "What do you do?" And our tasks from late childhood until now have been primarily tasks of doing—studying, establishing families and careers, getting ahead or getting by, making friends, supporting ourselves and our loved ones. Those are the appropriate tasks of the earlier life stages.

Now, this new stage of life gives us the opportunity to let go of some of those pressures. To make more time for *being,* amid the *doing.* More time for reflection, for relationships, for enjoyment of diverse activities. Choosing activities for the sheer pleasure or satisfaction of doing them, rather than as a means to achieve a goal, or for status, or recognition. We don't need to feel busy or productive to feel authentic anymore. Even when we are still working hard to care for parents or for a partner, or to earn income we badly need, we can still make time to enjoy the pauses. We can move more deliberately, take our time experiencing people, places, and moments more fully. We can explore our creative side, learn new things, or deepen our knowledge of things we love. We can teach from the stories of our lives, from our examples—not only from the place of our expertise. We can be less motivated by "shoulds" and "have tos," and more by "want tos." Often, a good phrase for now is, "I am old enough not to have to do that!"

Opening ourselves to spiritual or religious practices is another opportunity. Studies have shown that people who affiliate with religious communities experience more happiness than others, and it is not uncommon for older people to reconnect religiously at this time. Four women who had previously been alienated from their Judaism joined one of our wise aging groups because they hoped they would find comfort and inspiration from the Jewish teachings and from the community— something they had not felt since childhood, if ever. Very slowly they engaged with holidays, prayer and meditation, and study, even though they continue to struggle to find a meaningful sense of Divine presence in their lives. Three began to learn Hebrew, and all joined a synagogue. They have each found new friends, meaningful activities, and joy and purpose in their newfound community.

Learning to be satisfied with a more reflective life takes practice. When we are conditioned to be busy and to meet the needs of others, when we are occupied or distracted by our activities—by what we do—it is difficult to stop saying yes to more. But we can develop the skill of saying yes to saying no—to allowing ourselves to choose not to do something, simply because we would rather use the time for our own purpose. Rabbi Marcelo Bronstein calls this *holy chutzpah.*

As we do this work, we can view our need for autonomy and control from a different perspective; we see how fearful we are of relaxing and letting go. We can learn to notice when we are being driven by fear, or by anger, or by craving. We can learn to respond thoughtfully and deliberately to stimuli, rather than reacting out of instinct or habit. With practice, we can learn to find joy in the present even as we know that the joy must inevitably dissipate. We can learn to enjoy what we can do without longing for what we can no longer do. We can acknowledge regret without being stuck in it. We can inhabit the present, strengthened by memories but not trapped in them. In these ways, time has more meaning.

Rabbi Abraham Joshua Heschel, in "To Grow in Wisdom," reflects on the importance of being present in each moment:

> Most of us do not live in time but run away from it; we do
> not see its face, but its makeup. The past is either forgotten

or preserved as a cliché, and the present moment is either bartered for a silly trinket or beclouded by false anticipations. The present moment is a zero, and so is the next moment, and a vast stretch of life turns out to be a series of zeroes, with no real number in front.

Blind to the marvel of the present moment we live with memories of moments missed, in anxiety about an emptiness that lies ahead. We are totally unprepared when the problem strikes us in unmitigated form.... Time has independent ultimate significance; it is of more majesty and more evocative of awe than even a sky studded with stars.

Time to Strengthen Our Spiritual Practices

The ongoing task of being in the present requires more than pure thinking, more than finding new things to do. It requires that we adopt new practices of mindfulness.

Mindfulness Meditation—Seeing Truth in the Moment

A common misunderstanding about mindfulness meditation is that it means emptying our minds of all thoughts and creating a blank screen. But the goal is not to empty the mind; rather it is to cultivate calm alertness to what is going on in the mind so that we can pay closer attention to our experiences. Calm and alert are interesting qualities: we need both. Much of the time we are either so calm that we disengage, or so alert that we risk responding primarily to the agitation of daily, superficial matters.

Mindfulness meditation is an excellent tool for growing older well. Jon Kabat-Zinn, a pioneer in developing the medical field of mindfulness-based stress reduction, defines it as "paying attention in a particular way, on purpose, in the present moment and nonjudgmentally."

Mindfulness questions help us recognize our visceral, instinctive, and often unconscious responses to situations both ordinary and unusual. How am I feeling right now? What sensations are present? What emotions? What thoughts occupy my attention? As we develop the ability to bring our attention to the moment, and the feelings and sensations that are present in it, we can begin to distinguish between habitual, instinctive reactions that may lead to unproductive actions, and skillful responses that are based in reality. We may feel a pain and notice that we have pricked our finger and get a bandage, or we may feel that pain and become hysterical because we fear it is going to become infected.

With experience, we learn to notice bodily manifestations of emotional states. Perhaps we feel tension in the stomach, or weakness in the knees, or tight breathing. These sensations may be unpleasant, so we react to get rid of them, resorting to distraction, flight, denial, or blame. But if we can sit quietly and still, and *notice* the actual sensation of fear in the body, we can calm ourselves and see more clearly what is actually happening, whether there is in fact a threat, and how we might *choose* to respond. Just because we experience the physical sensation of fear or anxiety, which sets our mind reacting, does not mean we have to be afraid or anxious. Fear and danger are not the same. Danger is real. Fear is a state of mind that rises and can pass away if we let it.

In this way, mindfulness meditation can help us release the fears of aging that can grip us. We can notice how fear feels as it rises, as it settles into our body. We can see the stories that we create that cause it to proliferate: "Oh no, it's all downhill from here." "Oh, if only we had moved to Florida!" "Can I trust my children; will they put me into a good nursing home?" "Will I lose my mind?" "Who will I be when I am no longer who I was?" We can learn to see that sadness, anxiety, and fear are natural emotions, that they are states of mind that we can work with, and that with time and mindfulness they can pass.

When our fears or our anger are not founded in fact—when they are not healthy warnings—they rob us of clarity, they blunt strategic thinking as we strike out reflexively to protect ourselves. The anxiety keeps us from thinking clearly about effective responses to what troubles us. Mindfulness can help us transform fear into understanding, perhaps even into gratitude and compassion for ourselves and for others.

The story of the biblical Moses and the burning bush is a wonderful example of a mindful response. After having fled Egypt and the wrath of Pharaoh, living with the Midianites as a shepherd, Moses goes wandering in the desert. He walks along, not sure where he is going. Is he looking down, watching his footsteps? Is he looking to the horizon, hoping to find water? Does he feel lost or frightened? We do not know. But he is not lost in thought—he is fully aware. He sees a bush, off to the side; a fire is burning within it. He looks more deeply and sees that the fire is burning but the bush is not consumed by the fire. He walks closer; he wants to know what is true. "When God saw that he [Moses] had turned aside to look [at the burning bush], God called to him out of the bush and said: 'Moses, Moses.' And Moses answered, 'Here I am, *Hineini*'" (Exodus 3:4).

Moses's awareness allowed him to see the presence of God, and his "Here I am" lets God know that he, in turn, was fully present, ready to learn why God was calling and ready to follow God's command. God saw a mindful person, a trustworthy and humble servant.

Mindfulness meditation is a skill one can readily learn. It is called a practice because we must practice it regularly to become proficient and realize its benefits. In meditation, we develop the skills—like building muscles in a workout—to pay attention, to notice the truth of our experience in the moment. Sitting meditation is an excellent way to develop our muscle. But there are other ways to practice as well. We can practice it walking down the street or in the middle of a conversation. We can take three breaths while waiting at a traffic light or when the phone rings. We can remember to simply pause, take note that we have become distracted, and bring our attention back to the situation we are in.

Meditation

This meditation is a calming way to start the day. Try it for at least five minutes.

Begin by establishing a sitting posture where your spine is upright but not rigid, your shoulder blades are relaxed down your back, your feet are touching the floor or a mat, and where you are aware of the weight on your buttocks. Take a few breaths and feel the sensation of your body's weight on the chair or cushion, any spots of tension, perhaps tingling. Notice the sensations and try to let go of any tension—perhaps by imagining yourself breathing into it.

Take a few breaths and feel the expansion and contraction in your body. Put your hand on your belly to feel your breathing. Gradually bring your attention to your breath, noting the air as it comes into your nostrils and the warmer air as it leaves, or the expansion and contraction of your lungs, or the rising and falling of your abdomen.

Sit still and notice these sensations. When your mind has carried your attention elsewhere—as it inevitably will—perhaps out into the future, or over onto your desk, or back to something that happened earlier, notice that you are now

Blessing Practice—Bringing Attention to the Moment

Giving or reciting a blessing connects a particular moment with an action—the blessing. A blessing is a chance to notice what is true in the moment—I am about to eat a bite of bread. I see a rainbow. I am meeting an old friend on the street whom I have not seen in years. I am alive. Over time, a practice of saying blessings may increase your sensitivity to your surroundings and your place in them. You might "thinking." At this point you have the choice of continuing with the thought or of returning to your breath. Bring your attention back to your breath and see if you can take three breaths in and out without your mind turning to a new focus. When another thought arises, you might picture it as a cloud drifting in the sky or a feather floating in the air. You are not thinking about the breath or about how to breathe in some special way. You are simply feeling the breathing and noticing the thinking.

After establishing your concentration by paying attention to your breath, bring to mind a phrase. For example, simply "Thank you" or "Gratitude fills me." Or if you are comfortable, "I am grateful before You." Or in Hebrew, *Modeh ani l'fanecha* (for a man)/*Modah ani l'fanecha* (for a woman). Let the phrase float like a thought, on your breath, in and out. When thinking carries you away from feeling, come back to your breath or to your phrase.

After five minutes, gently open your eyes and notice how your body feels. With time, you will be able to extend the number of minutes you sit. See if over time you can extend it to fifteen, even twenty minutes. The longer you sit, the greater the impact of the meditation on your physical and emotional well-being.

become aware of how much is given to you simply because you happen to have been born. You might notice a feeling of humility when you understand that the gift of life is one you did not give, that you do not control. Blessing practice expands our awareness from the narrowly personal to a larger realm. See how many occasions during the course of a day you can find to make a blessing. Jewish tradition teaches that we should say one hundred blessings a day. You might learn traditional blessings, or make a list of blessing opportunities and create your own phrase to suit each occasion.

Perhaps the blessing most appropriate for celebrating this stage of life is the Shehecheyanu blessing that many Jews say when they do something for the first time ever, or for the first time that year (eat a seasonal fruit, put on a new piece of clothing, see a friend after a long absence, or celebrate a holiday): "Blessed are You, Adonai our God, who reigns sovereign in the universe, who has given us life, sustained us in life, and brought us to this very minute." (*Baruch atah, Adonai Eloheinu, Melech ha'olam, shehecheyanu v'kiy'manu v'higi'anu laz'man hazeh.*) Or, you can choose to make up your own "first-time" blessing.

Journaling—Giving Each Moment Import

Writing in a journal allows us simply to reflect on experience, and to create a record of our discoveries, insights, and challenges. When we write about an experience, it can help us recall details that all but passed us by. We have the leisure to remember what happened—in our mind, in our body, and in our emotions. Few of us can process that much stimulation all at once. Journaling allows us to stretch out that moment of time so that we can bring awareness to much more of what was going on. Journaling also stimulates levels of reflection; we ask ourselves questions about what we have felt and done. We observe how our responses as we write might differ from those that occurred in the moment.

A journal can also serve as a form of witness. We can go back to entries we have written in the past. Perhaps we will discover similarities and patterns of which we have been unaware. Perhaps we will notice how our responses and perceptions have changed over time.

In this book there are questions and exercises that are meant to serve as triggers for journaling. They are meant to open up new areas of thought and to help you connect the ideas presented in *Wise Aging* to your own experience. Your journal is also a good place to record favorite prayers, poems, or commentaries. You will find some in the course of this book, and you will discover others in your own explorations.

Time to Let Go of What We No Longer Need

At a certain time many of us become aware of how much stuff we have collected. Closets and drawers are jammed with clothes we rarely use. Magazines pile up. Then there are the old letters and photographs we meant to put in albums or digitally archive. At some point we start to ask ourselves: Do we need all this stuff? Want it? Will our children or friends want these things? Are we happier because we hold on to them? Now is a good time to consider our stuff—perhaps bringing our heirs into the conversation. We may need help making tough decisions.

With research, we can find places that collect the items we want to donate. Bonnie Fatio, director of a program called AgeEsteem, has a wonderful plan for getting rid of stuff when she moves to a smaller apartment. She will wrap up the things she does not want to take, hold a party for all her friends, and give them each a wrapped package containing some object she has loved, not knowing who will get what.

This is a time to let go of psychological baggage as well. What stories do you carry around that are no longer helpful or perhaps even true, which serve more to confine than liberate? Can you think of one story you could let go? A friend told us about the time she said to her husband that she had no such story. He looked at her and replied, "Do you know how often you tell the story about not getting into your first-choice college? How about letting that one go?" In carrying that story, she had adopted a negative judgment about her intelligence. She thought about it, realized that she had received a wonderful education anyway, and would never have met her husband of fifty-eight years if she had gone elsewhere. She turned a story of failure into a celebration of love.

And as we will discuss in chapter four, this is also the time to let go—however slowly and to the extent possible—of relationships that are draining our energy or weakening our spirit.

Time to Introduce the New

Writer and sociologist Sara Lawrence–Lightfoot sums up the wonderful possibilities for learning that we will encounter in these years of our lives, years that she calls "the Third Chapter": "For men and women in the Third Chapter, the process of learning something new feels familiar and strange, exciting and terrifying, mature and childlike, both in character and out of body, like returning home and setting out on an adventure to an unknown destination."

This is also a good time for a conscious effort to make new friends and renew valued friendships. And to cultivate relationships with younger people—both because we will learn from them and because they will be around in the years when many of our older friends will have moved, become ill, or died. This is a time when we can do more than serve younger people as mentors. We can also become their students. In the process, we become friends, and all lives are enriched.

As we look at the world around us, we also will see much that needs to change. We all have causes about which we care deeply. And we are also part of a collective that needs to speak up for the rights of our fellow elders to dignity, decent standards of health care, housing, and income security.

On the one hand we must ascertain how much time, energy, and passion to put into leaving the world a better place for the next generations. On the other hand, we now have time to pay attention to our own unfolding personal lives. Both hands can work together, with our personal experiences giving meaning to our concerns about the welfare of our friends, our community, and our world, and with our concerns about the broader world simultaneously informing our personal relationships.

Exploring the richness in this stage of our lives will take us to new places. It will enable us fully to say the blessing we learned above. "Blessed are You, Adonai our God, who reigns sovereign in the universe, who has given us life, sustained us in life, and brought us to this very minute."

Love after Love

The time will come
when, with elation,
you will greet yourself arriving
at your own door, in your own mirror,
and each will smile at the other's welcome

and say, sit here. Eat.
You will love again the stranger who was your self.
Give wine. Give bread. Give back your heart
to itself, to the stranger who has loved you

all your life, whom you have ignored
for another, who knows you by heart.
Take down the love letters from the bookshelf,

the photographs, the desperate notes,
peel your own image from the mirror.
Sit. Feast on your life.

—Derek Walcott

—2—

The River of Life

*The compensation of growing old, Peter Walsh thought,
coming out of Regent's Park, and holding his hat in his
hand, was simply this; that the passions remain as strong
as ever, but one has gained—at last!—the power which
adds the supreme flavour to existence—the power of taking
hold of experience, of turning it round, slowly, in the light.*

—Virginia Woolf, *Mrs. Dalloway*

At this stage of our lives we have the opportunity to reflect on our journey thus far. Where have we come from? With whom have we been traveling? What happened? How did we interpret those events and relationships? What lessons did we learn? Where to next?

Many of us love to tell stories: sharing memories of our family history, transmitting values, recalling funny or difficult or compelling experiences in our past. These stories provide glimpses of who we were. But now is the time when we can work with these important stories through intentional and systematic reflection to gain perspective on our lives today. Using a practice of "life review" we can document these events and then trace threads of connection between them, revealing our life as a flowing river that pools at times in basins of slow-moving deep water, and at other times races wildly over rocky rapids, turning and winding, sometimes calm, sometimes roiled.

Life review can help us see that in spite of its surprising turns and twists, it is all one story. First we recall specific events and construct a simple chronology without interpretation. When we've finished, we go back and look for high and low points, and for the threads that connect the events—threads we then pick up and weave together. Acknowledging our strengths and our blessings, witnessing our resiliency, we can look to the future with greater confidence and more optimism.

This potentially transformative work helps us to understand past events in the light of present experience. In doing so, we may be able to turn regrets about roads not taken into an appreciation of the paths we have chosen. Life review can help us identify the people, practices, and experiences that have been uplifting and meaningful. And with this awareness we can make more time for doing those things and spending time with those people that lift our spirits. With these insights, we can make choices to build lives of greater satisfaction in the years ahead.

At the same time, in mapping difficult times, we can become aware of—and appreciate ourselves for—the inner strengths and resources we displayed in living through and growing from them. We learn to trust ourselves to work through the trials and difficulties that are sure to challenge us in the years ahead. When we begin to see the patterns created by the interplay of all that has happened in our lives, we may develop greater equanimity about the way our lives have developed. Even those of us who feel sadness over the past may be able to overcome bitterness or blame.

The late Rabbi Zalman Schachter-Shalomi considered life review to be an integral part of "spiritual eldering." He taught that it "plays as crucial a role for elders as going from crawling to walking for children. Without it, elders retain the consciousness of a 45-year-old, measuring themselves against that level of productivity. It is an expression of 'an instinct for fulfillment, the longing to complete what feels like unfinished business.'"

We do not need to be approaching the end of life to do a life review. It can be helpful at any age to see more clearly what is meaningful, and to see what emotional, psychological, and spiritual work might bring us greater understanding and satisfaction. Now, rather than later, is the perfect time to do this work.

Stories Matter

Each photo in our album or on our wall records a particular instant. In our memories, we turn those instants into stories. Narrative is one of the primary ways in which we understand ourselves and the world around us. So the stories of our lives matter enormously, for they reveal to us and others something about who we think we are. Good stories help us face the challenges of growing older. They help make us resilient as they tell of ways we have found joy and overcome past adversity. In hindsight we can see how each life event has led to the next in one (often unplanned) chain. And with that lens we can often move forward in our lives with more clarity, confidence, and perspective.

At the same time, each story is partial, glimpsed in hindsight. We all have experienced hurt, rejection, pain, and loss, and we may be tempted to dwell on those themes in the stories we tell. But they can fill us with resentment, jealousy, bitterness, or despair. We may also believe things about ourselves and others that may not be true or that may leave us feeling helpless to change, and we risk turning those passing events into permanent structures. But in retelling them through the lens of life review, we have the opportunity to understand them in context, and we may be

As I write, I happen to be downloading 3,480 photos from my iPhone into my new laptop. Pictures of my life flash by. My heart fills with joy as I see a leaf uncurling in early spring and a gingko tree glowing a brilliant yellow in autumn. Two wonderful vacations zip by. A dear friend smiles, though now she has died of the cancer she was fighting then. My grandchildren age before my eyes—from birth to mini-superheroes, standing strong against life's anxieties—a once tiny girl is now a gymnast cartwheeling off a bench, and her eleven-year-old brother climbs up a steep rock face. A thousand pictures later two years have flown by; my grandson's wondrous bar mitzvah just happened. And there I am at my seventieth birthday party—looking younger than I look today. Important moments, prompts for good memories. Glancing at them from time to time makes me happy but does not tell me a lot about the seventy-three-year-old woman I am now. Here they are random events, but with the benefit of time for finding patterns and reflecting on significance, they could help me find a larger meaning in the context of a whole life.

— Rachel

able to reframe them, finding the elements we have missed before that make the stories more neutral or even redemptive.

It is time, then, for us to revisit those stories. Let us begin with a much older, more famous story: consider the biblical patriarch Jacob. His life stretches across the pages of Genesis, filled with drama. His younger years include violent competition with his brother, parental favoritism, and family deception. Later his beloved wife Rachel dies, his daughter is raped, his sons take revenge on the rapist's tribe, and ten of Jacob's sons gang up on his favorite son Joseph and sell him into slavery. They deceive their father by leading him to believe that Joseph has been killed. From this deception, Jacob never fully recovers.

Many years later, Jacob learns that the son whom he thought was gone forever has not only survived, but now holds a position of great power in

Egypt. Jacob and his family are invited to settle under Joseph's protection there. When they arrive, Joseph introduces his father to Pharaoh, who inquires simply, "How many are the years of your life?"

To this question Jacob replies, "The years of my sojourn [on Earth] are one hundred and thirty. Few and hard have been the years of my life, nor do they come up to the life-spans of my fathers during their sojourns" (Genesis 47:8-9).

There is no resilience here. Jacob speaks from a place of despair. He has a story, but hardly a strong one. It takes him seventeen years after this episode, living in Egypt, reunited with his beloved Joseph, surrounded by his children and grandchildren, to regain a positive sense of himself. Only as he lies dying is Jacob able to recall the blessings he received as a boy and to offer blessings to his sons. Some are generous; others harsh. Jacob is now, finally, speaking his truth, with all its complexity. Able to reconnect with his life story, he reclaims the role of patriarch and transmitter of blessings.

At the point Jacob responds to Pharaoh—when his resilience is so low— his self-understanding is limited by his suffering. He is stuck in a story that is all but over. He can envision no new chapters, no possibility of any change of circumstances or heart. In spite of being reunited with his favorite son, he cannot recognize the redemptive quality of what is happening.

What if, in that moment with Pharaoh, Jacob had perceived his life story as part of a greater narrative, more like the one we see today? What if he had remembered that he had inherited the blessing transmitted through Abraham and Isaac? What if he had trusted in the story that his descendants would become as plentiful as the sands of the desert and the stars of the sky? Would his one hundred and thirty years have been less bitter in spite of his losses?

Jacob needed a strong story to tell. We all do. But what constitutes a good story? How do we know when our stories are providing a more consistent, more productive, more truthful view of our lives?

The characteristics of good personal narratives reflect the tastes of a mature adult, one too seasoned to believe in one-dimensional characters, clear distinctions between good and evil, or guaranteed outcomes. We know that life can turn in a moment, good to bad and also from bad to good. Life experience has taught us something of paradox and complexity. Our stories can—they *should*—embody that complexity and nuance.

With the perspective of distance, we can reframe our life and soften our narrative. If we grew up with a parent or other relative who caused us to suffer, for example, it would have been impossible in the moment—as a child—to move to a place of understanding, let alone forgiveness. But with distance, we may be able to understand the circumstances that caused him or her to be that way. When we open our narrative, our perspective shifts, and we may find our heart softening. We may even be able to find moments of affection and connection amidst the darker places. Thich Nhat Hanh, the Vietnamese Buddhist teacher, invites us to go back as far as we can in imagining our parent at a stage when it would be possible to embrace him or her—perhaps if only as a small child. We may still be able to remember or imagine what might have caused our parent to be rigid, unloving, or irresponsible. We are not called to forget the dark times, but rather to remind ourselves of such good as was there as well. In finding those sparks, we may recognize a source of the hope or courage that enabled us to emerge from despair or darkness.

Reflection Questions

Thinking about "might-have-been" is a way of expressing disappointment or dissatisfaction. What is something you have at times wished had been different? What might be missing from your life or from whom you have come to be without this part of your story?

◈ At times when you have felt discouraged about life, what helped you regain perspective?

◈ What is a story about yourself that you love?

◈ Can you think of a story you might be able to let go of?

Reframing Our Narratives

Our stories, of course, seem fully true. And truth implies constancy. But the meaning we give them—our interpretation—changes over time. And so narrative reflection helps us see that the past is never fully settled; it appears differently to us when we stand at various distances from it. Thus our narrative truth is always on the move. And so it is in this wiser stage of life that we can deepen our understanding of the important events. Gerontologist Harry J. Berman notes, "Perhaps, we thought our life was a tragedy and all along, unbeknownst to us, it was a romance. Or perhaps we thought our life was almost over, at least in terms of the future holding anything new, and it turned out that we have much to look forward to."

The wholeness we seek depends on our ability to accept the past without holding onto the desire for it to have been different. Acceptance of our past, whether it was what we wished it had been or not, gives us enormous new freedom. It might mean a new and different love of our parents. It might mean acknowledging that somehow we found the strength to go on and rebuild our life after a profound loss, rather than continuing to live within the story of the tragedy.

When we resist accepting our *full* life—all of it—we risk being trapped by regret for what we could not *and cannot* change. The wish that we had had a better father, more money, lived in a different place, or gone to a different college can be gripping. Perhaps if those things had been true, we think, we would be happier now. We may even feel that we were cheated. Certainly if circumstance had been different our lives would be different. But our circumstances were what they were, and the choices we made were likely the best we could make at the time, with what we knew. Taking responsibility and accepting our past as it was is the best way to stay open to change and new discoveries. The only thing about the past that we can change is the way we interpret it.

Practicing a Life Review—Meditation

Before beginning the life review exercise, consider spending five to ten minutes bringing your awareness to the present moment, to how you are right now. This meditation for life review work is the "Here I Am/*Hineini*" meditation. You may remember that *Hineini* is Moses's response when God calls out to him from the burning bush. "Here I am"— present with attention, ready to learn.

The instructions for sitting are the same basic directions we gave in chapter one. It will help to repeat them until you feel comfortable with this practice. Begin by sitting in a comfortable position, one in which you can feel the weight of your body on your chair or cushion and the sensation of your feet on the floor. Bring attention to your spine, making sure that it is erect but not rigid. Your shoulder blades should be relaxed down your back, your hands lightly clasping each other in your lap. Scan your body, noting points where you are holding tension. Imagine yourself breathing into those points, warming and relaxing them. Then bring attention to hearing, to noting sounds in the room. Try to simply hear them, without interpreting or telling a story of why they are pleasant or unpleasant, welcome or annoying. Simply note "hearing is happening now," "sound is louder now," "softer now."

After a minute or so, bring that same careful attention to your breath and note, "breathing in" and "breathing out." When your mind begins to wander—as it will, over and over—when thoughts come in, or emotions rise, or you experience physical sensations in your body, bring your attention to them, noting "thinking," "remembering," " itching," "happy," "sad." Can you gently release them and return to the experience of presence in this moment? You may have to reconnect with your breath to strengthen your concentration. If the feelings persist, lean into them. What does "sad" feel like in your body? Explore it. Or "happy"? Or "thankful"? When you can release the feeling, come back to your breath.

After establishing your concentration by paying attention to your breath, try to magnify your concentration by repeating a phrase to yourself. Perhaps the word that Moses uses, *Hineini,* or the phrase, "Here I am." Or, "Breathing in, I am calm. Breathing out, I am awake." Or another of your choosing, which signifies to you that you are present. Repeat the phrase several times and settle into it.

Sit this way for the remaining minutes, knowing that every time you notice that you are thinking or feeling, you have the choice of continuing with the thought, or letting thinking stop and noticing breathing begin. Each time you make the choice to let go of the thought, you are choosing momentary liberation from habitual patterns of thinking. You are practicing mindfulness.

The Flowing River

We are indebted to Rabbi Zalman Schachter-Shalomi for his teachings about life review. We have fashioned this model, guided by his thinking. You will need a large sheet of paper (11 x 14, or even better, 16 x 20) and three pens (one regular, one felt-tip, and one highlighter).

Draw the edges of a river, at least five inches wide, flowing diagonally up and across the page, and then divide it crosswise into seven-year-long segments: 0 to 7, 8 to 14, 15 to 22, and so on, up to your current age, leaving room for the future. The river suggests the flow of life and a force that carries us into the future. Make sure there is plenty of space for writing.

After setting up your chart, sit quietly for a minute or two, then write on the river the events of your life that happened in each of the seven-year periods—as many as you can remember—and the people who were particularly important to you in those years. Pause before you fill in each section, thinking about your early childhood, your late childhood, adolescence, and so on.

When you finish, sit and read each section over quietly. Breathe in and out. Is there something else to add?

Next, highlight or circle the most significant events.

Then answer the following questions for each life period (it helps to write the answers on the river or in a journal):

- Who were the people who guided and influenced me during these times?
- Looking at the high points: What were the elements and emotions that made it such a high?
- Looking at the low points: What inner resources did I draw on to help me get through?

Then take more time to sit and consider your river. See if any other events come to mind. After reflecting, you may choose a few highs and lows to write about more extensively.

Next look to see if you can find a flow between events. Perhaps a low point leading to a high point or vice versa, or specific choices you made that led to multiple events and consequences, or a lesson you learned from one event that played out through later years.

- In what ways are you connected to past generations? In what ways to future generations?
- What can you learn from this work that can influence the decisions you make about the course of your life from this point on?
- What story or stories that you have told yourself about your past look less true as you reflect on the whole? Is there a story you would like to let go of?

Please remember that this is an exercise to encourage reflection and introspection, not a directive to write your autobiography. Enjoy it!

After finishing the exercise, write in your journal about the discoveries you have made. As you reflect on the strengths that you called on to deal with loss, pain, and other difficulties, make sure to recognize that they will be available for future challenges as well. Then, consider those individuals who have been important to you—perhaps you will want to give more attention to relationships with them in the future. You might choose to try to spend more time with them, or to stay in closer touch, or simply let them know how much you appreciate them or love them. And consider the things you have done that gave you pleasure; now is the time to think about ways you could bring more of that kind of experience into your life.

When finished, come back to your sitting meditation position. Spend at least five minutes in the simple meditation practice of observing your breath, focusing your concentration, noticing what arises.

You may be doing this review on your own. But if you are working in a group, when each of you is finished with your chart, divide up into smaller groups of three or four, where each person shares, for three or four minutes, something that he or she has learned. Then open the conversation to your small group. Can you together identify themes and lessons that may be helpful for the future? As your whole group comes back together, you can discuss what it felt like to do this work. Was it helpful, and if so, how?

Finding Your Thread

The Way It Is

There's a thread you follow. It goes among
things that change. But it doesn't change.
People wonder about what you are pursuing.
You have to explain about the thread.
But it is hard for others to see.
While you hold it you can't get lost.
Tragedies happen; people get hurt
or die; and you suffer and get old.
Nothing you do can stop time's unfolding.
You don't ever let go of the thread. (William Stafford)

Emerging from our life review, we may have glimpsed a thread we've followed. It could be a value or a guiding principle. Perhaps knowledge that we are and have been loved. A resilience that keeps us standing up or helps us rise back up when we fall. Or a capacity for friendship or for comfort in solitude. Most likely it will be several—our lives in fact are made of many such threads.

The poet tells us never to let go of the thread. Why? Because it protects us from getting lost, from forgetting who we most authentically are. A powerful way to remember our thread is to find or create an image that represents it. Sitting quietly, we can try to feel that thread in our body, to let an image emerge in our imagination and feel its strength. When an image does form, find or create that image in a physical form that you can place somewhere so you will see it often.

Something traditional may work for you, such as the *shiviti*, which some Jews hang on an eastern wall in their home to remind them of God's

When I did the imaging, a tree came to mind. I thought of a verse from Psalms:

For this one is like a tree planted near a stream
That gives forth strong fruit in season
And whose leaf doesn't wither
And whose branches spread wide.

—Psalms 1:3

I chose a photograph of ancient olive trees on a hillside in Israel's Galilee—still strong, still bearing fruit, while history keeps flowing on around them.

— Rachel

presence at all times. A statue of the Buddha or a Christian image may serve you in the same way, or a piece of calligraphy, a painting, or a photograph. You may discover that some piece of art on your wall is already serving that function. If no image arises for you, try writing yourself a note to remind you of something powerful you learned in the flowing river exercise and your intention to bring it more fully into your life.

We invite you to find your image, your thread, so you can always remind yourself of your strength and your beauty.

I Am My Body;
I Am Not My Body

The years have made up my face
with memories of love...
And the paths I have trod
have strengthened my stride—

—Leah Goldberg, "Toward Myself"

The body, according to ethicist William F. May, has a threefold meaning for human beings. It is an instrument for interacting with the world (hands for working, feet for walking, tongue for talking); a means of experiencing the world (the glare of sunlight, flavor on the palate, the hum of streets, a fragrance on the breeze, the feel of tree bark); and a means of revealing ourselves to others.

What has your body been to you? Has it been a source of comfort or discomfort, pleasure or pain, confidence or anxiety? When have you related to your body primarily in terms of how it looks, how it works, or how it perceives? Has this changed over time? Has your body been central to your overall sense of identity, or merely a container for who you really are?

Often, we first become aware of our own aging through some diminution of our health, vigor, or attractiveness. A glance in the mirror reveals new grey hairs; we experience breathlessness after walking uphill, or fatigue and pain in places that we hardly knew were places. All these experiences tempt us to equate aging with loss or decline.

Author and psychologist Dr. Vivian Diller writes of catching a glimpse of herself in the mirror as she was about to leave her apartment. "For a moment I thought I had forgotten to put on my makeup. Then I realized that I did have makeup on. I was just old and cosmetics couldn't cover my aging face. I realized that nothing would."

The physical process of growing older may leave us feeling as though we are living in an unfamiliar body. At the age of sixty-four, our friend Fran observed, "Suddenly I feel like my body is changing in very dramatic ways; like some transformation is going on over which I don't have any control, sort of like what happened in puberty.... Now, I feel astonished by my body; it doesn't seem recognizable—not like the body I've lived in all these years. Things that were once easy no longer are."

One of the reasons these moments take us by surprise is that aging may create a sense of disparity between the way we *feel* and who we feel we truly *are*. We may be perplexed to find that at seventy we still have the zest for life, the capacity for wonder, and the desire for adventure that we associate with being much younger. We may yearn to climb more mountains or jog great distances but find that our body says

Reflection Questions

◈ When was the first time you noticed your body changing in ways that you associated with aging? What other moments have triggered this awareness?

◈ How did you feel? How did you react? What thoughts and associations arose for you?

◈ In what ways have your reactions to these changes intensified or lessened as you have grown older?

"No! Not at this age." We may have dreams, goals, or projects we hold dear but that strike us as too ambitious for someone at our stage of life. Do we really have the stamina or focus to start a new business or get a PhD? We may indeed, but we also have to confront our surprise at being the one with the wrinkled face sitting next to fresh-faced classmates, or the owner of a slow-moving body trying to keep up with the pace of younger colleagues.

Relationship with One's Body Over Time

Truth be told, many of us never felt very good about our body at any age. That is why, in making peace with and appreciating our body now, it is helpful to begin by exploring the relationship we've had with it in the past. As you work on the exercise below, notice which memories and associations have greatest poignancy for you. Take special note of any surprising memories that arise; they may be clues to understanding how you related to your body.

Reader Practices

My Body Over Time

Make yourself a chart like the one on the right, or develop a similar format, for noting feelings and memories about your body at different stages in your life. For each period describe how you felt and see what memories arise for you. You may be able to do this right away, with little thought, or it may take several days of carrying these questions around with you before an old memory invites itself into your consciousness. Continue to add to your notes as memories that seem important come back to you. Feel free to use different divisions of time if they are truer to your experience. For example, you may have spent early adolescence feeling chubby or ill at ease on the athletic field but later adolescence being and feeling trim and fit; so you would need to break "Adolescence" into two time frames. Or, as an adult you may have suffered an illness or injury that shifted your relationship with your body or your understanding of it.

Reflection Questions

- Which are the most profound body changes you have experienced? What feelings arise for you about them?

- Why do you think these changes have been important for you, more important than other changes?

- Which changes have been positive? Have you taken time to appreciate changes for which you are grateful? Or those aspects of your body that are holding up well? If not, how might you do so?

	Feelings about My Body	A Specific Memory
Childhood		
Adolescence		
Early Adulthood		
Middle Adulthood		
Now		

Once you have recorded your memories about the various ways you have related to your body, spend some time noticing themes, consistencies, and contrasts between different periods of time.

Pay special attention to what is similar and what has changed in your body awareness. Are you more or less aware of your body now? Are your feelings about your body more positive or less? Are they more focused now on appearance or function, and how does that compare to past periods? In what ways does this history shape your thoughts, feelings, and actions today? You might want to record your reflections and insights in the form of a letter to, or conversation with, your body.

The Body as It Performs

Generally our bodies reach their peak in late adolescence or very early adulthood. Those who are engaged in competitive athletics, dance, and physically taxing labor may sustain their competencies longer. They may also be more aware of the body's subtle but growing resistance to being pushed so hard.

The losses we notice as our bodies age are a major focus of aging humor—in birthday cards, jokes, comedy routines. We rarely ask whether there might be gains as well as diminishment.

For blogger Rhoda P. Curtis, "That's one of the best parts of getting older. Coming to terms with limitations of physical energy means expansion of psychic energy. I find that the sharpening of awareness of small things brings great joy, including the taste of a great glass of wine." Curtis suggests that when our bodies are able to move with speed and expansiveness, much of our energy is diffused before we fully perceive it. With age, the energy that would once have been expended physically is transformed, held in the body and experienced with even greater intensity.

Can frailty then actually be perceived as a gift—a gift of more fully experiencing the strength of life's flow within us? Not all of us are sanguine about this transformation. Playwright and Jungian analyst Florida Scott-Maxwell finds it troublesome:

> Age puzzles me. I thought it was a quiet time. My seventies were interesting, and fairly serene, but my eighties are passionate. I grow more intense as I age. To my own surprise I burst out with hot conviction. Only a few years ago I enjoyed my tranquility; now I am so disturbed by the outer world and by human quality in general that I want to put things right, as though I still owed a debt to life. I must calm down. I am far too frail to indulge in moral fervor.

The reflections of these two women raise several questions. How do we maintain awareness of our aliveness in spite of our body's diminishing capacity to express it? Can we embrace physical frailty with the wonder and respect with which we respond to the fragility of an infant? Can we acknowledge and accept frailty without losing our dignity?

One possibility is a stance of irony—irony that is not cynical but that allows us to stand at a slight distance, to view things from the edge, to maintain awareness of the multiplicity of interpretations open to us. As professor of gerontology William L. Randall writes: "The aches and pains of later life bring out the disparity between impulse and ability, between what we want to do and what we can. The same disparity, I propose, inspires the irony-laden humor—the jokes—in which the elderly themselves so often delight, for the levity it allows, the perspective it permits on their infirmity . . . and mortality."

We embrace the importance of irony, and also wish to add *dignity*. "Age is more than a disability," Maxwell reminds us. It "is an intense and varied experience, almost beyond our capacity at times, but something to be carried high."

> *"Are you kidding me?" responded Elizabeth Roxas-Dobrish, a fifty-five-year-old artificial-hip owner and former superstar at the Alvin Ailey American Dance Theater. She had just received an invitation to come out of retirement to dance at a special New Year's Eve performance.*
>
> *Taking on the challenge, she returned to class and added physical therapy, massage therapy, acupuncture, and more intense Pilates to her preparation. She began to see the dance from an entirely new perspective, not just as a showcase for technique, but as an expression of "all the things that life has put into you." Each step, each turn of the wrist, each beat of the music was a new phenomenon to be savored. Her major concern was for her partner. Would he feel like he was "dancing with his grandma"?*
>
> *The experience for her partner held its own surprises. It was, Mr. Roberts implied, like dancing with a precious jewel that called on him for great delicacy. What most took him aback was the way Ms. Roxas-Dobrish met him eye to eye as they danced. "It wasn't flirtatious," he said, it was "wild, and it opened up a new dimension of the work to me that I want to explore."*
>
> —adapted from "With Willing Spirit, a Reprise for
> Ailey Dancers" by Sarah Lyall

Reflection Questions

❖ Think of a time when you experienced a disparity between the way you felt inside and the way your body could perform. Describe the feelings that arose for you.

❖ How aligned do the different parts of yourself—your age, your appearance, your physical abilities —seem to you? Where there is alignment, does that seem positive, neutral, or negative? Which aspects are not aligned?

❖ Do you feel that you will be able to reach equanimity about the physical changes that accompany growing older? What role can humor or irony play?

❖ When do you find humor or irony helpful in accepting the changes you experience? Are there times that they seem counterproductive?

Accepting Reality without Inviting Suffering

While we have limited control over how our bodies age, we have far greater freedom to fashion the meaning we make and the attitudes we hold. We can seek to accept our new limits, and from there discover and give meaning to the things we still can do.

Let us introduce a distinction: between suffering and pain. Pain is genuine hurt, physical or emotional. Suffering is the additional distress we experience as a result of the stories we tell ourselves about our pain: "It isn't fair; it's his fault; if only I had...; why does this always happen to ME?" Once we identify the feelings, attitudes, and assumptions behind these stories, we can choose to keep them or to let them go. If we let them go we free ourselves to cope with the genuine pain about which we may have little choice.

If we listen closely, our internal self-talk about growing older will give us hints about what the changes we are experiencing mean to us personally. We may discover that part of our distress is related to our ideas about how things ought to be rather than actual displeasure over what we are experiencing. Or we may realize that we are reacting not only to a genuine loss but also to the way it affects our sense of identity. For example, no longer being able to jog or needing to limit travel can be frustrating enough. However, if these limations also trigger our fear that we will become a couch potato like our father, the loss will feel much greater. Some losses, not to mention fears, tap into messages that come from our childhood or family history; some are influenced by our friends; others touch parts of our lives that still feel unlived.

Sometimes we can detect the false notes—the dissonance—of our internal dialogues on our own. Often it is friends or partners who can help us hear them more clearly—and shine a light on the places we are stuck. When Miriam realized that her gloomy mood and tendency to snap at people was related to her anger at being unable to hike anymore, something she had enjoyed much of her life, she realized how central being in the outdoors was to her sense of self. Up until then she had resisted having the hip replacement that her physician recommended. With the insight that she had lost not only the ability to hike, but also a key part of her self-identity, she decided to have the surgery.

But sometimes there is a loss that cannot be remedied; sadness or fear may be a clear-headed response to the reality of our new situation. Then we must adapt. Writing in her late eighties, author Mary Chase Morrison mused, "To preside over the disintegration of one's own body, looking on as sight and hearing, strength, speed, and short-term memory deteriorate, calls for a heroism that is no less impressive for being quiet and patient. Anyone who watches aging closely and with a sympathetic eye can sometimes be lost in admiration for the aging and their gallantry."

Part of accepting our changing bodies can be awareness of our capacity for courage. Had surgery not been an option for Miriam, she would still have had choices about other activities in which to engage and about the attitude with which she confronted her new limits. Indeed, Miriam did discover a leadership capacity that she had never imagined herself to have as she organized her neighborhood for political action. Discovering within herself this new power and capability was an experience of bemused wonder for Miriam. Her amazement struck us as no less profound than our student Fran's surprise at finding that her aging body suddenly seemed as unpredictable as it had been during puberty.

What Lies beyond Acceptance?

Wonder, appreciation, gratitude, patience, and compassion—for our bodies and for ourselves—help us to move beyond resignation, beyond acceptance. Fran, having realized that her body was her body and she couldn't change it, decided to spoil it instead. She bought oils and "just lathered herself with abandon." Her story made us laugh. Sometimes wonder, appreciation, and gratitude can be evoked by the simplest, everyday occurrence.

One of the most basic yet unusual prayers in Jewish tradition is often referred to as the "bathroom prayer." In the Talmud, Rabbi Abayei (fourth century) taught that, "When [one] exits the restroom, he says: 'Blessed are You…who fashioned man with wisdom and created within him many orifices and many cavities. It is obvious and known before Your throne of Glory that if one of them were to be ruptured or if but one of them were to be blocked, it would be impossible to stand before You. Blessed are You, Who heals all flesh and acts wondrously.'"

A friend shared his appreciation of this blessing in the light of men's experience of an enlarged—or removed—prostate. It's not uncommon in the men's room, he said, "while we're waiting for something to happen, that one older man looks over at another and says something like 'at this age…a good pee is as important as good sex!'"

Anyone who has experienced ruptures, blockages, or other malfunctions of the body immediately understands the impulse to express gratitude when the body is working as it is meant to. The problem is that when our health is fine, we forget to notice. Mark, a friend with multiple sclerosis, bemoans how easy it is to readjust to "normalcy" within a month or two of remission. "I always think that *this time* I will continue to be grateful for the days I feel good, that I will continue to rejoice in the days free of pain. But, every time…I lose it."

In the bestseller *Tuesdays with Morrie*, we hear Morrie, in conversation with his former student Mitch Albom, preparing himself for the next step in his decline:

> "Do you remember when I told Ted Koppel [in a television interview] that pretty soon someone was going to have to wipe my ass?" he said.
>
> I laughed. You don't forget a moment like that.
>
> "Well, I think that day is coming. That one bothers me."
>
> Why?
>
> "Because it's the ultimate sign of dependency. Someone wiping your bottom. But I'm working on it. I'm trying to enjoy the process."
>
> Enjoy it?
>
> "Yes, after all. I get to be a baby one more time."
>
> That's a unique way of looking at it.
>
> "Well, I have to look at life uniquely now. Let's face it, I can't take care of the bank accounts, I can't take out the garbage. But I can sit here with my dwindling days and look at what I think is important in life. I have both the time—and the reason—to do that."

William F. May suggests that we consider aging to be a mystery rather than a problem. Often, he says, the question we need to ask is "How are we going to behave toward it?" rather than "What are we going to do about it?" May contends that along with the virtues of wonder, patience, gratitude, and compassion that we have acknowledged, the elderly need the virtue of humility to overcome the sting of humiliation that often accompanies aging.

Reciting Rabbi Abayei's prayer can act as a reminder that, as poet Jane Kenyon notes, "It might have been otherwise":

Otherwise

I got out of bed
on two strong legs.
It might have been
otherwise. I ate
cereal, sweet
milk, ripe, flawless
peach. It might
have been otherwise.
I took the dog uphill
to the birch wood.
All morning I did
the work I love.

At noon I lay down
with my mate. It might
have been otherwise.
We ate dinner together
at a table with silver
candlesticks. It might
have been otherwise.
I slept in a bed
in a room with paintings
on the walls, and
planned another day
just like this day.
But one day, I know,
it will be otherwise.

Reflection Questions

◈ When are you most aware of the workings of your body? In health? In illness? When taking on a physical challenge? When have you experienced your body's strength as a wonder or as awesome?

◈ What is implied by the statement in the "bathroom prayer" that without the body's ability to function we could not stand before God? See if you can answer this even if you consider yourself to be nonreligious. Substitute *Life* for *God*.

Patience, compassion, and perhaps a touch of humor are also among the ingredients that are helpful to stir into the acceptance mix. We were touched by the undertone of compassion with which Susan Moon, in *This Is Getting Old,* wrote about her changing body:

> My knees talk to me, and I have to respond. The old bones provide a kind of companionship. It's not really me that needs things like handrails and hiking poles, it's my knees. I make these arrangements for them, because we're family.... I used to take my bones for granted, but now that I am paying attention to them, I see that they are a great invention. When young people's bones are growing, for example, cells get added to the outside of the lengthening bone at the same time that cells are subtracted from the inside, in order to enlarge the hollow place where the marrow lives, in a complex engineering project....Now I'm shrinking. Under the soft flesh, the bones are shorter, lighter, more porous than they used to be, with spurs here and there that were not part of the original design. But they are still good bones—hinges and sockets, ball bearings and cables. I love their names: humerus, tibia, scapula, fibula.

Aging may present an opportunity for befriending our body in new ways, or for making peace with a body that has never lived up to our wishes for it. Linda Weltner writes:

> The history of a life is here, written into cells and carved into skin. My body has memories of its own carried in the tension of my shoulders, in a characteristic way of holding my head, in a crease of concentration between my eyes. My body, absorbing pain and pleasure with equal ferocity, has kept a careful record of the passing time....My age is visible in the way I rise from sitting on the floor, the way I collapse into bed at night, in my losing battle with sagging stomach

muscles....Yet though I am determined to face the ravages of time, when I look into the mirror I feel touched in the most profound way by the sight of this old flesh-and-blood

Walking Meditation—Who Guides a Person's Footsteps

Many of us are aware of our bodies only when something is amiss, paying little attention to the way our body feels when it is functioning as we expect it to. In a walking meditation, we use the feel of our body as our focus.

Start by selecting a space in which to walk. There is no destination. You will be taking ten to twenty steps in one direction, turning around, and walking back to your starting point. You will repeat this motion throughout the meditation. This is not about getting somewhere, it is simply about walking. Decide in advance how long you will meditate; ten to twenty minutes is a good amount of time in general, but you might want to begin with just five or seven minutes.

Start with your feet together and take a moment. Build your intention to fully experience "just walking."

Experiment with your pace. Walk more slowly than you usually do—you can vary your pace from a slow, browsing walk to a pace that is deliberately in slow motion.

As you begin to walk, concentrate on sensing your whole body. Notice the movement of your arms, the feelings in your hands, your back, the bottoms of your feet as you take each step. After a few minutes shift your attention to your legs, friend....It has introduced me to every pleasure, shared in every wondrous discovery. It fits me. And despite all its shortcomings, it has been a comfort to me more times than not.

noting each sensation as it becomes apparent as you walk, step by step. Continue to walk.

Finally bring your attention to your feet. Notice the parts of a step. What does it feel like to lift, move, and place each foot in turn? Notice the pressure, the balance, the sensations in the bottom of each foot, in your ankles, in your toes. Notice what it takes to change direction.

When your focus wanders, pause, stand still, and then gather your attention back to your body. Reaffirm your intention to be "just walking"—to walk with presence and attentiveness to each step as it unfolds.

The sensation of walking becomes your doorway into the present moment. Pay close attention to each step. Absorb the sensations. Let each step reveal itself to you. Notice the miracle of walking.

What did you notice about sensations in your body?

As you reflect on the experience, can you feel an openness to gratitude for the gift of your body? If so, you might like to know this blessing, which expresses appreciation for the "preparation" or "guidance" of each human step.

Blessed are You, Source of Life of the World,
who guides my step.

*Baruch atah, Adonai Eloheinu, Melech ha'olam,
hameichin mitzadei gaver.*

The Body as It Perceives

The body perceives the world in two different but interrelated ways. The first way refers to our five senses. We touch something and it feels soft, hard, cold, prickly. We see something and it appears red, blue, bright, dark. We taste something and experience it as sweet, salty, bitter. All of this can happen without our putting these perceptions into words.

The second way our bodies perceive the world is more subtle; it involves the interaction between our five senses and our mind; it is the way we interpret physical sensation. In the meditation above, for example, when you considered the "miracle of walking," you went beyond pure physical sensations and interpreted the meaning of those sensations, the *meaning* of walking.

When we distinguish between these two we can better appreciate both. We can come to appreciate that our bodies affect our understanding of the world in ways that inhabit a spectrum from purely instinctive to highly thoughtful and intellectualized. We can understand that everything we know of the world results from complex interactions both within our brains, and between our brains and all the other parts of our bodies. After all, our bodies are the source of raw material—the information—out of which our brains make meaning.

The Body as It Perceives through Our Senses

Aging may be accompanied by the dulling of our senses. Taste, touch, and smell may lose some of their sharpness and pleasure; glasses and hearing aids can usually maintain our vision and hearing at acceptable levels, but not always. But there's another side: slowing down can help us savor the world around us and the feeling of our own bodies. By refusing to be overly busy or overstimulated, and through conscious mindfulness practice, we can cultivate greater sensitivity to our physicality. Thus we can become more acutely aware of wine on the palate or a fragrance on the breeze.

Reflection Questions

◆ When do you consciously take notice of physical sensations? Think about small events such as drinking a cup of tea or less ordinary ones such as being caught in a storm.

◆ What signals does your body provide when something is amiss? When something feels right? That you have hit a true insight? That you are anxious? What are the key differences between those different signals?

◆ In what particular settings or activities are your senses most alive? In what ways could you seek pleasurable physical experiences more frequently?

Our experiences of our bodies are personal; they vary dramatically from individual to individual. Some of us are aware of even small fluctuations of how we feel physically; some of us are less attuned to our physicality.

In the mid-1950s, Dr. Eugene T. Gendlin investigated why psychotherapy was sometimes successful and sometimes not. He concluded that successful patients were able to intuitively focus on subtle internal bodily awareness, which Gendlin came to call the "felt sense." The felt sense provides clues that can help patients reach a deeper understanding of themselves and the issues they bring into therapy. This attunement to felt sense was more important, Gendlin believed, than even the most sophisticated intellectual understanding of the roots of their distress.

This kind of somatic knowing is not easily put into words. Those who are more oriented toward thoughts than raw sensation may need practice or coaching in order to learn how to pay attention to this sensory wisdom with an open, welcoming curiosity. The good news is that we *can* learn to pay attention to our body, become familiar with the way it speaks to us, and understand what it is saying.

An Exercise for the "Felt Sense"

Sit in a comfortable chair. Get the feel of how the chair is supporting you. Now check each part of your body for tensions, aches, or other forms the body's messages may take. Turn your head slowly from side to side a few times. Then, rest your head on your neck and shoulders in such a way that you don't have to consciously carry it.

Take a deep breath and let it out. Are your neck and shoulder muscles loose, resting easily on the frame of your body as it rests on the frame of your chair?

Exhale deeply and ask yourself, "What stands between me and total physical well-being? Is my body informing me that there are still things to be taken care of?"

The message from your body will consist of a feeling that may or may not be translatable into words. If words do form, there will be only one or two; try to remember them.

Next, ask yourself how to acknowledge the body's message. What step is necessary to move from the place and condition

The technique of focusing, as developed by Gendlin, helps us do just that. Once we can recognize sensations, knowing they are clues to underlying emotions we are experiencing, we gain fuller access to our body's wisdom, wisdom that goes beyond the physical world, extending to our thinking and feeling as well.

The exercise above, adapted from Rabbi Zalman Schachter-Shalomi's *First Steps to a New Jewish Spirit*, helps us get in touch with what Gendlin called the felt sense.

in which you are now, past the obstacles indicated by your body, to a place of well-being?

Wait for the answer. When it comes, it will be a body sense concerning something that can be done now (like relax the muscles in your forehead, take off your shoes, release the tension in your calves).

When you have done this, check with your body once again. Has the action you've just performed taken care of the immediate problem? Is your body at ease or is there still something else in the way?

If there is still something in the way, repeat the procedure. Repeat it until your body is content, until every fiber and cell begins to hum.

◈ If you reached the place of well-being, what did it feel like? Is this state familiar to you?

◈ Rabbi Schachter-Shalomi suggests that, "When you have reached this state, you've given your body to God and your soul is sure to follow." What do you think he means?

Eros and Intimacy

Theologian Ronald Rolheiser writes beautifully about the power of eros:

> Sexuality is an all-encompassing energy inside of us. In one sense it is identifiable with the principle of life itself. It is the drive for love, communion, community, friendship, family, affection, wholeness, consummation, creativity, self-perpetuation, immortality, joy, delight, humor, and self-transcendence. Sexuality is...experienced in every cell of our being as an irrepressible urge to overcome our

incompleteness, to move toward unity and consummation with that which is beyond us. It is also the impulse
to celebrate, to give and receive delight.

If sexuality is such a basic dimension of our capacity for sensuous-
ness, a way of knowing ourselves and discovering the depth of others,
we would certainly want to remain sexual beings until our final breaths.
That may mean learning new ways to express and satisfy our need to stay
connected to that all-encompassing life energy. It may entail adjusting
to the new realities of what our body is and is not able to do. It may
mean revisiting the beliefs and attitudes about sexuality that we have
lived with thus far. It may mean finding an outlet like massage for the
lack of physical contact in our life. Some gerontologists speak of "skin
hunger" and encourage us to indulge in pedicures, to walk arm in arm,
to use a vibrator, to express affection with a hug or a pat on the shoulder,
to spend time with a pet.

For some, it is not so much the sex that we miss but relationship and
intimacy, and we may need to renew our skills in pursuing those things
that connect us to others and put us in touch with our own aliveness. We
may need to relearn how to bring new people into our lives or how to date.
It may mean doing more with words, touch, holding, and kissing. We
may choose to read love poetry or allow a racy film to fire up our desire,
even if it cannot be fulfilled. At least we know that that part of ourselves is
still alive. We can write passionately, or paint wildly, or put on music and
dance with abandon, even in solitude.

When the prolonged decline of a partner and the isolation and stress
of caretaking leaves us feeling lifeless, how do we entertain a life-renewing
relationship without violating our marital commitment? Several American
rabbis have discussed the possibility of conducting ceremonies to sanctify
and honor a loving relationship between two people when one or both
of them has a still-living spouse in the late stages of Alzheimer's. They
acknowledge that the elders with whom they have discussed this possibility recognize the ambiguity of their situation, and yet feel guided by their

own inner wisdom to rediscover life's goodness. They are traversing new territory. But then, so are we all.

The AARP has published a number of articles about this dilemma. In one, geriatric psychiatrist William Uffner, medical director for the older adult program at Friends Hospital in Philadelphia, writes, "Most of the people who do those things are not abandoning their spouse. It can actually be something which allows them to maintain the caretaker role in the most responsible way possible. It stops them from getting depressed, and it stops from being too isolated." Such an arrangement can also provide caregivers with positive feedback. They have someone who thinks they're attractive or interesting, someone to talk to about daily life, continues Uffner. "Those are the things which keep us going as human beings."

Dr. Ruth Westheimer, in her highly praised book, *Dr. Ruth's Guide for the Alzheimer's Caregiver*, takes a firm stand, saying, "Though it's not your spouse's fault, you've been abandoned. If you need the love, the companionship, and yes, the sexual gratification of a relationship, then by all means seek one out."

Alternatively, sometimes a new love relationship can occur at the initiation of the partner with Alzheimer's. Former US Supreme Court Justice Sandra Day O'Connor stepped down from the court in order to care for her husband, who was suffering from Alzheimer's. As his disease progressed, her husband became depressed, introverted, and barely recognized his own family. Eventually, however, he developed a new romantic relationship with another resident in his assisted living facility. According to her son, Justice O'Connor was "thrilled" and relieved to see him so content. She often visited with the new couple as they sat on a porch swing holding hands.

Some couples are beginning to discuss their feelings about such relationships during the early stages of Alzheimer's in order to provide permission or spare their partner's guilt should he or she desire to enter into a supportive relationship.

Take a few minutes to consider where eros is alive for you:

◆ What do I remember as the significant sexual experiences and transitions of my life?

◆ When am I most in touch with the eros of which Rolheiser writes?

◆ What could I do to welcome more eros into my life? What holds me back?

The author Joyce Wadler was "messing around" on the couch with an old boyfriend when she sensed things were about to heat up.

> "There's something I have to tell you," I say to the fellow.
>
> "I've had breast cancer, and my new breasts, while spectacular, will be different from others you have known.... They're really gorgeous—but I haven't, you know..."
>
> "You're telling me I'm the first person who's going to see them?" he says. "I'm the first guy to see the new breasts? You chose me? I am really honored."
>
> You see what I'm saying? The first time I had sex, when I was a teenager, I didn't really know the guy, though I thought I did? Deeply disappointing. The first time I had sex as a 65-year-old woman with a 66-year-old man, and we'd both had illnesses that could have killed us and left us scarred and that we had to talk about?
>
> That was trust, that was intimacy, that was real connection.

The Body as It Perceives through the Mind

As human longevity has been extended, we have become more aware and fearful of the diminution of our mental perception. For nearly a century, the unchallenged assumption was that the cells of the brain did not regenerate. We thought that after young adulthood, the brain developed no further and indeed began to deteriorate. Now we know that the changing dynamics of the brain are much more complex than that. Scientists hold that whereas some regions of the brain do decline with age, others continue to develop throughout the life-span; new neural connections continue to be made, reinforced, and strengthened.

Although performance on paper-and-pencil tests that rely on speed and the immediate use of new learning decline after middle age, everyday problem solving and verbal abilities improve. Cognitive functioning may slow, but the quality of information that an older brain can process and generate is more nuanced. Neuroscientists have recently explained such phenomena by noting that older people's brains have stored more information than the brains of younger people; consequently, like a computer, processing time is greater. More than compensating for the lack of speed, they say, older people show "greater sensitivity to fine-grained differences," which is an important component of what is universally regarded as wisdom.

In *The Wisdom Paradox,* Dr. Elkhonon Goldberg explains the difference between the particular or descriptive knowledge that resides in the right hemisphere of the brain, and the generic knowledge that resides in the left. Generic knowledge involves recognition of broader patterns, what Goldberg calls "prescriptive" knowledge, which helps us solve problems and know what to do. While the right hemisphere tends to decline with age, making it harder to learn and remember facts, Goldberg argues that with age we rely more on well-developed patterns that have formed during a lifetime rich with experience. Using the left hemisphere more actively stimulates its continued development.

Interestingly, the right hemisphere tends to hold our negative emotional associations, while positive emotions are correlated with the left side. This may help explain why people actually seem to be happier and more resilient as they age. Yet, this "mental armor" is not an entitlement of aging; it is the reward of maintaining a vigorous mental life. Just as we need to exercise our bodies, we need to continue to exercise our minds with activities such as learning to play a musical instrument, taking up a new art or craft, working crossword puzzles, or studying a new language.

Psychologist and author Louis Cozolino, who emphasizes the ways in which, from infancy on, our brains are socially constructed, recommends that we engage in new kinds of interpersonal activities to stimulate our minds and avoid what he calls "hardening of the categories." He suggests buying a new gadget and asking a young person to instruct us on its use, adopting an irresistible puppy and getting to know the people who stop to play with it, or adopting a new cause and learning to advocate for it with others.

We've been particularly intrigued by the way that recent discoveries about the neuroplasticity of the brain also help us understand the transformative nature of the spiritual practices in which we have been engaged. While some of these practices appeal to our rational mind, they are simultaneously working at a deeper, neural level to repattern our perceptions and responses.

Increasingly, studies that use magnetic resonance imaging (MRI) document meditation-produced changes over time in the brain's gray matter. A 2011 study conducted at Massachusetts General Hospital was able to document measurable changes in brain regions associated with memory, sense of self, empathy, and stress after participants engaged in an eight-week mindfulness meditation program.

These studies affirm what spiritual teachers have known for millennia. When we meditate, pray, or chant, we are creating and reinforcing new patterns of behaving, thinking, and feeling. When we cultivate or enhance certain qualities of character (as we will elaborate in chapter six), we are consciously directing our growth toward becoming the kind of elders we want to be. A number of studies have begun to focus on the cultivation of empathy and compassion through meditative practice.

The Body as It Appears

When older people complain about being invisible, some sense that because of their wrinkled skin or their need to walk with a cane, they are being regarded as used up, finished, and worthless, when in fact they know themselves to be as engaged and engaging as ever. A friend who let her hair go grey for a few years and then began to color it said that the way she was treated in public settings was distinctly different depending on the color of her hair. "Having grey hair," she said, "was like not being there."

Of course for some, invisibility has its advantages. Political commentator Kristine Holmgren writes, "Once upon a time, I was a show-stopping 'looker,' a major babe....Then, I grew old and became invisible....Overnight, I became someone people overlooked, ignored. I spoke, and no one responded. I entered a room and no one (especially men) noticed." In her essay "Five Reasons to Enjoy Being an Old, Invisible Woman," Holmgren reports that invisibility gives her freedom to stare, to interfere, to fight back, to love, and to pass it on.

Ninety-three-year-old sports writer Roger Angell is less sanguine:

> We elders...have learned a thing or two, including invisibility. Here I am in a conversation with some trusty friends—old friends but actually not all that old: they're in their sixties—and we're finishing the wine and in serious converse about global warming in Nyack or Virginia Woolf the cross-dresser. There's a pause, and I chime in with a couple of sentences. The others look at me politely, then resume the talk exactly at the point where they've just left it. What? Hello? Didn't I just say something? Have I left the room? Have I experienced what neurologists call a TIA—a transient ischemic attack? I didn't expect to take over the chat but did await a word or two of response. Not tonight, though. (Women I know say that this began to happen to

them when they passed fifty.) When I mention the phenomenon to anyone around my age, I get back nods and
smiles. Yes, we're invisible. Honored, respected, even loved,
but not quite worth listening to anymore. You've had your
turn, Pops; now it's ours.

Beauty and Virility

The message that being beautiful is important starts in early childhood with
the compliments and assessments offered by relatives and strangers. Girls are
told, "My, aren't you pretty! What a pretty little girl!" Young boys, even tod-
dlers, are likely to be greeted, "Hey, buddy, let's see those muscles!" Meant as
compliments, these are also messages about how one ought to appear. Living
as we do in an era in which we are exposed to thousands of images of ideal
body types, the impact of being judged from the outside is great. The effects of
this may play out differently for men and women, but none of us is immune
to having our self-image shaped by cultural standards that are difficult to meet.

With the rise of second-wave feminism in the 1960s, we have become
more insightful about how the cult of beauty works for women, and
understand that it is the observer's eye that matters. Professor Frida Kerner
Furman, in her anthropological study of women's beauty-shop culture,
reported one of her interviewees saying, "I knew I was pretty because
people told me I was pretty. But I didn't tell myself that I was pretty." In
The Beauty Myth, Naomi Wolf contends that, "What little girls learn is not
the desire for the other, but the desire to be desired." As a result, some girls
choose to become passive in the hope of becoming objects of male desire.

Beauty can often lead to power. Economists Daniel S. Hamermesh
and Jeff Biddle of Michigan State University have studied the effect of
appearance on earnings potential for a large sample of adults. Like many
other desirable commodities, "beauty is scarce," Hamermesh says, "and
that scarcity commands a price."

Ironically, even as beauty may be regarded as a source of power for
women, it is also the means by which they may be disempowered. While

needing to make themselves appear attractive in order to capture attention and achieve status, women are, at the same time, belittled for their shallow and narcissistic preoccupation with appearance. Achieving the goal of beauty may thus register as a double-edged sword.

For Bonnie Lee Black, there has been greater comfort in aging than in the beauty of youth.

> When I was young and considered beautiful, men pursued me, as if playing a competitive sport for which I was a winning trophy....The face I see in the mirror—now that I've reached my sixties—is the face of the older woman I've always been. At last I feel whole, connected to this now-weathered outer shell....I feel, finally, light and free. To men, I've become invisible; from other women my age, I no longer sense jealousy. But to me, quite honestly, I've never looked more beautiful.

We see the ambiguity of beauty play out around the ambivalence many women feel toward cosmetic procedures or surgery as they struggle with the competing values of growing comfortable with the natural changes that come with aging or bowing to the cultural demand that they maintain youthful attractiveness. Our friend Sharon cancelled several appointments with a surgeon before deciding to let nature take its course. On the other hand, our friend Sue chose facial surgery because she could not bear to look at herself with the deep wrinkles that, she felt, robbed her of her sense of self. Both are comfortable with their choices.

Much less research has been done on men's relationship to body image. What we do know is that men now make up 10 percent of the cosmetic procedures performed in the United States. In addition to less invasive procedures like Botox, hair plugs, and laser skin resurfacing, plastic surgeons report that men are increasingly opting for surgery to address beer bellies, "man boobs," and sagging eyelids. In one study, 38 percent of men said they would sacrifice at least a year of their life in exchange for a perfect body—a higher proportion than women in the same study. Reflecting on the current bulked-up male image with rippling abs, Dr. Helen J. Fawkner, a senior lecturer in social psychology, notes that traditionally, a male's role in society has been more clearly defined than it is today. The "ideal" man demonstrated strength by providing both economic and physical security; today, men are less frequently relied upon to be the sole provider of livelihood or a primary source of physical defense. Given that, Fawkner suggests, men feel the need to display masculinity through physical appearance; "their body is one of the few remaining ways in which they can differentiate themselves from women." The consequent rush for the gym has also created a new and rarely talked about phenomenon identified by health experts as "muscle dysmorphia" (occasionally referred to as "bigorexia"), which involves dissatisfaction with the extent of one's muscle mass. For some, the need to work out can become so exaggerated that it interferes with productivity at work or the maintenance of social relationships, and for others it can lead to steroid abuse.

In spite of the increased cultural attention being given to the male body image, the physical impact of aging is still more easily overlooked in men than in women. The lines that adorn women's faces are perceived to be wrinkles but may be described as "character lines" for a man. Gray hair on men is often referred to in the press as "silver" and is perceived as "distinguished."

Ram Dass, formerly Dr. Richard Alpert, left his position at the department of psychology at Harvard and set out as a spiritual seeker. He became a major spiritual teacher and was awarded the Peace Abbey Courage of Conscience Award in August 1991. He writes:

> For forty years, I fought with myself in the area of extra fat...every milkshake and dessert brought guilt; every goody resisted brought feelings of deprivation....Then I had an experience that changed this preoccupation.
>
> I was teaching for a week at a Jewish family summer camp, and late one Friday afternoon, I joined all the men for a mikva, or purifying [ritual] bath, that involved immersing ourselves in a hot tub and then a swimming

pool en masse, naked. There were men and boys of all ages, and looking around, I suddenly saw myself reflected in many of the bodies around me, descended, as I was, from Eastern European peasant stock. I saw in that moment that the contours of my natural body, which I'd been fighting most of my life, were genetically ordained! I felt my compulsion to be thinner start to shift, and soon my body weight had stabilized at 215 pounds with no diet involved. Statistics say this is a bit too high, but I ceased caring, and shed the attachment to a thinner body-image. I learned to appreciate my tummy rolls rather than fight them....

As we grow older, body image may take on different meanings. Research suggests that many women may feel less stress about body image as they age. Some women, concluding that they no longer want to attract a man's attention using their appearance, express relief at the freedom they feel to carry around a few extra pounds or leave the house without makeup. Others, having entertained that possibility, understand their conscious choice to continue tending their appearance to be an expression of what makes them feel good rather than a response to societal pressure. Thus the body can become an instrument of aesthetic display for women who enjoy the artistry of earrings, scarves, color, and texture.

Recently, Ari Seth Cohen published a series of photographs of stylishly dressed women in their eighties and beyond who live on Manhattan's Upper West Side. Reminding him of his beloved grandmothers, who dressed with panache, he began to stop women on the street and ask to take their pictures. Their styles range from smart to wild, discrete to flamboyant. "It's a matter of enjoying it, and creating a painting. When you get dressed, you create something," explained one. Asked what she would tell a younger woman who was afraid to be different, ninety-one year old Royce Smithkin replied, "I would say, look in the mirror and find your own beauty. Look how wonderful your eyes are, and they can see! Look at your ears, they can hear…your mouth, it eats, it can whistle, can sing, it can kiss. You have so many beautiful things—use them!"

Uncovering Our Own Ageism

Many of us can remember the television soap commercials of the 1960s that featured mothers and daughters who looked so alike they could barely be told apart. The mothers' astonishing youthfulness

When I began to reflect on the way our bodies change and the way we feel about it, I found myself noticing the way I reacted to the physicality of the older people with whom I was sharing a subway car. Sometimes I was surprised by how visceral my reaction was. I don't want to be old like that! or That's an attractive old person; maybe I could grow old to look like that.

Recently I made a long-awaited trip to the Galapágos Islands, a remarkable and enchanting place with red- and blue-footed boobies (sea birds), unbelievably large tortoises, graceful sea lions, and brilliantly colored fish. The most prevalent creature, however, was the marine iguana. And every time I came across these dragon-like creatures I thought, That is a truly ugly animal. Talk about a visceral reaction.

It turns out that the marine iguanas of the Galapágos are wonderfully and uniquely adapted to their island environment. Over millennia, they have developed the capacity to dive to great depths, hold their breath for up to forty-five minutes, feast on ocean algae, and return with enough nutrients to feed their young—and that after making their way up an impossibly rugged and steep mountain of lava rock.

For quite a while after coming home, I thought about that reaction, about how often and how immediately it arose. Why did I want the iguanas to conform to my aesthetic sensibility?

— Linda

Reader Practices

Your Response to Images

Spend some time looking through magazines or on the Internet contemplating images of older men and women. If you use the Internet, which will give you many images to consider, you may want to try different browsers and enter different prompts, e.g., "older women," "elderly man/men," "old woman's body," "old man's hands," "portrait of old woman," etc. See which images stand out for you. You may want to copy and save them for contemplation, or share and reflect on them with a friend or group. Note your inner responses when you first glimpse an image, when you study it more contemplatively, and as you find some way to relate to it personally.

◈ What surprised you?

◈ Where can you find beauty in the aged face, body, skin?

◈ What kinds of shifts took place as you deepened your contemplation of a picture? Were there any discoveries? Insights?

◈ Do any memories from your youth arise as you notice your response to images of older people?

seemed to promise that using the proper face soap, lotion, or even dish detergent could be the long sought-after fountain of youth.

According to activist Cynthia Rich, alienation from our aging bodies derives from attitudes we developed when young. "Alienation from the body comes from the fact not only that we weren't always old, but also that we were ageist when we were young. We shared society's revulsion of aging flesh. We internalized the ageism."

Examining Our Judgments: A Story from the Talmud

Physical appearance is not an important value in most spiritual traditions, but the ancient rabbis were acutely aware of our judgments about people's appearances, as we see in this story, "The Caesar's Daughter."

> Because of his great wisdom, Rabbi Joshua was a welcome guest at the home of the caesar, who very often had discussions with him about the Jewish religion. In contrast to his great "beauty" in Torah, his outward appearance was by no means handsome.
>
> Once the caesar's daughter asked him: "How could it be that such marvelous wisdom is kept in an ugly vessel?!"
>
> Rabbi Joshua said to her: "Your father puts his choice wines in plain earthenware vessels."

Reflection Questions

◆ Consider when in your life someone whom you found physically unappealing turned out to embody another form of significant beauty (kindness, wisdom, artistry, intellect, etc.). Once you became acquainted with this other form of beauty, what happened to your original judgment?

◆ When are you most likely to have a visceral, negative response to someone's physical appearance? What physical characteristics or situations are likely to trigger this response? Think both about the pictures on the Internet that caught your attention and possible reactions you may have to the way young people present themselves (red mohawks, tattoos, piercings, etc.).

◆ What are the dangers in storing wisdom in a *beautiful* human container?

"What else would we put them in?" she said.

"You, who are so important, should by all rights put your wine in vessels of gold and silver."

She went and conveyed this to her father. He put the wine in vessels of gold and silver. It soured.

Only then did the caesar's daughter realize what Rabbi Joshua had been trying to convey to her. Wisdom does not always lead to outward beauty, and vice versa. (Talmud, *Ta'anit* 7a)

Reader Practices

Taking Note of Physical Appearance: Blessings

In Jewish prayer some blessings are said with regularity—for example first thing in the morning or over weekly Sabbath candles and wine. Others are recited when something unusual occurs. Examples of the latter include things like seeing a king or a volcano, and included in this category is a special blessing for seeing exceptionally beautiful people, trees, or fields:

> Blessed are You, Lord our God, King of the universe, who has such things in His world.
>
> *Baruch Atah, Adonai Eloheinu, Melech ha'olam, shekacha lo b'olamo.*

And one recited upon seeing exceptionally strange or unusual looking people or animals:

> Blessed are You, Lord our God, King of the universe, who makes creatures different.
>
> *Baruch Atah, Adonai Eloheinu, Melech ha'olam, m'shaneh hab'riyot.*

> ### Reflection Questions
>
> ◈ How does reciting a blessing when seeing something strange compare to reciting a blessing upon encountering something beautiful?
>
> ◈ How do you understand the different purposes of these two blessings?
>
> ◈ What do you think it would be like to adopt one or both of these blessing practices? What could it do for you?

It's not uncommon as we grow older to catch a glimpse of ourselves in the mirror and indeed feel we are viewing something strange and surprising. It's not quite the face we remember or imagine that we still wear. Or it may be a remembered face—but that of a parent or other relative.

Body and Soul

How are the mind and body related? How do they interact? What is the self—is it body or mind? Or, as Buddhists would suggest, is there really no such thing as self? The discussions generated by such questions may engage us from time to time, but most often they go in circles or they explain one mystery by creating another. There are no clear answers.

Consciousness and thought (themselves so very difficult to define, let alone understand) seem very different from anything physical. Yet they are related to the body, which responds to the prompts of our thoughts as surely as it shapes what we perceive and think and feel. Sometimes our experience seems bifurcated between thought and physicality; yet we also know ourselves as unified beings.

The dilemma becomes all the more profound when we consider the spiritual dimension, regardless of what we call it: the soul, or the authentic self, the divine spark, or one of so many other terms. But whether we consider our physical mind and body to be the sum total of who we are, or regard the body as the vessel for a transcendent soul, respect and care for the body is a part of almost every religious tradition.

> Once, Hillel the Elder, at the end of a lesson with his students, walked along the way with them.
>
> "Rabbi," they asked, "where are you going?"
>
> "To perform the will of my Creator."
>
> "What is it that you are going to do?"
>
> "To bathe in the bathhouse."
>
> "Is that a Divine precept?" they asked.
>
> "Yes, it is," he said. "Consider the following: The one who takes care of the statue of the king that stands in theaters and circuses, who cleans and polishes and makes offerings of food to it, is ennobled in its company and by this service to the king. Insofar as we are created in the Divine Image, we must take care of ourselves." (*Leviticus Rabbah*, 34:3)

Although primarily interested in a person's soul, Jewish teachers have never disregarded the importance of the body or the role it plays in connecting us to the divine. Blessings draw attention to the connection between embodied actions in the world and our spiritual yearnings. The Chasidim called this service "worship through our materiality." Bathing, eating, even sex, performed with conciousness, were considered forms of serving God.

Sixteenth-century kabbalist Isaac Luria taught that the body itself transforms energy from the material world and reunites it with the spiritual world:

You can mend the cosmos by anything you do—even eating. Do not imagine that God wants you to eat from mere pleasure or to fill your belly. No, the purpose is mending.

Sparks of holiness intermingle with everything in the world, even inanimate objects. By saying a blessing before you enjoy something, your soul partakes spiritually. This is food for the soul….So, when you are about to eat bread, say Hamotzi…then by eating, you bring forth sparks that cleave to your soul.

—4—

Cultivating Nourishing Relationships

At its core, life is not about things,
it is about relationships. It is the hands we
go on holding in our hearts at the end that
define the kind of life we have led.

—Sister Joan Chittister, *The Gift of Years*

From infancy we are shaped by interactions with others—first with our mother and father, then other family, and then with an expanding circle of friends, teachers, and acquaintances. In *The Healthy Aging Brain*, Dr. Louis Cozolino suggests that the brain is a "social organ" and confirms what we all know intuitively: that our relationships play a key role in maintaining the well-being of our bodies and our minds.

Relationships with family and close friends can be our most reliable and comforting bonds even as they can cause us the most anguish. One way or another, these are often the relationships that matter most, that help to form our sense of whether our lives have gone well or poorly.

At this time in our lives, many of our relationships may be changing. We may be caring for aging parents while we parent our own children. We may not have children and therefore worry about who will feel responsible for us as we grow older. We feel the loss of friends and family members who move away, become ill, or die. We may move to a place where we have no community. Or discover that those once close to us are no longer in our inner circle: perhaps the interests we once shared no longer hold the relationship together; perhaps a misunderstanding or misdeed damaged the relationship in a way that remains unhealed.

For all these reasons, this stage of life is an ideal time to reassess our current relationships. We can begin to ask ourselves new questions: Are we able to devote more time to nurturing relationships with those we love most? Can we let go of relationships that drain us, that fail to provide support or care in turn? Where will we find the energy and courage to make new friends? How can we dare be open to intimacy when loved ones have passed away? How can we learn to trust and enjoy our own company?

Friendship

The busy lives we have led—raising children, building careers, caring for older parents, participating in our community—have most likely loosened our ties to people with whom we were once close. At this point, we may want to recultivate these relationships. School reunions often precipitate the renewal of such friendships, and so does picking up the phone and making an unsolicited call, or reconnecting through social media. We may have to refresh our skills for developing new friendships, learning to reach out and take the initiative, making ourselves available again—perhaps even interesting—extending invitations, making an effort to find both the places that attract people our own age and events at which different generations interact.

Debra Rapoport, writing for the *Huffington Post* says:

> I am sixty-eight. I keep myself stimulated by maintaining
> my old friendships and also making a strong point to create
> new friendships with young people, twenty-five- to forty-
> year-olds, because they are young enough to know what is
> happening in the world and mature enough to appreciate

people in their seventies, eighties, nineties, and older. My partner Stan and I love to invite friends of different age groups over for fun and stimulating gatherings. We find that it's a way to keep the community diverse, growing, and engaged.

Reflection Questions

Ask yourself the following questions. Then write about the thoughts that come to you.

◆ Which of my friendships do I most cherish? Why?

◆ Which of my friendships feel more burdensome than fulfilling? Why? Do I have any desire or responsibility to maintain these friendships in spite of their burden?

◆ Am I continuing to make new friends? How and where do I meet new people? When is this easy for me? When is it difficult?

◆ What do I enjoy doing with friends?

◆ Do I have friends younger than myself? Older?

How Important Is Friendship?

The rabbis of the Talmud placed enormous importance on friendship. These sages lived during a time of tremendous upheaval, when values and sources of authority were shifting and unstable. Friendships were critical structures of support and meaning, just as they are for us today, when extended families no longer live in close proximity and when we are exposed to an ever-increasing variety of perspectives and values. A sad tale is told of the sage Choni Hame'agel, a sort of Jewish Rip Van Winkle.

In his time, Choni was greatly revered for his wisdom. One day he fell asleep for seventy years. When he awoke, no one of his own generation was left, and no one recognized him for who he was. Indeed, he was ridiculed for claiming to be Choni, whom everyone assumed had died many years before. Isolated and without anyone to affirm his identity, he prayed, "Either friendship or death" (Talmud, *Ta'anit* 23a).

Theologian Richard Rohr, in *Falling Upward*, notes the paradoxical quality of the way our relationships can change in the second half of life. "If you are on course at all, your world should grow much larger.... But I must tell you that, in yet another paradox, your circle of real

Reflection Questions

I have learned much from my teachers, but from
my friends even more than my teachers.
—Talmud, *Ta'anit* 7a

Consider a valuable lesson you have learned from a friend—either something your friend told you or something you learned from his or her behavior.

◈ Among your current friends, who is a teacher and friend at the same time? Can you articulate how this relationship might be different from other friendships you have?

◈ To whom are you or have you been a teacher and friend at the same time?

◈ In what ways do your friends affirm your identity? Challenge it? How does their friendship strengthen your sense of self? Which friends particularly do this for you?

◈ Besides affirming your sense of self, in what other ways are friendships important for you?

confidants and truly close friends will normally grow smaller, and also more intimate."

Author Andrew Sullivan contends that the importance of friendship is largely unappreciated as "a critical social institution" and "as an ennobling moral experience" that helps us become more fully realized human beings. He suggests that the gift of friendship is far greater than that of romantic love. Friendship, unlike most other relationships, is characterized by equality and autonomy; mutuality is inherent.

> A condition of friendship is the abdication of power over another, indeed the abdication even of the wish for power over one another. And one is drawn to it not by need but by choice. If love is about the bliss of primal unfreedom, friendship is about the complicated enjoyment of human autonomy. As soon as a friend attempts to control a friend, the friendship ceases to exist. But until a lover seeks to possess his beloved, the love has hardly begun.... [Friends] provide an acknowledgment not of the child within but of the adult without; they allow for an honesty which doesn't threaten pain and criticism which doesn't imply rejection. They promise not the bliss of the womb but the bracing adventure of the world. They do not solve loneliness, yet they mitigate it.

Three Levels of Friendship

The great medieval commentator Moses Maimonides identified three levels of friendship. The most basic level is a friendship based on mutual benefit, such as the relationship between two business partners. The intermediary level he describes as one of mutual trust, consisting of friendships based on pleasure (those with whom we can share interests and have a good time) and friendships based on trust (those with whom we can let down our defenses, express our opinions, questions, doubts, and fears without concern about being judged). Maimonides describes the highest level of friendship as one in which two people are united in their commitment to each other's growth or in shared ideals. In such a friendship, both friends aspire to grow in goodness, and they feel mutual responsibility for helping one another pursue that goal.

In his *Tales of the Hasidim*, Jewish philosopher and educator Martin Buber recounts a story in which Rabbi Moshe Leib of Sasoy is pondering an exchange he observed between two friends. One of the men had challenged his friend with the following accusation: "You say that you love me, but you do not know what I need. If you really loved me, you would know." Moshe Leib concludes that true love of a friend entails knowing the needs of the other and bearing the burden of his sorrow.

Reflection Questions

Try the Maimonides typology on your own friendships.

◆ Do you consider the first level—relationships explicitly based on formalized give-and-take—truly a friendship? When is it, and when is it not?

◆ Who among your friends would fall into the middle category, mutual trust, friendship based on enjoying time together?

◆ Do you think that the middle category—pleasure and trust— should be split into two categories? Are they fundamentally the same or different types of friendship? Among your friends, do some provide pleasure and others provide trust?

◆ In what ways does the highest level—friendship based on a mutual commitment to support one another's spiritual growth—differ from the others? Do you have any friends who fit this description?

Reflection Questions

- Do you agree that the measure of true friendship is being able to discern unstated needs, or is that too much to expect? How do *you* perceive really being known and really knowing another? When have you felt fully seen, genuinely known?

- Which of your friends or people in your family do you feel that you truly know?

- Are there people who are happy to be your friend but don't bother to get to know who you really are? (This could be a family member as well as a friend.) How do you feel when you are with him or her?

- Which relationships are important enough that you want to consciously nurture or revitalize them? Why?

- What is your experience with bearing a friend's sorrow? In what ways have friends been helpful—or unhelpful—in your own times of sorrow.

What Is Spiritual Friendship?

Most faith traditions place a great deal of importance on the company we keep. The journey to live a more conscious life can feel lonely without companions who share our questions and concerns. Growing into our best selves requires conscious attentiveness to all aspects of our lives, and our friendships can either foster or undermine us. People who become more attentive to spiritual interests in midlife often find that friends of longstanding are puzzled and sometimes even distressed. When this happens, we may discover that the concerns closest to our hearts cannot be shared with those who once supported us, and there is a period of spiritual loneliness until we connect with people who understand the new direction our life is taking. This is often when we feel most keenly the distinction that Maimonides was making. We continue to count on our old friendships for trust and for pleasure, but slowly begin to establish friendships based on supporting our mutual growth. In *Called to Question*, Sister Joan Chittister states, "I have no doubt whatsoever that being loved by someone is what gives us the ground we need from which to launch our lives beyond their small arenas."

Rabbi Nachman of Bratslav, an eighteenth-century Chasidic master, encouraged his followers to develop friendships with people who could share their deeper insights and questions:

> Talk over spiritual matters with your friends. Each of us has
> [our] own unique good point. Thus when two friends have
> a discussion, each can benefit from the other's good point.
> Sometimes your friend's good point may shine to you
> during a conversation that is outwardly about mundane
> topics—because at times even mundane conversations
> may give rise to new ideas and inspire you spiritually....
> By discussing spiritual matters regularly with your friends
> you will all be able to benefit from each other's good points.
> (*Likutei Moharan* I, 34)

The friendships we are considering now—those in which each party is committed to the refinement of the other—are rare and precious. Old friends, even perhaps our life partners, may be on different life paths. Some may be puzzled or even threatened by our new inwardness, and we may find that it has become harder to engage in the more superficial chitchat of social exchange. Maimonides's acknowledgment of different types of friendship is a helpful way of letting go of unrealistic expectations. We can continue to enjoy friendships based on pleasure and trust, or even maintain some because we feel responsible to the other, as we seek out spiritual friendships that will help us grow.

Reflection Questions

◆ Who has loved you in a way that encourages you to be your best, most authentic self? As you think about your current relationships, are there people you genuinely love and whose love for you feels transparent and trustworthy?

◆ Who invites you to grow, helps you reach self-understanding, supports you through dark times, and can tolerate your periods of regression?

◆ For whom are you that sort of friend or relative? What is it about you that allows you to fulfill that role?

Sometimes we may believe that it is too late, or it feels too awkward, to reawaken a dormant relationship. In his book *Unfinished Business,* Lee Kravitz recounts his experience of doing this repeatedly over a year that he devoted to reconnecting with both friends and relatives with whom he had lost contact. Initially it seemed like a daunting task; each "dead" relationship had its own point of discomfort, regret, confusion, or curiosity: a condolence call unmade, a small loan that had not been repaid, the poignant memory of an experience shared, a dispute among family members of the previous generation. In addition to discovering that it was not too late to make up for past failures in these relationships, Kravitz learned that while he had sought closure, the fruits of his efforts were many new openings. We invite you to experience this form of reviving the dead.

Reader Practices

A Spiritual Practice for Cherishing Relationships

Blessings generally remind us to be grateful. Beyond adequate food, shelter, and health, relationships are often our greatest treasures. How odd that we so rarely take time to feel or express gratitude for them.

Judaism brings us a blessing to recite when encountering someone we haven't seen or had contact with for a long time (traditionally thirty days). For such an occasion, we use the *Shehecheyanu* blessing that we introduced in chapter one:

> Blessed are You, Adonai our God, who reigns
> sovereign in the universe, who has given us life,
> sustained us in life, and brought us to this very minute.
>
> *Baruch atah, Adonai Eloheinu, Melech ha'olam,*
> *shehecheyanu v'kiymanu v'higi'anu laz'man hazeh.*

◆ Try saying this blessing when seeing a friend. How do you imagine it would feel to know that a friend is reciting this blessing upon encountering you?

◆ In previous eras, in which people often lived in smaller communities and relationships were generally face-to-face, thirty days was a long time to go without contact. What, for you, seems like a long time to be out of contact with a friend?

◈ In what ways is e-mail, texting, or social media "seeing someone"? In what ways is it not?

◈ What would your own personal blessing be for reconnecting with a friend?

There is also a blessing for a friend one has not seen in over a year:

Blessed are You, Adonai Our God, who reigns sovereign in the universe, Who revives the dead.

Baruch Atah, Adonai Eloheinu, Melech ha'olam,
m'chayeih hameitim.

Although we understand the phrase "revives the dead" to be used metaphorically here, it is nonetheless startling. And, we may indeed feel startled when we find ourselves reunited with someone who has been absent from our life for an extended period. Think about examples of this kind of reunion in your own experience. What feelings do they evoke?

◈ What relationships might be "dead" to you that you want to revive? Think about calling or arranging to see someone whom you haven't seen in a year. Consider reciting the Shehecheyanu, or a blessing of your own, either aloud or to yourself, when you meet or speak.

◈ Whom in your life do you need to tell that they are important to you, even if you see them often?

Family

Family relationships are complex, and expectations can run high. We have years of shared experiences and most likely different memories of those very same experiences. Deep in our hearts we believe that family relationships should be positive and that families should provide safety, caring, and love. As Robert Frost wrote in "The Death of the Hired Man," "Home is the place where, when you have to go there, they have to take you in."

Yet we all know how many opportunities there are for disappointment, misinterpretation, and anger mixed in with sweet memories, gratitude, and generosity. The patterns of behavior chiseled out of that long history don't always allow us to change or, even if we do change, to be recognized by others as having changed. In many cases the dramas that play out may truly belong to previous generations. And then there are families in which relationships are toxic and the rifts wrenching. These too need to be tended, although our choices of how to do so may be extremely limited. Sometimes all we can do is reconcile our own feelings, work on forgiveness, or pray for someone's welfare even though we are no longer in contact.

Life Brings Change

Whether or not Leo Tolstoy was correct when he wrote "Happy families are all alike; every unhappy family is unhappy in its own way," there do seem to be an infinite number of ways that family relationships challenge us, particularly as we enter new stages of life.

Not everyone in a family wants the same thing. Adolescents may seek to claim increased independence quite some time before parents are ready to relinquish their authority. Young adult children may expect continuing support—financial or emotional—longer than their parents had anticipated or consider appropriate. And so it is with the adjustment to growing older; we slide into these older years at different rates. These shifts affect sibling relationships as well. Does responsibility for aging parents fall to one child disproportionately or is it shared? If it is unequal, how comfortable is everyone with that arrangement? Can it be discussed openly?

When I was sixteen, I visited a friend who lived about an hour's drive from my family. We were at her synagogue when her rabbi approached me and asked, "Do you have an Uncle Sam and an Uncle Abe?" "Yes," I replied cautiously.

"And an Aunt Rose?" he asked.

"Yes."

"And is your father Morrie?" I nodded, feeling strange and a little frightened.

"I think we are cousins," he said.

It had never occurred to me that there were relatives whom I did not know. And a rabbi in the family!

When I got home and reported the conversation to my parents, my father replied, "That must be Dave! I haven't seen him since I was about eleven and he was six. There was some kind of argument between our fathers." That's as much as either Dave or my father knew.

My parents called Dave and his wife, and for the rest of my parents' lives the two families socialized and attended one another's simchahs (joyous celebrations). I stay in touch with Dave's children, though we live three thousand miles apart. Recently one of my daughters and her family moved to within half an hour of Dave's son, Mike, and his wife and children. Mike's children are close in age to my grandchildren. The two families now meet frequently for play and picnicking on weekends.

What was the argument about? No one seems to know. Whatever it was, we all grew up with far fewer cousins than we might have had—pieces of family history were lost.

— Linda

Reflection Questions

Take time now to think about your family relationships. Include in-laws, aunts, uncles, and cousins if they are part of your family web.

◆ With whom are you in frequent touch? How satisfying are these relationships? Are there expressions of closeness, caring, and love? How much tension or unpleasantness comes with these relationships?

◆ Are there parents, children, siblings or others with whom you have less contact than you would like?

◆ What often goes badly in your family interactions? How much of this stems from issues from childhood? How much from family members' temperaments and personalities? How much from yours?

◆ Who takes responsibility for what in your family? Who initiates and hosts family gatherings? Who takes care of aging parents? Who keeps family members in touch with one another? Are these responsibilities shared or spread among members in a satisfactory way? Are there struggles or resentments over this?

If you have family relationships that are toxic or severed, but you want to work on them, a good place to start is with your own feelings of sadness or disappointment for what is not as you would want it to be. Acknowledging these feelings will help you think about and plan more wisely for how you might initiate healing.

◆ What feelings arise when you think about the state of these relationships? Is there room for you to get past the anger and hurt?

◆ How much room for compassion do you have for those who may be most responsible for the rifts? (If your answer is little room, don't judge yourself harshly; just entertaining the question may be sufficient for now.)

Reflection Questions

◈ What significant changes have occurred in your family relationships that might be worth reflecting upon, either because they went smoothly or because they did not? What lessons can be learned from the past?

◈ What changes are you experiencing or do you anticipate? How have they affected or how will they affect your relationships with family members?

◈ What relationship changes do you hope for? What do you fear?

Spouses and Partners

Marriages and partnerships that have served us well may be tested as the focus of partners' lives shift. When children leave the nest, or work no longer provides a central identity or consumes the majority of a couple's time and energy, it is not uncommon for partners to gaze at each other and wonder, "Who is this person? What are we doing here?" Established patterns are gone—no car pools, soccer games, or late-night work sessions. Weekends, and perhaps daytimes too, require us to decide over and over again whether to spend more time together or pursue separate interests and relationships.

Some couples find that without the pressures of mid-adulthood they can rediscover a companion. Others realize that the years of pursuing separate interests and responsibilities have left them with little to share other than the routines of maintaining a household and social calendar. Now he wants to move to Florida where his golf buddies have relocated, and she has just been accepted into the prestigious docent-training program at the local art museum. He feels entitled to live his hard-earned leisure as he

As my husband approached retirement, I was treated many times to one version or another of the old saw, "I married him for better or worse but not for lunch!" I had my own set of concerns that seemed a bit more serious than lunch. I was still working, and my office was at home. If I was writing, I didn't want to be interrupted. If I was with a client, my husband would have to stay in his study and time his bathroom breaks between appointments. He talked incessantly about foreign travel; I had regular weekly commitments. I was also accustomed to his being out of town for work, and I relished the breaks from maintaining our two-person routines. He was so eager to move into this new stage of life; I worried that my ambivalence was disloyalty.

The transition turned out to be easier than I expected. My husband stays rather busy and handles his confinement when I am with clients with grace. It turns out that I am now the one who leaves town more often for work commitments. I haven't yet, however, found a good replacement for the periods of solitude I had when he was away.

— Linda

chooses; she fears having to choose between her marriage and the culturally stimulating urban life that she never had time to pursue.

For couples, retirement may shift many dimensions of a long-term relationship. If one partner but not the other is retiring, does the balance of responsibility for cooking, paying bills, and waiting for repairmen shift? Does decision-making power shift because one partner is now providing the primary income? Does one partner want to move to a warmer climate or be near the grandchildren, while the other is reluctant to leave the friends and lifestyle to which he or she is accustomed? Even more than retirement, illness or disability shakes up many of the patterns a couple has developed over their life together, all, of course, in the context of the anxiety and fear likely to accompany poor health.

Psychologists suggest that our expectations of marriage have changed. Until around 1850, American marriages revolved around food production, shelter, and protection from violence. While many couples established an emotional connection, that was not marriage's central purpose. In the century that followed, Americans had the new luxury of looking to marriage primarily for love and companionship. Now, expectations have shifted once again, and Americans look to marriage for self-discovery, self-esteem, and personal growth.

Meeting these new expectations requires insight and involvement with each other. It requires investing time and energy in the partnership, and this is hardly easy when both members of the couple are working and raising children. Without time and intentionality, couples may grow apart. Discontent may not become apparent or be articulated until later in life, when we begin to ask ourselves how we want to spend the rest of our days. This new stage of life offers the opportunity to reformulate a marriage, and through personal growth and hard work to create a new arrangement that nourishes both parties in ways they may not have imagined at an earlier stage of life.

A number of us enter into new romantic relationships after divorce or a partner's death. Inherent in such decisions are the complexity of blending the lives, families, interests, and assumptions of two fully formed adults. Much has to be given up or negotiated. Benefiting these later-in-life relationships is the likelihood that we know ourselves better than we did when we were younger. We may also know more about being patient and compassionate than we did in our youth. Harriet Rosen, a lay leader of the Jewish Women's Learning Center, interviewed older adults who had entered into later-in-life marriages for a study conducted by the Department of Jewish Family Concerns of the Union for Reform Judaism. To her surprise, she reported, the biggest problems that these couples said they had encountered were related to the reactions of their adult children.

Our Family of Origin

The Bible does a better job of demonstrating how siblings should not behave toward one another than it does of modeling ideal behavior. Think about it! The first pair of siblings is Cain and Abel. Cain kills Abel when he sees that Abel's sacrifice has been accepted and his has not. Jacob's wives, sisters Rachel and Leah, competed for Jacob's sexual favors and over fertility. Jacob's sons consider murdering their brother Joseph and ultimately sell him into slavery.

Even the relationship between Moses, Aaron, and Miriam, siblings who support one another and work toward a common goal, contains a story of Aaron and Miriam gossiping about their brother. How odd to have Biblical heroes who teach us less about how to get along than how hard it can be for siblings to support and befriend one another!

If we look at these ancestral stories, we also see that parents often play a role in these troubled relationships. Isaac's favoritism and Rebecca's duplicity set up the competition between their sons Jacob and Esau. Jacob shows unchecked favoritism toward Joseph and sets the brotherly contention in play.

Perhaps the point of these stories is that every family, no matter how whole, has its share of resentments, misunderstandings, and painful patterns of behavior. We all know parents we consider loving, intelligent, and attentive who have one or more deeply troubled children; and we also know individuals who emerged from seriously dysfunctional families intact and well adjusted. The more we learn about the complex ways that nature and nurture interact to form personality, the more we should release ourselves from the guilt or anger that often accompanies our disappointment in the way that relationships in our family have unfolded.

Turning problematic relationships around requires hard work. Sometimes that hard work creates change—mends the troubles of the past—and sometimes we must surrender, concluding that the rifts of the past simply cannot be healed. Acknowledging that family relationships are often delicate and require careful tending can help us to appreciate and celebrate those that do fulfill our expectations of closeness, mutual caring, and loyalty.

Relationships with parents, children, brothers, and sisters go through different phases; they can worsen or improve, grow more intimate or more distant. These shifts often occur in tandem with major life events. For example, illness or the need to care for aging parents may bring siblings together, motivating them to let go of old stories and resentments as they work together. These same situations may trigger discord, sometimes based on old patterns of family interaction, long-held jealousies, conflicting personality traits, or disagreement over basic values. It can be helpful to develop a clear assessment of both the benefits and the challenges that result from a changing family structure and the need for everyone to attempt to adjust to the resulting new relationships.

Grandparenthood

There is an old saying that grandparents and grandchildren get along because they have a common enemy, and it may be equally true that adult children and their parents often get along better because they so deeply share their love and hopes for the next generation. Grandchildren give both generations a joint project. How life affirming and fulfilling it can be when this joint project allows us to align ourselves with our adult children and their children.

Grandchildren also create much room for disagreement about roles, values, strategies, and power. We surely do not want our grandchildren to be pawns in the reenactments of old parent-child battles. As the elders in these multigenerational relationships, we can more consciously bring patience, empathy, and self-insight to interactions that are challenging. We hope for the wisdom to open the doors of healing when necessary and remain humble about our ability to see truth and to know what is needed.

For the first six months after I became a grandparent, I lived in a state of radical amazement. The world looked sunnier than I had ever remembered it. One of my friends observed that I was "besotted." Six years later, I would estimate that this is still my primary state when I am with my now four grandchildren. At least 80 percent of the time! Sometimes the cleverness of their meltdowns and manipulations evoke wonder too, but it's mixed with dabs of frustration, puzzlement, and occasional anger. I get to practice all over again those lessons that I learned as a parent and see that I am indeed more patient and less reactive than when I was younger. I marvel at how much wiser my daughters and sons-in-law are than I was at their stage of life, and that makes me feel hopeful in spite of the greater difficulty of raising children now than thirty years ago.

— Linda

Becoming a grandparent means seeing one's own children step into their positions as custodians of the future. Linda recalls the rabbinic story that she recited at the ceremonies celebrating each of her daughters' births:

> When God was about to give the Torah to the Jewish people, God said, "Present me good guarantors, and I will give it to you." The people of Israel said, "We will give you our ancestors, Abraham, Isaac, and Jacob, Sarah, Rebecca, Rachel, and Leah; they'll vouch for us and be our guarantors." God said, "Your ancestors are not sufficient. Bring me good guarantors that you will keep it, and I will give it to you." They said, "Lord of the Universe, our prophets will be our guarantors." But God said, "Your prophets are not sufficient. Bring me good guarantors that you will keep it, and I will give it to you." When Israel was about to receive the Torah, God said to them: "I am giving you the Torah.

Present me good guarantors that you will keep it and I shall give it to you." They said: "Indeed, our children will be our guarantors."

The Holy One said: "Your children are good guarantors. For their sake I give the Torah to you." (*Song of Songs Rabbah* 1:24)

Seeing our children and grandchildren as custodians of the future shifts our role and self-understanding; we move into the stage of life that Erikson spoke of as generativity. If we are wise and humble we will ask ourselves what we can do to support their growth and well-being without imposing our own sense of what their futures should look like. We see how easy it is to intervene too much, and on the other side to fail to step in when help is genuinely needed. It may feel like a delicate balance to turn adulthood over to our children, and if we are wise we will ask ourselves why: If they are the guarantors, why do we still sometimes feel like we should be the guardians? What ego investment do we have in what remains of our role as parents? Are we reluctant to relinquish our role in their upbringing because whatever comes next for us is so ill-defined?

Grandparenting is actually a role that affords us great liberty. We can be playful. We can turn our own passions—for camping, or dancing, or word games—into joyful teaching. In grandchildren we may enjoy an audience for personal and family stories, and eager ears for our sage advice. We model our values—whether the importance of family cohesion, love of books and learning, or a commitment to social justice. We give and receive unconditional love.

Perhaps it is the enormity of the generational difference that allows grandparents and grandchildren to listen to one another with wonder and curiosity. We can more easily express bafflement at each other's lives and experiences. And while as grandparents we provide a personal link to the past, our grandchildren give us a glimpse into a distant future that we will not live to see.

Single and Childless

Being single in a society built largely around marriage comes with its own set of challenges, particularly if one is without a primary intimate relationship. Remaining single has generally meant not having children, though this is becoming less the case.

People who have been single for a substantial part of their lives are likely to be adept at initiating, investing in, and sustaining relationships

Reader Practices

Looking at Relationships

Answer these in your journal. Pick two family relationships in your life, one that is troublesome and one that is rewarding. Go through the following steps with one and then the other. (Consider doing this at two different times so that you are able to contemplate each more fully.)

◈ Describe the relationship in as much detail as you can. Emphasize your feelings and the thoughts that come to mind more so than the concrete details of the story. Try to capture the dynamics of this relationship.

◈ When you are satisfied with what you have written, take a few breaths. Then, try to write about this relationship from the other person's perspective. What would he or she write?

◈ What steps might you take to improve the relationship that is troublesome and to further acknowledge and honor the one that is rewarding?

◈ Consider making a plan to work on one or both of these relationships.

with family, friends, and others who share their interests. Many create interlocking circles of friends who know one another well and act much as an extended family, celebrating holidays together, looking out for one another in times of sickness, motivating each other to grow. For those newly single, relearning the skills of making new friends can be a challenge. Sometimes it is possible to be welcomed into an already established circle of family-like friends.

Networks of relationship and support exist in many arenas of our lives, but they are particularly likely to develop with siblings, cousins, nephews, and nieces. Many singles act as the adopted aunts and uncles to friends' children, adding to the number of people who shower love on a child. They introduce children to activities and interests outside their parents' realm, and model alternative ways of seeing and interacting with the world. Later they may become the people to whom a young adult can turn without the history and baggage of the parent-child relationship. Wherever there is an opportunity to expand family relationships—biological or chosen—it provides an opportunity to enhance the richness that the nuclear family cannot offer on its own.

Parents and Adult Children: Honor, Reverence, and Their Limits

Parents are powerful shapers of our sense of self and self-worth. They provide our first relationships; on some level we never stop wanting their unconditional love. Because these bonds are so primal, our interactions with our parents have greater impact than any other, save perhaps with a spouse or life partner. Moreover, though it may seem otherworldly, these relationships continue long after our parents have died.

These relationships also have enormous societal importance, and they come with both explicit and implicit expectations. For many, these relationships have the resonance of the commandment "You shall honor your father and your mother."

The sages of the Talmud recognized the potential complexity of this seemingly simple exhortation and had many discussions about its meaning. Their analysis began with the observation that when the commandment is proclaimed in Exodus and repeated in Deuteronomy, the verb used is *honor*. However, when the obligation toward parents is reiterated in the book of Leviticus, it switches to *revere*. What, the rabbis asked themselves, was the difference? "What is reverence and what is honor? Reverence means that he [the son] must neither stand nor sit in his [father's] place, nor contradict his words, nor tip the scale against him. Honor means that he [the son] must give him [the father] food and drink, clothe and cover him, and lead him in and out" (Talmud, *Kiddushin* 31b).

In other words, the rabbis concluded, reverence is about maintaining a parent's dignity, and honor has to do with providing for his or her concrete needs.

We can imagine times when taking care of a parent's physical needs conflicts with attending to his or her dignity, as when children believe that a parent's safety may be jeopardized by living alone, and the parent insists on remaining in his or her home rather than moving to an assisted-living facility. Such conflicts are often viewed as power struggles between parties who are stubbornly holding onto irreconcilable views. In most cases, it is more helpful to ask ourselves how we can find a way to balance worthy but competing values. With that clarity, it may be easier to make a decision about which value needs to be compromised for the sake of the other or how both can be at least partially fulfilled.

We have seen this kind of dilemma play out between one of our students, Henry, and his father. Henry was concerned with honor, his father's physical well-being; his father was seeking reverence, the dignity of making his own determination of how he wanted to live his remaining years.

Henry was very concerned when he learned that his aging parents were planning a long cruise. His father's cancer was in remission, but Henry still tried to dissuade them from taking this extended trip to exotic ports, knowing that medical resources would be limited. Henry was dismayed at his father's stubbornness and ran through his arguments against the cruise again and again, hoping that his father would see the light. Finally, Henry set up an appointment with his father's physician. Only then did he learn of his father's decision to cease further treatment. His father was aware that this would be a final voyage, but he had chosen to live out whatever time he had left "enjoying life," rather than taking on another round of chemotherapy. Henry's parents were approaching the trip from a wholly different framework than Henry imagined. The parents had hoped to spare their son an extended period of sadness over his father's impending death; they had not understood how anxious their decision had made him. Once all these feelings and considerations were shared, it became easier to make a joint decision about which value needed to be compromised for the sake of the other. Henry was able to give his blessing to the trip. The postcards he received from around the world recorded his parents' delight at being able to spend their last months together on this "dream trip."

Reflection Questions

◈ As a child, what do you do for your parents that would be a sign of reverence and what as a sign of honor? (If your parents are deceased, think about the ways you interacted with them when they were alive.)

◈ As a parent, what do you need or want from your children? To what do you feel entitled? Are you reluctant to accept either signs of honor or concrete help when they are offered? If so, why? If not, why not?

Honoring the Desires of Others

See if you can identify a conflict with another person in your own life—any person—from a values point of view. Ask yourself what, at the deepest level, are you really trying to achieve and what seems to be important to the other person involved. Find a way to have a conversation with that person so you can assess the validity of your assumptions. Sometimes, by compromising or even a simple acknowledgment, we can honor the desires of others, even if we cannot find a way to meet them.

Conflicting Obligations

The twelfth-century sage Maimonides was keenly aware of the potential for conflicting values and emotions in the parent-adult child relationship, and he tried to provide guidance for such situations. For example, Maimonides ruled that if one's spouse cannot abide one's parents, the primary obligation is to the spouse.

> A man who tells his wife, "I do not want your father and mother, brothers and sisters to come to my home" is to be obeyed. She should visit them in their home monthly and on every holiday, and they should come to her only in circumstances such as illness or birth, for a man is not to be forced to bring others into his domain.
>
> Also, if the wife says, "I do not want your mother and sister to come to my [home], and I will not live in a shared courtyard with them, because they cause me grief," she is to be obeyed. (*Mishneh Torah, Hilchot Ishut* 13:14-15)

Maimonides also suggests that children should be able to set limits on their obligations if their parents are too difficult or too severely incapacitated for them to provide the needed care: "If the mind of his father or mother is affected, one should make every effort to indulge the vagaries of the stricken parent, until God will have mercy on the affected. But if the condition of the parent has grown worse and the son is no longer able to endure the strain, he may leave his father or mother provided he delegates others to give the parent proper care" (*Mishneh Torah, Hilchot Mamrim* 6:10).

But when is the strain great enough for a child to legitimately decide, "This is too much for me; I need help"? That is the question that torments so many of us with parents who are aging and increasingly infirm.

Where Is the Line, and Who Draws It?

Although the traditional focus is on children's obligations toward their parents, the obligations in fact run both ways. Parents are expected to restrain themselves. As Maimonides explains: "The parent is forbidden to impose too heavy a yoke upon [the children], to be too exacting

Reflection Questions

◆ Have you ever experienced a conflict between your obligation to one of your parents and to a spouse, partner, child, or sibling?

◆ How did you handle your conflicting loyalties? Did you fully understand each of the conflicting values you were trying to balance or did you make an instinctive decision under pressure?

◆ How do the choices you made at the time look to you now?

◆ If those choices felt wise, how can the experience help you with similar dilemmas in the future? If you feel that you could have handled the situation more skillfully, what could help you do so in the future?

with them in matters pertaining to his honor, lest he put a stumbling block before them. He should forgive them and shut his eyes, for a parent has the right to forgo the honor due him" (*Mishneh Torah, Hilchot Mamrim* 6:8-9).

Family situations can be extraordinarily difficult to sort out. Here are some poignant examples that our students have shared with us over our years as wise aging leaders:

- "My parents rejected me when I married a non-Jew. Years later my mother let me know that she was sorry for the way they had behaved, but my father has never relented. He's dying now. My mother wants me to come—without my wife. I don't feel I owe my father anything. And what about my wife's feelings?"

- "I showed a collection of my poetry to a friend. He called my poetry deeply moving. He said, 'Aviva, although you do not make it explicit in any way, some will read this and know your father abused you. It is likely to be mentioned in reviews of your poetry.' I take the commandment to honor your parents very seriously. I've decided that I can't publish these poems while my parents are still alive."

- "My children only see one another when they come for my birthday. I know that their resentment of each other goes back to their childhoods. I wish I had done a better job of getting them to be friends with one another. Should I ask them to promise me that they will see each other at least once a year after I die? I wonder whether I'll just be adding to their list of resentments."

- "My parents have decided to move from their modest home of many years to a luxurious assisted-living facility, far nicer than the house they have lived in. They have asked us for a substantial contribution to the monthly fee. If we agree to anything close to this amount, it will mean that we cannot help our children purchase their first homes. My parents seem to think that we are obliged to help them finally live in "such a lovely place." We feel enormously torn. We want to help our children, but we also want to show respect to our parents."

Talking these situations through with trusted family members or friends can provide support and guidance. But there are often no adequate answers to questions of conflicting loyalties.

When You Don't Know What to Do: Try a Clearness Committee

A clearness committee allows one to access one's own deepest wisdom with the gentle and compassionate support of others. The process has its origins in the Quaker community, dating back to the mid-1600s. It developed because Quakerism is nonhierarchical; there is no rabbi or priest from whom to get the authoritative answer about how to handle a problem. Each person is responsible for his or her own judgments. In addition, the Quakers were a tight-knit community, dedicated to helping each other gain clarity about challenging issues. One might imagine that when Moses gathered up the seventy elders in the Tent of Meeting because the burden of leading the Israelite people alone was too great, he was really calling a clearness committee. It is a remarkable resource for addressing personal problems, questions, and decisions that just seem too big.

The premise of the clearness committee process is that we all have the inner resources, an inner teacher some call it, to find our way through complicated problems. When we are confused, conflicted, anxious, sad, or even overly excited, however, these emotions block our access to our own wisdom. We are likely to be overwhelmed by unexamined assumptions, judgments, and the myriad of conflicting advice that we have received from others or from our own divided mind.

A clearness committee, which is described on this book's website, http://www.behrmanhouse.com/wise-aging, provides a structure within which we can call on our own inner wisdom with the guidance of others, who are not there to analyze or advise, but rather to help us access our own values and inner resources.

Loneliness and Solitude

Loneliness, which involves feelings of separation from others, isolation, even abandonment, is often cited as one of the worst problems afflicting older people. It can affect our physical as well as emotional health. Loneliness can range from slight sadness to devastating depression.

Especially when severe, it's important to consider its sources. If we are grieving a death or a move or a divorce, loneliness is a natural part of that process, and natural healing eventually will help us regain our equilibrium. For those with a genetic inclination toward depression, there are a variety of helpful forms of therapeutic aid available. But if you are simply lonely, consider reaching outward as a spiritual practice, much as reaching inward is a form of practice.

Acknowledging the problem of loneliness in our later years, Rabbi Abraham Joshua Heschel wrote: "the way to overcome loneliness is not by waiting to receive a donation of companionship but rather by offering and giving companionship and meaning to others." In the later stages of life, even though we may be more limited, there are many ways to combine our desires to be of service and to connect with others. Rich relationships often develop as we work together to promote political causes we care about or engage in hands-on service to others, such as preparing food in a soup kitchen. Mentoring someone younger in a field we know about is a way of developing intergenerational relationships, and in many mentoring programs mentors meet together to share common interests and observations.

Let us also distinguish solitude from loneliness, for they are quite different. In solitude, we enjoy our own company, and that can be deeply satisfying—sometimes soothing, sometimes stimulating. In our younger years, some of us often longed for more solitude than our lives allowed, crowded as they were with the demands of other people. Others of us have never quite known what to do with ourselves when alone. And some of us have virtually run away from solitude.

Reader Practices

A Spiritual Practice for Solitude

Rabbi Nachman of Bratslav introduced a powerful practice that is still followed by Jewish seekers of all denominations today. He called it *hitbodedut,* which is best translated as "self-seclusion" or "being alone with oneself," although the awkwardness of the English hardly conveys its power. This practice involves being fully alone, either in an outdoor setting or indoors, and speaking out loud—with no witnesses or listeners—about the issues, concerns, troubles, or opportunities on one's mind. This practice is a form of stream-of-consciousness communication, which Nachman referred to as "pouring out one's heart."

Find a secluded place (your car, your backyard, an open field, your bedroom, the shower) to talk out loud. Speak, out loud, about your most private thoughts and feelings, frustrations, and hopes. No subject is too mundane. Just keep talking, even if all you are saying is "This is ridiculous. I don't know what to say." Just be with the experience. Allow your words and your emotions to go wherever they need. Sighing, crying, shouting, and weeping were all forms of expression that Nachman assumed might accompany a person's words. That's why finding a safe, secluded place was an important part of his recommendation. It is remarkable how this practice can lead to unexpected insights and cathartic release.

Although Nachman prescribed *hitbodedut* as a daily practice, it can be very powerful as an occasional practice done for twenty minutes. It is likely to feel awkward at the beginning, and so it is important to provide enough time to get through any initial resistance. And of course allow yourself to engage for longer if you are in the flow.

Turning Solitude into a Practice

While formal *hitbodedut* may be too intense as a regular practice for most of us, there are many other ways of turning solitude into a spiritual practice. Simple forms of self-seclusion can have a profound impact on our sense of calm and wholeness.

◈ Fix your favorite beverage and sit in a space you particularly like—a comfortable chair, opposite a favorite painting, among family photographs. Simply sit and enjoy the space, the quiet, the sounds from outside, the patterns of light and shade, the colors around you.

◈ Prepare a bath that feels slightly luxurious. You might turn down the electric lights and light candles. Use soaps, gels, or lotions with fragrances you enjoy. Take your time.

◈ Walk your dog mindfully. Notice the various smells outside, the sun and the shadows, the temperature and the breeze. Smile, nod, or say hello to whomever you pass. (Of course you can do this without a dog too!)

◈ Take a book you enjoy to a restaurant and savor the meal as an experience, not just a way to ward off hunger. Try to fully taste every bite of food. Enjoy noting the variety of people around you. Pay attention to any negative self-judgment that arises, especially if you are unaccustomed to eating out alone. If your self-talk voice is a critical one, consider its origin rather than taking its message at face value.

◈ Use your journal. Write about some of the reflection questions in this book or use your journal as a form of written *hitbodedut* or stream-of-consciousness writing.

The truth of the matter is that as we grow older, solitude may no longer be just a choice. Friends die or move away, we relocate to new communities ourselves, and physical frailties keep us from activities that formerly brought us into contact with others. Consequently, it may be wise to befriend solitude so that we know what to do with it when it is forced upon us. Even if we have wished for more solitude at earlier times in our lives, some of us may be surprised to find that we now experience it with a sense of emptiness and face a steep learning curve in appreciating being alone with ourselves.

Theologian Richard Rohr suggests that solitude "is necessary to unpack all that life has given and taken from us." Aging is a time for integrating our life experience. That process often requires periods of aloneness and silence, which need not mean being lonely. We need this time alone, frequently in relative silence, to discover our innermost thoughts and feelings. What would our heart really say if it were given the chance to speak in its still, soft voice? How do we find our own depths and listen to our soul's inner wisdom?

It is likely that we will experience both loneliness and comfort in our solitude, as we may have at other times in our lives. The journals of poet and writer May Sarton testify to the way we may experience alternating feelings about the time we spend alone. Sarton's six published journals were written over a period of two decades, from age fifty-nine to eighty; consequently we see her go through many cycles of intimacy, loneliness, and solitude. At times she craves solitude to "sort things out," which feeds her work as a writer. We hear her luxuriate in solitude: "I am here alone for the first time in weeks to take up my 'real life' again at last…. When I am alone the flowers are really seen: I can pay attention to them." "There are compensations for not being in love—solitude grows richer for me every year."

We also read of her fear of loneliness. "My need to be alone is balanced against my fear of what will happen when suddenly I enter the huge empty silence if I cannot find support there." Loneliness, she claims, can be "like starvation," and she takes note of the bareness she feels at receiving an advance copy of a book of her poetry but having no one with whom to immediately share it.

Sarton recognizes that loneliness is not necessarily the result of being alone but can also result from not being in touch with oneself: "Because I am well I no longer suffer from the acute loneliness I felt all spring and summer until now. Loneliness because in spite of all the kindnesses and concerns of so many friends there was no one who could fill the hole at the center of my being—only myself could fill it by becoming whole again. It was loneliness in essence for the *self*."

Here Sarton reminds us that there is an existential form of loneliness that we may occasionally dip into. Centuries of philosophers, writers and poets, and others have described it, often suggesting that it is an inescapable dimension of human life lived most deeply. Theologians tell us that only connection to the divine—or the divine within—can fill this felt void. Rabbi Joseph Soloveitchik described it as the experience of "the lonely man of faith." Many of us never, or only rarely, encounter this depth of

Reflection Questions

◈ How would you characterize your own history with solitude? Does it feel fruitful? Is it difficult? What do you enjoy doing in solitude? What do you do with your loneliness when it arises?

◈ Do you need more solitude or more company in your life? How could you go about fulfilling either of these needs? What part of you might have to stretch to do so?

◈ How do you understand what it means to be in—or out of—touch with oneself? What memories do you have of times when you have experienced these states?

loneliness, but should we happen upon it, there is solace in knowing that this too is part of the human experience.

Rabbi Nachman considered this a most important form of prayer. But one need not believe that there is a listening God for it to be a powerful practice. We can call out to the source of life, or to the universe, or into the nonjudgmental silence. The point is to let go of whatever inhibitions might prevent us from voicing and thereby discovering what is true for us in that moment.

Holding the Larger Picture: Interdependence

Albert Einstein had an understanding of the interconnectedness of time and space that few of us can truly grasp, but his insights into how we are all interrelated in daily life was beautifully simple:

> What an extraordinary situation is that of us mortals....We exist for our fellow-men—in the first place for those upon whose smiles and welfare all our happiness depends, and next for all those unknown to us personally with whose destinies we are bound by the ties of sympathy. A hundred times every day I remind myself that my inner and outer life depend on the labours of other men, living and dead, and that I must exert myself in order to give in the same measure as I have received and am still receiving.

We live in a web of dynamic relationships and interdependence—we live within the natural world and with each other. Yet our society prizes individualism. As we grow older, fear of dependence causes many of us to struggle, sometimes unreasonably, to maintain our sense of independence. Being able to do things for ourselves can provide a feeling of control and normalcy; it affirms our strength and continued vitality. We imagine that so long as we don't rely on others, we can fend off feeling helpless or irrelevant.

Stories abound of people whose denial of aging extends to refusing to take medication, wear hearing aids, or stop driving. The wisdom of age teaches us to let go of these bids for false self-sufficiency.

As difficult as it may be to accept a seat from a stranger on the subway, we may struggle much more with accepting the help offered by those closest to us. And even more problematic can be asking them for help.

It is difficult to have the tables turned. Having spent the better portion of our adult years nurturing and supporting our children, it feels strange to be on the receiving end. It can feel painful to have so little to offer our independent children, just as they begin to have more and more to offer us. Hasn't that been *our* role? Getting old doesn't diminish our desire to be the nurturers. Consequently, when our children insist on

The first time a young woman stood up to offer me her seat on the subway I was horrified. Do I look that old? Catching my breath, I smiled and said, "No thank you, I am fine." The next few times the same thing occurred, I had the same reaction. But then I accepted with a big smile, feeling genuine gratitude. Sitting comfortably in the seat, my bag in my lap and not straining my shoulder, I realized that even though I was perfectly capable of standing, this was actually a relief. After all, seventy is not the new fifty. As I reflected further I saw that in fact I was allowing this young person to practice generosity and respect for her elders. By accepting the offer graciously I was also modeling reciprocity. And I realized that for many, many years I had stood up to offer my seat, my arm, my time, my concern to an older person, and now it was my turn to be on the receiving end.

— Rachel

◆ When do you find yourself reluctant to accept offers of help? Why do think that is?

◆ Is it easier or more difficult for you to be dependent on family members, on friends, or on people in helping professions? Why?

helping, we may react just the way Rachel did on the subway: "No thank you, I'm fine," or even "How dare you think I need...?" But of course, we *do* need. The lack of independence is what feels so frightening.

Philosopher Sara Ruddick includes "wise independence" in her essay on the virtues of age, which she defines as "independence joined with willingness to acknowledge one's limitations and accept help in ways that are gratifying to the helper." She sees wise independence not as a virtue to be achieved and then simply lived out, but rather as an ongoing struggle between two temptations: on the one hand to give up, become passive, stop making or carrying out plans, and turn ourselves over entirely to the care of others; and on the other, to deny our limitations, refusing help when it is needed, insisting on maintaining control over everything, and asserting our will over even small matters. Neither path is wise. Neither respects the fact that two are involved—the elder and the helper—both of whom have needs, feelings, concerns, and goals.

The elder needs to recognize that the consequences of refusing help may extend to the helper as well as oneself. If our rejection of help results in a fall, a burn, or other injury, those who love and care for us are likely to suffer guilt, frustration, and the pain of seeing us in pain—and our care may then require more of their time. Likewise the helper also needs to find a balance between hovering, which disempowers the elder, and allowing an elder's "willful assertiveness" to result in injury. That is why

A Spiritual Practice for Asking

Ask yourself the following questions.

◆ Where in your life is there an opportunity to relinquish independence?

◆ Think about an area in your life in which you could accept or ask for help. What kind of "sacrifice" would you be making to receive help? What would be the incentive for asking?

Then make a commitment to try asking for help, for something that would be meaningful to you. At least a limited amount of help for a limited time. Take note of how you feel and what you learn from your reaction to asking.

Ruddick understands this kind of virtue to be relational; we achieve wise independence when all parties remain aware of the desires and the consequences for others as well as themselves.

This requires ongoing effort and negotiation, especially as circumstances change and relationships require adjusting. Uncertainty in this kind of relationship is inevitable, and thus it is important to regard what Ruddick calls "outlaw emotions—impatience, resentment, anger, disappointment"—as part of the process rather than failures of the relationship. These emotions tell us that the parties need to find a new balance between holding on and letting go, assertion and acceptance, intervention and letting be.

Although some adult children offer their parents help in a patronizing way, perhaps out of their own discomfort with shifting roles, or perhaps out of lack of skill, most offer out of loving concern and the genuine desire to help. Do we realize that when we refuse help, our children may feel frustrated or even fearful of the consequences? When we meet their

well-meaning attempts to help us with anger or resistance, the help originally offered from a place of generosity may begin to feel to them more
like grudging duty.

And adult children may feel as fearful and confused as we do; we are
all wrestling with changes that no one welcomes. Here is where we, the
elders, can assert our parental role. How can our children know what it
feels like to be growing older? They are at a completely different stage of
life, not even close to ours. At least we know something about that, and
we can help. We can't expect them to understand our feelings and concerns unless we take the lead and speak openly.

We may find ourselves wanting to raise these issues with our children
now, while we are healthy and self-sufficient, while we have the luxury of
beginning the conversation "in theory." We want them to know that we
do worry about being a burden, to tell them what we have done to secure
our financial future so that we will be able to pay for the care we might
need, but that we may become dependent in other ways. We want to
acknowledge that we will need them to be forthright with us so that we
are not haunted by fears of being resented or becoming a burden.

Two of our teachers in this area are women we have never met, Sheila
Solomon Klass and her daughter Perri. Sheila Klass was a professor of
English at Borough of Manhattan Community College, City University
of New York. Below is an excerpt from one of her online posts, "A Very
Ungrateful Old Lady," which was printed in the New York Times.

> I am a legally blind octogenarian. I have wonderful adult
> children who often help me, but I can never accept their
> help gracefully.
>
> It is a terrible thing to be a burden. They say I am not,
> but I know better....
>
> ...My busy children are kind beyond measure, but I am
> uncomfortable in these situations. And being uncomfort-
> able makes me sharp and unpleasant....
>
> My children try so hard....

So why can't I just be grateful? Why am I so resistant, so irrational, so difficult and unpleasant? Because burdens aren't grateful, any more than they're graceful.

It is not that I am unaware of all that is being done for me. Quite the contrary, I am painfully aware of it....

...My life is now directed by other people the way it was when I was a child. That they are people who love me is irrelevant.

Sorry, kids....

Shortly after she died, her daughter Perri wrote her own blog post called "She Wasn't So Ungrateful After All."

...I'm not sure that everyone is ready for certain kinds of honesty from people toward the end of life....

And my mother's character was fixed; she was one of the most interesting people I've ever known, and one of the toughest. She was irreducibly and completely herself— indomitable, admirable, and intermittently irrational. And she would probably have said the same about me. We recognized each other, and we argued, and though I am younger and stronger and possessed of a medical degree that she regarded with all the awe that goes into that large repertoire of Jewish doctor jokes, I didn't win most of the arguments....

...The gratitude I feel now, and felt then, [is] for getting the chance to be there. Man, I loved her. Man, I loved taking care of her. I wish I had been able to do it better, and I certainly wish I had been able to do it longer....

...I didn't want a different kind of gratitude, or anything else that would have compromised her voice and changed the conversation....

Reflected in the longer versions of these essays, others by Sheila, and a book the two women wrote together is a wonderfully open dialogue that acknowledged their frustrations, their capacity for wise introspection, and the enormity of the love and respect they had for one another.

Over and over again, the accounts of adult children who serve as their parents' caretakers confirm that although it is difficult and painful to accompany parents on this journey, most are grateful for the opportunity to do so. They write about the intimate conversations they had, and what they learned about a parent's or their family's past. They talk about the preciousness of stroking an arm with papery skin or being able to give a foot massage to distract their loved one from pain. They express gratitude for learning that they have the capacity for loving service, and, perhaps most important, they express gratitude for being brought into touch with the beauty and the fragility of life.

We do need each other—physically, psychologically, emotionally, and spiritually. None of us is whole without others. Wouldn't it ease both the process of aging and serve as a model for those younger than ourselves if we could acknowledge this gracefully? Can we learn to see ourselves embedded in a fulfilling cycle of interdependence, living in a flow of

Reflection Questions

As we do this work with ourselves, it can be helpful to look at the roots of our feelings about dependence and independence.

◈ Think back, first on your childhood and then on adulthood. Where have you fallen on the spectrum of dependence, independence, and interdependence in different dimensions of your life?

◈ Have you always been fiercely independent, happiest when collaborative, or varied in the extent of your independence by necessity or by the nature of your work?

relationships throughout our life stages? We were once the caregivers, the providers, the teachers; now we are entitled to be given care. At the same time, we may indeed be continuing to give, albeit in very different ways. As Thomas Merton said, "The whole idea of compassion is based on a keen awareness of the interdependence of all these living beings, which are all part of one another, and all involved in one another."

Ruth and Naomi: Interdependence over Time

One of the most instructive texts on the beauty of interdependence is the book of Ruth. One of the many different ways it can be read is as a tale of the shifting pattern of interdependence between Ruth and her mother-in-law Naomi. Through that lens, it is a remarkable tale of compassion.

Because of a famine, Naomi, her husband, and two sons move to the land of Moab. Her sons marry Orpah and Ruth, women from Moab. Shortly thereafter, Naomi's husband dies, followed by their two sons. Naomi decides to return to her native land and bids her daughters-in-law farewell, saying to them: "'Go—return each of you to her mother's house. May the Lord deal kindly with you, as you have dealt with the dead and with me....' Then she kissed them; and they lifted up their voices and wept" (Ruth 1:8-9).

Orpah and Ruth assert their intention to follow Naomi, but she urges them again to leave her, for she has nothing to offer them. Orpah gives in and leaves, but Ruth refuses and in one of literature's most beautiful statements of loyalty and devotion says: "Entreat me not to leave you, or to return from following after you. For wherever you go, I will go. Wherever you lodge, I will lodge. Your people shall be my people, and your God, my God. Where you die, I will die; and there will I be buried" (Ruth 1:16-17).

Ruth's refusal to leave shifts our sense of where the strength lies in this relationship. By casting her lot with Naomi, Ruth takes on the role of provider. Ruth sets out to glean the leftovers in the fields that remain for

Reflection Questions

◆ How do you see the dance of both emotion and interdependence in this story? What is Ruth able to provide because of her youth? What is Naomi able to provide because of her age?

◆ Do you participate in any relationships in which the give-and-take goes back and forth in a way that is reminiscent of this story?

the poor. Unbeknownst to her, she ends up working the fields of Boaz, a kinsman of Naomi.

When Naomi realizes that Ruth has reconnected them to family, she is reenergized and instructs Ruth on how to cultivate Boaz's attention. Ruth becomes the beneficiary of Naomi's network and intelligence. Ultimately Boaz takes Ruth as his wife; she conceives and bears a son, which further restores Naomi to life and projects her own life and legacy into the future.

In an Interdependent World, Receiving Can be Giving

We have all heard the admonition, "It is better to give than to receive." We are taught from a young age the value of offering concern and care. But how practiced are we at gracious receiving? And, do we ever think about receiving as an obligation?

We are inextricably connected—with each other, with our communities, with our Earth, and with God. What each of us does makes a difference for the other. This truth becomes more apparent as we grow older. The work of wise aging involves coming to see ourselves from this larger perspective. As the generations that came before cared for us, so we care for the next. And as generations before us received support from others, so can we receive support. Our ability to model that for the next generation can be one of the most powerful aspects of our legacy.

One of my own lessons in receiving came at the end of shiva for my father. Each night of that first week, friends from around the city gathered at my home for a brief evening prayer service, which concluded with the recitation of Kaddish, a prayer said in memory of one who has died and which can only be recited when at least ten Jewish adults are present. The shiva week formally concludes the morning of the seventh day, so the evening before we tallied how many people could make an early morning service the next day. We had a count of nine "for sure" and several who would do their best. But when the morning came there were only nine of us. To my discomfort, my husband proposed calling a man who lived just half a mile away to see if he could come at the last minute. We had only met him the week before.

Not only did he arrive within minutes, he thanked us profusely for calling. It was as if we had done him a favor!

It was only then that I understood how rarely we are called upon to give what is needed, to respond without hesitation when asked, to feel included in and obligated by a community. I was moved by his instinctive response and by the realization that by virtue of our membership in a community, both he and I were included in a web of relationships that could be called upon so naturally. I am still more comfortable being the one who responds to need rather than the one who needs and asks, but I am trying to learn that when I ask or receive, I am also contributing to the dance of interdependence.

— Linda

Reader Practices

A Meditation for Becoming Aware of Interdependence

Sit comfortably with your spine erect. Hold yourself upright, in a dignified position but not rigid. Relax your shoulders. Hold your hands gently in your lap or place them on your thighs. Relax your jaw.

Focus your attention on your breathing. Each in-breath takes oxygen into your lungs. You are breathing in air that has blown over the surface of the Earth. Most of the oxygen comes from phytoplankton, from the sea. When you breathe out, you are releasing carbon dioxide that will nourish trees and plants on our planet. Trees and plants will transform it back into oxygen, and we will receive it back in our bodies. As you breathe, notice the sensations; relax into a sense of flow.

Breathe in. Breathe out.

Breathe in. Breathe out.

We also breathe in smoke and chemicals—we are never separate from the output of human activity. The Earth's foliage purifies the air so that we can fill our lungs with life-sustaining breath.

Breathe in. Breathe out.

Breathe in. Breathe out.

Our bodies are composed of the same minerals as other living beings. Most of our body is composed of water. The ocean stirs within us.

There is no way we are separate from each other. No inside, no outside. A Möbius strip of impact.

Allow yourself to sit, holding that awareness. Feel the barrier that holds yourself as a separate entity slowly relaxing.

Say to yourself with the in-breath, "Breathing in I receive from all," and with the out-breath, "Breathing out I give to all."

—5—

Forgiveness and Reconciliation

Any fool can criticize, complain,
and condemn—and most fools do.
But it takes character and self-control
to be understanding and forgiving.

—Dale Carnegie, *How to Win Friends & Influence People*

ometimes, an important relationship can be a troubled one. The
discord that it creates can keep us awake at night, sleepless and
perhaps seething, maybe even swept into a whirlpool of anger,
hurt, and self-righteousness that we cannot seem to escape. Perhaps we
keep replaying the scene, trying out new retorts we wish had come to us
in a moment of confrontation. Perhaps we nurse visions of revenge. We
analyze and reanalyze: What was that *really* about? How did it come to
this? What if I had…? What if he had…?

After a while—a week, a year, a decade—our memory of what occurred
loses much of its vigor; our feelings grow cold. But that knot in our soul
remains, sapping energy, restricting freedom.

Sometimes we find that the dampened sparks of anger are all too easily rekindled. This not only is debilitating for our soul; some researchers
suggest that it is destructive of our health.

At this more reflective time of life, we begin to think about people
whom we once loved but from whom we have become estranged, people

with whom our relationship is ongoing but more problematic or fraught than we would like, people who have wronged us or whom we sense we have wronged. Even if we are not tossing on the pillow in distress, we may nevertheless find ourselves harboring uncomfortable memories of relationships that have disappointed us. There may be people we no longer see or speak with; there may be people who no longer speak to us. Sometimes the break came suddenly, over an incident we both remember; sometimes we're not quite sure what happened that caused the fraying of ties. Not all of these relationships can or need to be repaired, but some may call to us loudly, inviting us to attempt resolution, if not with the person him- or herself, at least with our own feelings and memories.

There is often deep sadness when it seems impossible to heal broken relationships or to let go of old regrets and resentments. It is not uncommon to hear of reconciliations that occur on someone's deathbed. Those are wonderful and healing, but we imagine that the participants must be left with the question: Why did it have to wait so long?

Maybe it doesn't.

Reflection Questions

◈ Ask yourself, "With whom do I remain angry, resentful, or alienated?"

◈ Picture that person or group in your imagination and note any feelings you experience.

◈ Reflect on how long you have carried these feelings. How have they changed as time has passed?

◈ Where does the wrong lie? Could there have been shared responsibility for how events unfolded? If so, how?

◈ Have you attempted a reconciliation? If so, what happened? If not, why not?

Forgiveness and Its Practice

There are no magic formulas, no easy guarantees. Jewish tradition teaches that even God sometimes struggles with forgiveness. Moses argued vehemently to wrest forgiveness from God for the Israelites' faithlessness and rebellion. In the Talmud, a rabbi asks God what prayer he could recite for God's well-being. The prayer that God requests may be surprising; "May my compassion exceed my justice."

Forgiveness, as we will see, is a complicated matter, nuanced and layered. When we are able to discern the multifaceted nature of forgiveness, we are more likely to find a way to soften our resistance or at least understand what is keeping us from moving toward forgiving.

Religious Traditions: "Forgive, for Goodness' Sake"

> If you want to see the brave, look to those who can return love for hatred. If you want to see the heroic, look to those who can forgive.
>
> —Bhagavad Gita

Why do religious traditions pay so much attention to forgiveness? The simple answer is: because we are human.

These characters are all depicted in stories from the Bible: Adam and Eve, Cain and Abel, Jacob and Esau, Rachel and Leah, Joseph and his brothers. They all are depicted in stories of jealousy and misunderstanding. But by the end of Genesis, there is a new story in which humans display the capacity for reconciliation. Joseph forgives his brothers for selling him into slavery. The brothers verbally acknowledge the shame of what they have done and, by behaving differently in similar circumstances, demonstrate their transformation. In its subtle way, the Bible suggests that there is hope, that people can grow and repair relationships that have been damaged.

Most world religions include teachings on the nature of forgiveness, although the emphasis varies from one tradition to another. Exhortations and parables about forgiveness abound in the New Testament. Some, like the parable of the prodigal son, provide assurance of God's forgiveness, while others admonish Christians to emulate divine forgiving: "Then Peter came to Him and said, 'Lord, how often shall my brother sin against me, and I forgive him? Up to seven times?' Jesus said to him, 'I do not say to you, up to seven times, but up to seventy times seven'" (Matthew 18:21-22).

Accepting Christ as one's savior and believing that Jesus died for one's sins (along with those of all humanity) provides assurance that God will forgive a Christian's transgressions.

Neither interpersonal relationships nor relationships with a deity are of primary concern with respect to forgiveness in Buddhism. Followers of Buddhist teachings are urged to practice forgiveness because it protects them and others from the effects of ill will, which can set off chains of additional suffering. When one is hurt or angry, Buddhist tradition teaches that the proper response is to practice a form of meditation in which one sends wishes for well-being to those who have hurt or angered you.

Jews have developed a somewhat different perspective on forgiveness, one that couples it with active repentance. Jewish tradition teaches that before God forgives sins committed against another person, an individual must seek forgiveness from the person who has been harmed. One is entitled to such forgiveness only after taking the following steps: apologizing with sincerity and asking for forgiveness, repairing the damage caused or paying restitution, and committing to behaving differently in the future. This system places emphasis on restoring justice and upholding a core Jewish value that people should be held responsible for their harmful deeds.

Jewish tradition, though, includes another mode of forgiveness. The Jewish bedtime ritual provides an opportunity to extend forgiveness to everyone, regardless of whether or not they have expressed regret or redressed the injury they have caused. It begins: "I now forgive all who have hurt me, all who have done me wrong, whether deliberately or by accident, whether by word, by deed, or by thought, whether against my pride, my person, or my property, in this incarnation or in any other. May no one be punished on my account." (A fuller version of this ritual can be found at the back of the book in "The Bedtime Sh'ma") This statement is immediately followed by the expression of desire to be released from one's own wrongdoings, suggesting that the inclination to forgive others wholeheartedly is in part the result of our awareness of our shared status as flawed humans.

This notion is explicitly expressed in a passage from Baha'i writings that urges love, acceptance, and forgiveness for God's sake, in spite of humanity's flawed nature and imperfect behavior.

> Love the creatures for the sake of God and not for themselves. You will never become angry or impatient if you love them for the sake of God. Humanity is not perfect. There are imperfections in every human being, and you will always become unhappy if you look toward the people themselves. But if you look toward God, you will love them and be kind to them, for the world of God is the world of perfection and complete mercy. Therefore, do not look at the shortcomings of anybody; see with the sight of forgiveness.

Reflection Questions

- Which religious ideas do you find compelling? Interesting? Puzzling? Distasteful?
- What religious ideas about forgiveness did you grow up with?
- In what ways do they still inform your thoughts and actions around forgiveness?
- In what ways have your ideas changed?

A Mindfulness Practice for Forgiveness

(based on a meditation from the Fetzer Institute)

When we assign blame to another and envision ourselves as the righteous victim, we often make judgments about the character of the other. It then becomes easy to lose sight of the many ways in which we all have similar experiences and feelings, desires and foibles.

Practice noticing your own judgments when they arise in the normal course of your day. When you find yourself judging, add the phrase "just like me" or "sometimes I am too." For example, "My partner is so stubborn; sometimes I am too." "My friend holds too many grudges…just like me." Do this with positive qualities as well: "My friend is so generous with his time; sometimes I am too." "That person is so creative…just like me." Over time you may begin to sense that we all share strengths and flaws, that we are more similar to the person from whom we feel alienated than we generally imagine. The compassion that can flow from this practice can move us toward becoming a more forgiving person.

Obstacles to Forgiveness

Even as we consider forgiveness, it is often difficult to know quite what our goals should be. Are we accepting an apology, letting go of our hurt or anger, and/or reestablishing a relationship? When our notions of forgiveness are overly broad, our resistance to it grows stronger. Here are some of the mental traps that can make the consideration of forgiveness more difficult:

- **Forgiveness is the same as forgetting.** No. Sometimes we do forget, but if we choose to, we can forgive without forgetting. We are entitled to remember; often it is wise to remember in order to protect ourselves from experiencing a similar hurt in the future.

- **Forgiving is the same as excusing or condoning.** Not at all. We can continue to find a person's behavior inexcusable but still let go of the anger or hurt we feel when we think about it. We can separate our negative judgment about the action from our feelings of being personally injured.

- **Forgiving is the same as reconciling.** Not necessarily. Hurt in a marriage is a good example. A person may maintain a cordial relationship with a former spouse for the sake of the family but not be willing to continue in the marriage. Or a person may decide to remain in a marriage for the sake of the children without having let go of the hurt associated with a breach of the relationship.

- **Forgiveness makes us vulnerable and weak.** This is most assuredly wrong. Forgiveness actually makes us stronger. Some people fear that forgiving is like giving in, and that if they forgive, they concede a battle and set themselves up to be hurt again. On the contrary, says Rabbi Harold Kushner: "Forgiveness is something you can do when you're strong enough to let go. When you are strong enough to say, 'you, because of what you did to me, don't deserve the power to be the ghost inside my head.'"

- **Forgiveness can only occur when there is an acknowledgment of wrongful behavior.** This belief is a trap, for it gives the wrongdoer all the power. If we have spent time thinking about what happened as objectively as we can, why do we need to wait for the other person to conclude that he or she was in the wrong? Perhaps it would add to our satisfaction and make reconciliation easier, but we do not need to be held back from our own internal process by the other's disagreement or recalcitrance.

If forgiveness does not depend upon forgetting, excusing, reconciling, or apology, then how do we think about its essence? Psychologist Robert Enright says that forgiveness is "giving up the resentment to which you are entitled, and offering to the persons who hurt you friendlier attitudes to which they are not entitled."

An Exercise for Moving toward Forgiveness

You can do the following exercise in several ways: solitary journaling, in dialogue with a trusted friend, or in contemplative solitude.

◈ Picture in your mind a person about whom or a situation about which you remain significantly angry. Note any physical sensations that may arise for you. Do any of your muscles tighten? Has your jaw clenched? Do you detect other internal sensations — in your stomach, throat, head?

◈ Ask yourself, "How long ago did this insult or incident occur?" Then notice that it is not happening now. All that is happening now is that you are thinking about it. It is your own thoughts that are constricting your body, making you feel physically uncomfortable, and triggering your brain's synapses of anger.

◈ Ask yourself whether you would like eventually to be free of uncomfortable thoughts and feelings around this incident. If your answer is yes, how ready do you feel to work on letting go? If your answer is no, or not yet, what feels like it needs to be worked out in order to move toward a yes?

There are many reasons to work toward forgiveness, but most experts say the most important is simple: it's good for us. Forgiveness releases us from forces that weigh us down: feelings of anger, resentment, and powerlessness; fantasies of revenge; and preoccupations with the past. All of these work to displace our energy, energy we need to move into the future. When we allow these feelings and preoccupations to fester, it hurts us. One friend describes the reasons for forgiving as follows: "Holding on to resentment is like drinking poison and then waiting for the other person to die."

Shlomo Carlebach, the charismatic singing rebbe, came to America as a teenager fleeing the Nazis. Before he died, he returned to Austria and Germany to give concerts. Someone asked him: "Why are you doing this? Don't you hate them?" His answer: "If I had two souls, I'd devote one to hating them. But since I have only one, I don't want to waste it on hating."

Forgiving as a Process

Most of us need a bit of time to work toward forgiveness. The kind of inner work that helps us grow is a process. And it's not formulaic; each of us needs to navigate our own unique assortment of obstacles, and each situation is different.

Before attempting to forgive, spend some time reflecting on exactly what happened and how you feel about it. Dr. Frederic Luskin, director of the Stanford Forgiveness Project, suggests that forgiveness is on a continuum with grief: "The way I understand it now is that when you're offended or hurt or violated, the natural response is to grieve. All of those problems can be seen as a loss—whether we lose affection or a human being or a dream—and when we lose something, human beings have a natural reintegration process, which we call grief. Then forgiveness is the resolution of grief."

In the long run, it doesn't help to bypass feelings associated with hurt. Eventually those feelings tend to catch up with us, often at unexpected times and in unexpected ways. Dr. Luskin advocates sharing our story and feelings of hurt with at least one other person, but he also cautions against overtelling it. If we tell our story repeatedly, to ourselves or to others, both the story and our feelings may get frozen in place.

Another strategy that can be helpful is to examine what has happened from a less personal perspective. Consider how the history or personality traits of the person who has hurt you may be a primary cause of his or her behavior. Did you expect too much? Consider how you might have contributed to the situation. Perhaps you might conclude that the situation was complex, with too many unknown factors for you to fully understand what happened.

Remind yourself that the most important part of forgiveness is letting go of *your own* preoccupations. Mindfulness practices can help you to distinguish what has actually occurred from the interpretation you have created by your reactions to the situation and the behaviors of others. Once you have identified what has actually occurred and your reaction to those events, you can choose what to keep and what to let go.

Sometimes letting go of thoughts and feelings that we have deemed untrue or unhelpful requires deliberately distracting ourself with something else. The distraction can be small and superficial, like picking up a gripping book, calling a friend, or looking for a late-night movie. Sometimes we just need a quick escape from unproductive thought patterns. But we can also diminish the power of hurt and anger over the long term by choosing to focus on more significant distractions, and deliberately putting energy and attention into the many things in life that give us pleasure and over which we do have control. For example, we can seek out people and situations that are most likely to surround us with kindness, beauty, and love. We can concentrate on the many aspects of our lives for which we are grateful. In this way we tip the balance of our experience toward the positive. When our lives feel weighted toward the good, negative thoughts weaken their grip.

Another Way to Work toward Forgiveness: In Your Journal

Think of a situation in your life for which you would like to be forgiven or would like to forgive. Write or record a short description of the situation from your perspective. Now imagine that you are the other person in the situation and write or record a short description from that person's perspective.

How are the two stories different? Have you ever thought about the situation from the other person's perspective? Does it make you more willing to consider forgiveness in this situation?

Now imagine yourself as a wise elder to whom the two parties in contention have brought their stories. What questions would you ask each of them? What would you hope they could offer one another?

If you can, write a dialogue of reconciliation. If you were both functioning from your higher selves, what might you say to one another?

Growing in Forgiveness

Forgiveness can become a part of the way we live. The more we practice forgiveness, the more we can learn to understand and control our angry responses to things, and keep them from being easily triggered. We can notice signs of distress within ourselves as they arise, name them, and choose to focus elsewhere or turn to stress reduction techniques. We can remind ourselves what we are grateful for and choose not to dwell on hurts unless we can learn from them constructively. Not surprisingly, it is

I will always be grateful to have witnessed a remarkable family healing in which a painful past was transformed into a fruitful and loving future.

A man came to me for direction in order to focus more attention on his emerging spiritual life. As I got to know him, I witnessed his deep sadness over his estrangement from his children. I watched him struggle with his desire to reconnect with them and his hurt and frustration when they would not respond positively to his efforts to reconcile.

One day he arrived hurt and angry about the distrustful tone of the most recent letter he had received from his oldest child. His therapist had urged him to reply with honesty about the feelings the letter had stirred in him, but I kept hearing his longing for reconciliation. I suggested that we sit in silence and see what would arise in him. I urged him to try to access the deepest part of himself, the part that lay beneath the conflicting tangle of emotions with which he was grappling. Perhaps he could contact the wisdom inherent in his most authentic self. I had no sense of what, if anything, might come of this, and I prayed that he might find whatever wisdom he needed.

After ten or fifteen minutes, he opened his eyes and said, "What is clear to me is that my love for my children is the most important thing in the world to me."

"Then let that be your guide," I said. "Whenever you make contact with one of your children, tap into that love, the love you just felt so powerfully. That will help you decide what to do, what to write, what to say."

Over the next few years I witnessed him reach out in love, rather than from a place of frustration or hurt, accepting the pain of whatever happened as the price of keeping open the possibility of reconciliation. Tapping into that place of love that was stronger than hurt or anger guided his decisions about whether this was a good time to communicate with them and what he wanted to say. Being mindful of the love has, over time, brought a profound healing. It is now possible for this family to enjoy a warm relationship, one that is grounded in mutual love, respect, and understanding.

— Linda

easier to forgive small offenses than larger ones. Consciously forgiving a rude comment or someone cutting in front of you in line is good practice for the bigger challenges.

There are also spiritual practices that help us keep forgiveness in mind. Interestingly, both Jewish and Buddhist prayers for forgiveness place our need to forgive alongside our need to be forgiven. They both emphasize our commonality with others and the fact that we all sometimes need forgiveness.

When We Are the Ones Who Need Forgiveness

Apologizing is a manifestation of dignity, even though it may make us feel that we are putting our dignity aside. Asking for forgiveness can be as difficult as granting it. It means acknowledging that we have offended or failed. It's often easier to shift blame or make excuses than to admit that we have not lived up to our own or another's standards. Facing that in ourselves can be painful; humbly acknowledging it aloud to another, more so. It requires courage.

Reflection Questions

◆ What is your personal history with apology? How were apologies and forgiveness handled in your family of origin? Did parents as well as children apologize when it was appropriate? Were apologies pro forma? Forced? Accepted? Rejected?

◆ To whom is it easy for you to apologize? To whom is it difficult for you to apologize? What makes the difference?

◆ When have you needed to apologize for something you considered serious? How difficult did you find it? What helped you move forward and decide how to go about asking for forgiveness? Or, what held you back?

A Jewish Forgiveness Practice

As we mentioned earlier, Jewish tradition offers a nighttime prayer ritual that focuses on both granting and asking for forgiveness (see "The Bedtime Sh'ma," page 307).

Try the Jewish bedtime prayer or fashion something similar in your own words. After reciting it a few times, write down whatever you experienced. Who came to mind? What was the story behind the memory? How did you feel about requesting forgiveness for the other person? For yourself?

We have a colleague who struggled with this bedtime practice because she often knew that she was not really done with her anger at someone, and it felt disingenuous to claim that she had already forgiven that person. She resolved this conundrum with the following practice. She would say something like, "Okay, God. We both know that I'm not really done with this. But I'm handing it off to you to hold for the night. I'll take it back in the morning and keep working on it."

A Tribute of Forgiveness

This exercise taught by Rabbi Zalman Schachter-Shalomi, called "A Testimonial Dinner to the Severe Teachers," is another helpful way to gain perspective on your need or desire to forgive:

First, list the people who have hurt you. Then, for each one, describe the apparent injustice they committed against you. Finally, think of some way(s) in which you have actually benefitted from what happened.

Then write a short tribute to each person on your list. (Unless you have a very short list, do this over time, or do it as you find yourself with stirred up feelings and resentments toward someone.) The tribute might go like this: "I understand now that you did me a great service by your actions when you _____. Although I did not understand at the time, and it was difficult for me and possibly for you, I now want to thank you. I am grateful for the contribution you made to my life. I forgive you and wish you well."

Zalman suggests that in addition to freeing up the energy that has been bound up in holding on to resentments, "forgiveness work challenges us with the evolutionary task of ennobling our sufferings, transmuting tragedy and sorrow into understanding," and enhancing our capacity to love.

A Buddhist Forgiveness Meditation

If I have harmed anyone in any way
either knowingly or unknowingly
through my own confusions
I ask their forgiveness.

If anyone has harmed me in any way
either knowingly or unknowingly
through their own confusions
I forgive them.

And for all the ways that I harm myself

by judging or doubting or being unkind
through my own confusions
I forgive myself.

What makes for a good apology? First of all, we examine our intent. Apologies are not meant to provide an easy escape. A good apology involves sincere regret and a genuine attempt to understand the hurt we have caused. When we apologize, we are truthful and specific. We acknowledge without excuse and without shifting responsibility. We do our best to make amends, and offer to repair the situation or provide a form of restitution if that is possible. We also ask directly for forgiveness: "Please forgive me," rather than, "I'm sorry I hurt your feelings."

Sometimes an apology is best conveyed in writing. It can be helpful in repairing a relationship to take time to explain that we didn't set out or deliberately mean to be hurtful. We may want to convey how we feel about what happened, why we want to be forgiven, what we have learned from this experience, or what we are willing to do to apologize or repair the damage we have caused. Such a letter can include a request to meet or speak to continue the process of apologizing and seeking forgiveness. If it seems best to apologize in person, it still may be helpful to have written out what we might want to say.

Remember, too, that asking to be forgiven requires patience. We do not always get the response for which we hope. Instead of a quick "Yes, I forgive you," the person may say he or she needs more time, or he or she may decide to forgive us but acknowledge that the hurt we have caused remains.

Even after several heartfelt attempts at apology, sometimes a person can't or won't forgive. Then it is time to move on. Jewish tradition teaches that if the person we have offended refuses to forgive us, we should return and make the request two (some say three) more times, this time in the company of others. If the apology is heartfelt and accompanied by a commitment to behave differently in the future, the offended person is obliged to accept it and forgive with a willing spirit. After the third apology, the onus shifts to the person who was wronged; he or she becomes responsible for an unwillingness to be appeased (Maimonides, *Mishneh Torah, Hilchot T'shuvah*).

Repentance Poem #4

Of all the people I don't think about anymore
you're the one i miss the most

The last night we spoke
I knew the combination of words
I could have said
to make things better again,
but I didn't.

—Matthue Roth

Self-Forgiveness

Holding on to anger with oneself can be as toxic as clinging to grudges toward others. Yes, we need to acknowledge our mistakes with as much straightforwardness as we can muster. But no, we need not wallow in them or take on an exaggerated sense of guilt. Beware: do not confuse deed with essence. When we berate ourselves without clarifying how we will change our behavior or work on a character flaw, we risk contributing to a general sense of unworthiness from which too many of us suffer. This is counterproductive to our desire to grow in goodness.

Rabbi Alan Lew admonishes us "to give up one of our most cherished beliefs—that there is something wrong with us, that we are bad, inadequate, somehow defective, and lacking in goodness. Disciplining ourselves, rejecting ourselves, beating ourselves, leads us farther away from this goodness, not closer to it."

Rabbi Nachman of Bratslav, who suffered from self-doubt, realized that many of us judge ourselves even more harshly than we judge others. Consequently, he began his teaching with the following counsel: "Judge all people favorably." After instructing us to search for the "point of good" in others, he added:

You must also find the good in yourself. A fundamental principle in life is that you should always try to keep happy and steer well away from depression. When you start looking deep inside yourself, you may think you have no good in you at all. You may feel you are full of evil, and the negative voice inside you tries to make you depressed. Don't let yourself fall into depression. Search until you find some little good in you....The good you find inside you will give you new life and bring joy to your soul.

Judaism is adamant about the essential goodness of human beings. The morning liturgy states that, "the soul that you have implanted within me is pure." Even when our intentions and deeds are despicable, Judaism insists that our innermost core, our God-given soul, cannot be distorted and that, consequently, we can always return to that pure and holy essence. Genuinely embracing that belief, according to Rabbi Nachman, is central to our ability to find the proper balance between regret and self-respect.

To fully appreciate the profundity of this teaching, we need to know more about the way Nachman and his companions understood the dynamics of being human. From their perspective, each human is created in the divine image, and is a vessel through which divine energy passes. The energy itself is pure, but as it is given shape by the vessel, it may be directed toward good or ill. From this perspective, lust may be seen as misdirected love, fear as overextended respect, vanity as uncontained aesthetic appreciation, promiscuity as the unbounded desire for intimacy.

This view is congruent with the Jewish understanding of sin, or *cheit*. Translated literally, *cheit* really means "missing the mark." Our mistakes and failures generally result from misdirecting our energy rather than our being essentially evil or flawed. Adopting this perspective can encourage us to be more gentle with our self-criticism and more forgiving of ourselves when we have misdirected our energy.

- How prone are you to fall into unhelpful self-judgment (I did it again! Why can't I ever get things right? If anyone knew the real me...)?

Reader Practices

Practices For Self-Forgiveness

These are steps you can follow when you are unable to forgive yourself and let go of negative self-judgment.

◈ Review what has happened as truthfully as you can and distinguish between moral failures and mistakes due to unskillfulness. Try to trace misdirected behavior to its root and ask yourself how you can redirect that same kind of energy in a more appropriate way.

◈ Make amends and repair things where you can and appreciate the seriousness with which you are trying to work through this.

◈ Try to get in touch with the feeling of being cared for. Remember a parent, friend, partner, or even a pet, who has acquainted you with a tender and trustworthy love. Imagine what he or she would name as your good qualities—patience, determination, empathy, fairness. Take in both the love and the sense of yourself as embodying these qualities.

◈ When you have done all you can to repair what has been broken and to learn from this experience, say— in your mind, aloud, in writing, or to another—"I have taken responsibility for my actions and done what I could to rectify the difficulty I caused. I forgive myself for _____ and _____. I will no longer dwell on the bad feelings that surround this incident."

Learn to recognize this kind of self-talk when it begins so that you can prevent it from spiraling downward.

♦ Think about whether there are particular situations in which, or issues around which, you are relentlessly self-critical. What triggers these feelings of worthlessness?

Divine Forgiveness

If you are struggling with extending forgiveness to yourself or to another, be gentle with yourself; don't judge yourself for only being able to get so far. Rabbi Jonathan Omer-Man offers the following consolation, "I don't know if anyone has a PhD in forgiveness. I don't. It is a struggle to forgive. We never fully can; but we can approach it....[Only] the Divine One forgives totally, a hundred percent."

Judaism recognizes different levels of forgiveness. According to Rabbi David R. Blumenthal, the first involves "forgoing the other's indebtedness" (*m'chilah*). This is the kind of forgiveness we offer when the offender has met the standards of repentance: acknowledging the wrongdoing, expressing remorse, making restitution, and taking steps to prevent repeating the offense. This does not necessarily involve a change of heart toward the offender, but we relinquish our claim against him or her.

The second kind of forgiveness is an act of the heart (*s'lichah*). We still might not embrace or even reconcile with the offender, but we can feel empathy for the troubledness of the other. We identify with our shared human frailty.

The highest level of forgiveness is atonement or purification *(kaparah tahorah)*. This is the total existential cleansing of the misdeed. It is said that this ultimate form of forgiveness is granted only by God.

One of the major sources of support in working on forgiveness is a spiritual friend. Such a friend, with whom we can speak about our deepest concerns and doubts, can let us know when we are being too hard on ourselves, when we need to turn from acknowledging wrongdoing to reconnecting with our best selves. A spiritual friend is someone who can reflect our goodness back to us and can also challenge us when it is necessary, offering well-meaning and constructive criticism.

Constructive Criticism

If you propose to speak, always ask yourself, is it true, is it necessary, is it kind.

—Gautama Buddha

"Now that I'm forty…Now that I'm sixty…Now that I'm eighty…I'm going to say what I think!" Who hasn't said that from time to time? But while we may want to claim the right to say whatever we'd like, the first thing that pops out of our mouths is not always a demonstration of our wisdom.

In the book of Genesis we read that the world came into existence through speech: "God said, 'Let there be light'; and there was light." So too is our world of understandings created largely through speech. Jewish tradition recognizes the awesome power and the extraordinary delicacy of our speech. We create with speech, but we can also destroy with words. Of the many sins enumerated in the Yom Kippur confessional prayer, eleven are sins committed through speech. The Talmud suggests that the tongue is an instrument so dangerous that it must be kept behind two protective walls (the mouth and the teeth) to prevent its misuse.

There are those who caution against speaking up too hastily or too much. There are also those who warn against silence:

I am very little inclined on any occasion to say anything unless I hope to produce some good by it.

—Abraham Lincoln

If I were to remain silent, I'd be guilty of complicity.
—Albert Einstein

Speak only if it improves upon the silence.
—Mahatma Gandhi

Just as it is a mitzvah to say something that will be heard,
so it is a mitzvah not to say something that won't be heard.
—Talmud, *Yevamot* 68b

Immediately preceding the Bible's instruction that we should not bear a grudge but rather forgive and "love thy fellow as thyself," we read, "Thou shalt surely rebuke thy neighbor." At first this seems like an odd juxtaposition. Forgiveness generally leads to the softening and healing of a relationship, while rebuke frequently results in contentiousness.

Why is rebuke so important? When we are in a relationship with someone, and we withhold criticism, we can contribute to the fraying of our bonds. When we fail to speak up, we lose the opportunity to better understand what has happened and the other person's actual intentions. Letting our assumptions stand may lead to a misunderstanding that simmers and undermines the good feeling and trust we have for another. By not speaking up we may take on a degree of responsibility for the other person's actions. We become complicit in wrongful behaviors. At the same time, offering constructive criticism is something of an art.

When relationships go awry, the damage is often the result of poorly chosen or ill-timed words. Sometimes they burst out of our mouths in anger; sometimes we hurt each other with well-intended but unskillful criticism. As elders, we want to contribute to the way our families and communities face challenges by offering thoughtful, calming words rather than complaints, nagging, or blame. We want our speech to reflect who we are and who we are choosing to become at this stage of life: patient, kind, and compassionate. Regardless of any diminishment of our physical powers, our ability to contribute wisdom and care through our words is unlimited.

Reflection Questions

❖ In what situations and with whom do you offer (or have you offered) constructive criticism with relative ease and success? With extreme caution? Without adequate prior reflection and self-examination? What have you learned from these experiences?

❖ When have you refrained from offering rebuke out of self-protection? Out of the belief that it wouldn't make a difference? Out of concern for the other's feelings or well-being?

In Ecclesiastes 3 we read, "To everything there is a season…a time to keep silent and a time to speak." Knowing when and whether to offer constructive criticism requires wisdom and discernment. We all know people who are difficult to satisfy or who are slow to acknowledge the good in something without adding a qualifying remark. Still others let moments of discomfort, unfairness, or injustice pass without objecting, perhaps out of a desire to avoid discomfort, angering a friend, or risking being wrong. Most of us walk a delicate path that meanders through both speech and silence, wishing we had better signage to guide our choices.

In the previous chapter, we took note of the way our relationships may be shifting at this time of life. As parents of school-aged children we had greater experience in the world and unquestioned responsibility for our children's well-being. Now our children are adults themselves, no doubt more savvy about certain aspects of the world than we are, and perhaps concerned with our welfare and their responsibility for it as we grow older. How do those factors change the manner in which criticism is offered and received? Might they, or we, be tempted to criticize too hastily? Might these changes in our status trigger defensiveness, in us or in them?

When do we offer the wisdom of our life experience? How do we respond when our advice goes unheeded? When do we listen to, and even follow, those whom we once had authority over, especially when our views and theirs differ? When do we maintain silence in order to avoid upsetting our relationships?

Wendy Lustbader writes tenderly about the struggles she observes her older patients facing as they become dependent on others for their everyday lives. For example, one complains that her daughter vacuums the kitchen for her but always misses the crumbs under the table. It disturbs her deeply to look at those crumbs all week, but how can she express anything but gratitude when her far-too-busy daughter comes to clean for her? Another, paralyzed on one side by a stroke, describes the utter helplessness she feels when her home aide simply swishes water around the sink instead of scrubbing it with cleanser and disinfectant as she has always done for herself. "I want to jump out of the wheelchair and do it myself. But I am trapped in this chair, in this body, and I am supposed to be glad that I have help. But I'm not glad. I'm furious." A third describes sneaking downstairs to the basement to do an extra load of laundry between visits from the woman hired to do her wash. "My son says he'll throttle me if I ever go down there....It's my house, my basement, my washing machine, and my life. That's the way I feel."

On the other side, we can imagine that the son who forbids his mother from going downstairs fears that if she falls, his caretaking responsibilities will overwhelm him. The daughter who unintentionally overlooks the crumbs is aware of her mother's judgment that she's never been much of a housekeeper. She's doing her best, and it's true that if her mother spoke up about the crumbs it might tear the scab off old wounds. The home aide would like just a bit of gratitude for the heavy lifting she does, but there's rarely positive acknowledgment of anything; what she experiences is her client's resentment of needing her help.

If everyone weren't doing such a good job of controlling themselves, we might hear words such as these flying back and forth:

"What's the matter with you? Can't you see those huge crumbs under the table? What am I going to do if they attract mice/roaches/ants! I tried my best to raise you to...."

"Mother! The basement door's unlocked! Did you go down there again? How many times do I have to tell you that if you fall and break your neck or need a hip replacement I'll lose my job if I have to take care of you. You're worse than a child!"

The sentiments are understandable, on both sides, but the words that may slip out would be painful, and their impact destructive.

Similar challenges arise in sibling relationships. Old hierarchies, often based on age, have evolved. Now we are all adults. Perhaps we are now equals, and if not we are probably closer to it. Nevertheless, what lingers from our childhood roles, our relationships with each other and with our parents, will inevitably color the way we relate to one another today.

For many years we may have lived our lives independently of other family members. We may have applauded the lives they have constructed, or puzzled over them, or worried. Suddenly we may need to collaborate, perhaps on the care of aging parents. Different life choices, our history as siblings, the different kinds of relationships we have had with each other during our adult years may suddenly matter again. Do we know how to discuss sensitive situations openly? Do we know how to disagree without being critical? Do we know how to listen to disagreement without growing defensive?

Relationships with our spouse or life partner may also shift. We may resent the lost capacities or interests of a partner who seems to be aging faster than we. We may have lost patience with our partner's foibles, or they with ours. Have we softened with one another or become more contentious? Do we hide our annoyance under an unconvincing veil of "joking" but wound nevertheless?

Constructive Criticism and Love

If we examine Jewish wisdom, we find both support for offering criticism and caution about the circumstances under which we should proceed.

In Proverbs 28:23, we are told, "One who rebukes a person shall in the end find more favor than one who flatters with the tongue." In the

Talmud, we hear from two of the sages: "Rabbi Yosi bar Chanina said: 'Rebuke leads to love…Any love that does not include rebuke is not really love.' Reish Lakish said: 'Rebuke leads to peace…any peace that does not include rebuke is not really peace'" (*Genesis Rabbah* 54:3).

Additionally, Jewish tradition advocates for persistence when it comes to offering critique. With respect to forgiveness, we are instructed that once we have made three requests of the person we have offended, we are clear of the obligation. In contrast, in the case of rebuke, there is no limit to the number of times one should raise an issue. Rabbi Esther Adler refers to this as "sacred nagging" and sees it as a sign of love. "If I decide that there is no point in raising the issue because I won't be heard or because 'she'll never change anyway,' I am writing that person off, forgetting that she, too, is created in the image of God."

But the book of Proverbs (9:8) also advises caution, "Do not rebuke a scoffer, for he will hate you; reprove a wise man and he will love you."

This may strike us as rather commonsense guidance, but don't we often violate these simple instructions? Don't we frequently persist even when it is clear that our sacred nagging is simply going to be resented? The Talmud records an insightful conversation between two rabbis:

> Rabbi Tarfon: "I wonder if there is anyone left in this gen-
> eration who knows how to take criticism?"
> Rabbi Elazar ben Azaryah went even further: "I wonder if
> there is anyone in this generation who knows how to give
> criticism!" (*Arachin* 16b)

Most important in any discussion of criticism—both offering and withholding it—is that it be done with love. Indeed, the rabbis, who often enjoyed delivering their message by playing with the root letters of the Hebrew words with which they were conversing, suggested that we read the Hebrew word for rebuke, *tochachah*, as if it were actually two Hebrew words, *toch ahavah*, which translates as "inside love" or "from a place of love." This was their way of suggesting that getting in touch with our respect, affection, or love for the other individual is the best way for us to determine whether, how, and when to offer rebuke.

This kind of deep love, expansiveness of spirit, and risk taking can often open up new possibilities. We turn to another example from Wendy Lustbader's *Counting on Kindness,* one that deals with the delicate negotiation of dependency and caretaking that often happens between parents and adult children.

A daughter found that four years after her mother's death, her relationship with her beloved father had turned sour. Her father was still despondent over his wife's death and his daughter was growing impatient trying to cheer him up and comfort him. Each phone call sounded much the same as the last, as he expressed his loneliness and sadness. Nothing she could say seemed to make a difference, and so the calls began to feel more and more futile. Moreover, the time her father tended to call was right around bedtime, just as she and her husband were settling down for their own time together.

When she finally stepped back to pay attention to the pattern that had developed, to acknowledge her growing resentment and incapacity to rescue her father, and to recognize that the timing of her father's calls was related to his missing her mother most in the evening as he prepared to go to bed alone, she realized that she had to take the situation in hand.

She began by telling her father that although she knew that he was unaware of it, the timing of his nightly calls was making it difficult for her and her husband to nurture their own relationship, something that they had always done consciously, partly in response to what she had learned from the way her parents had lovingly tended to theirs. She engaged him in conversation about what might help him deal with his sad and lonely evenings, and she made a tape for him to listen to of her childhood memories of their family's happy times together. They arranged for him to call her earlier in the evening when it was more convenient for her.

Shortly thereafter, her father thanked her for speaking up. He had been unaware of the intrusiveness of his calls and was grateful that she had not allowed him to continue to interrupt her precious time with her husband. He took comfort from knowing that the legacy of his happy marriage was appreciated and being extended by his daughter, and he was impressed with the creativity and forthrightness she had exhibited in finding some solutions. Meanwhile, her resentment of her father receded dramatically.

Responding out of love, this daughter was able to step back from her frustration sufficiently to imagine what was really going on for her father and find a gentle way of discussing the situation as a mutually shared problem that they could solve together.

When Love Is Not Enough

Sometimes we can't depend on love to direct our hearts toward wisdom. Sometimes it just isn't there; sometimes it is caught in a web of jealousies or mistrust; sometimes we run out of patience or good will. A student of ours reported that her sister said, "I thought cancer was supposed to change you for the better; you haven't changed a bit!" When we can't call on love or even goodwill, here are some principles on which we can lean in deciding when, how, and whether to offer rebuke.

- Offer criticism privately and at a time when it can be talked about fully.
- Probe your motives for offering rebuke; are there elements of self-interest, competition, or mean-spiritedness?
- Focus on things that can actually be changed; for example, behavior rather than a character trait.
- Try to understand the other person's perspective; how do things appear to him or to her?
- Invite discussion of what has happened; emphasize description over judgment. Invite collaborative discussion of consequences rather than offering advice.

- When making a judgment, offer it tentatively, allowing it to be open-ended.
- Don't offer rebuke in a moment of anger or frustration. Gain some distance, let your emotions cool down, and give yourself time to look at the situation from multiple perspectives.
- Allow the discussion to flow both ways.
- When in doubt, ask yourself: Is it true? Is it kind? Is it necessary? Sometimes silence is the wisest action.
- Rabbi Sheila Peltz Weinberg offers a helpful acronym to guide us in speaking: WAIT—**W**hy **A**m **I** **T**alking?

Some of the qualities of spirit that are important in nurturing and healing relationships include: patience, compassion, generosity, and equanimity. It takes patience to still our reactive inner voices and to hold our words until we have had time to consider the other's intention. Cultivating patience can help us create a mindful gap between our reactivity and our actions. Generosity of spirit helps us give other people the benefit of the doubt, to approach them with the assumption that their intentions were good. Equanimity helps us maintain a sense of balance and inner calm; we offer help as best we can but let go of our need to control or to be right. This is what we are trying to grow toward, and for most of us that is the work of a lifetime. We will not always get it right, but only by stretching our capacity for openness and authenticity do we continue to grow in wisdom.

Accepting Criticism

A good friend will always stab you in the front.
—Oscar Wilde

Growing older—and hopefully wiser—doesn't exempt us from being the recipients of criticism. We may be the mother whose son berates her for going downstairs to do the laundry, or the father whose daughter calls to gently suggest he change the time of their nightly call. We may be the parent whose child complains about our letting the grandkids have too many sweets when we are babysitting, or the sister whose sibling is always angry about the way we are handling our parents' finances but never offers to help himself. Perhaps it is our spouse or life partner whose criticism has become more frequent or less kind.

Although we may pay coaches and consultants to critique our work, athletic, or personal skills, it is hard not to begin from a place of defensiveness, or at least sensitivity, when criticism comes unbidden. The temptation to deflect or ignore it is strong. All the more so if it is offered unskillfully. We may be tempted to respond in kind, shouting back our denial or turning the tables to fling a comparable zinger back at our critic. In some families the cold-shoulder response prevails.

So perhaps the first piece of work to be done is to look at our patterns of response, both what happens inside us and how we tend to react, in different situations.

- In which of your relationships do you find criticism hard to take and in which is it relatively easy? Is the difference related primarily to the way it is offered, to the nature of your relationship, or to some other factor?
- What feelings arise based on who is offering the criticism and their manner? Defensiveness? Anger? Fear? Curiosity? Concern? Gratitude?
- What is your personal history with criticism? How was criticism offered and received in your family of origin? In marriage or in other intimate relationships? At work? What has changed, and what has stayed much the same for you?

Whether offered lovingly or with hostility, we can choose to respond with the wisdom of our years. Just as it is wise to step back and gain perspective when we offer rebuke, so too, we need to create spaciousness around our response to rebuke. It is always possible to say, "I need some time to think about what you have said." Then it is our task to determine whether we indeed have something to learn from this critic, and whether we can separate the message from its source or its inelegant delivery.

Rabbi Avi Shulman recounts an unusually creative response to criticism in spite of it being delivered in a rather nasty way. He recalls meeting a cantor whose clear enunciation of each word in prayer he greatly admired. Asked how he had developed such clarity, the cantor said that when he began leading prayer he was quite unskilled and stumbled. Several members of that prayer service taunted him. He turned the situation around by taking on the challenge: he offered the group's ringleader a dollar for each mistake they spotted in the future, suggesting that the arrangement could benefit both of them. Within a few weeks, he said, his prayer leading was perfect!

The cantor chose to take on the criticism as a dare, to hear the message as "you can be even better" rather than as "you're no good." It takes courage to ask our critic to elaborate so that we can really understand what changes we might want to make. In the classic Jewish morality text, *Pirkei Avot* (*The Teachings of the Sages*), the authors ask, "Who is wise?" The reply is, "The person who can learn from everyone."

When the criticism we receive does not seem warranted, stepping back to gain perspective gives us time to assess the situation apart from the natural responses of our hurt or angered ego. We ask ourselves, What's going on here? Have my words or behavior been misunderstood? Is this a simple misunderstanding, easily cleared up, or is it something more basic to our relationship that causes this person to interpret my words or actions this way? Within families, it is not uncommon for people to respond as if they were still in roles that have been long discarded. The child who never felt understood may, especially when under stress, revert to old ways of interpreting a parent's well-meaning suggestion. Again, it may help to try standing in the other's shoes before determining how we want to respond.

It is often possible with some time and distance to reopen the subject in a way that can lead to both clarity and a deeper relationship. We may say, "I've been thinking a lot about the exchange we had last week, and I need some help understanding what you meant....or why you were so angry....or what you thought I had done." We invite a discussion in which both parties, working together, try to unravel the incident or the issues that loom beneath it. In some cases, this may require a level of skillfulness that may be difficult to reach by ourselves. It is helpful to know to whom we can turn: a thoughtful and discerning friend, a spouse or partner, a child, a therapist. Sometimes we can simply shrug off what seems like unwarranted criticism, but occasionally it is worth the hard work of pursuing it for the sake of an improved relationship.

With thought we create our inner world; with speech we create our world of interpersonal relationships. Laura L. Carstensen, a psychology professor and founding director of the Stanford Center on Longevity, says that if you are wise, "you're not only regulating your emotional state, you're also attending to another person's emotional state...you're not focusing so much on what you need and deserve, but on what you can contribute."

Reflection Questions

◈ Who in your life can you depend upon to gently set you straight when you have erred? What makes their criticism effective for you?

◈ For whom do you provide loving and supportive criticism? What have you learned about providing effective criticism for this person?

— 6 —

Cultivating Spiritual Qualities for Well-Being

We all need models for how to live
from retirement to past 80—with joy.

—George Vaillant, MD

One who has aged well is a person whom people *want* to visit, not just someone they *have* to visit. Who comes to mind when you think of someone who has aged well? More than likely it is a person whose character stands out. Maybe her eyes really do twinkle and her wrinkles spread out when she smiles, revealing an inner joy. Or maybe he is self-contained and upright—sticking to his principles and values, aware of how they manifest in his actions. Maybe he tells wonderful stories, or invites you over for tea just to talk, sharing the perspective and wisdom of a lifetime. Maybe she is crusty, even grouchy, but has a certain generosity within. But whatever the distinctive qualities, she or he is likely to be a resilient, compassionate, loving person.

People who have aged well have developed important character traits over the length of their years. They are likely to be people who easily feel and express gratitude, finding the good in others and in events. From this sense of abundance they are less frightened, less angry, and more accepting of their situation. And they are more generous, finding pleasure in giving in many ways and thereby building relationships and community. They have learned to be patient and trusting, though not passive—allowing events to unfold more slowly, accepting other people's foibles and not rushing to judge or blame them. They are joyful, though not necessarily ebullient, so they find more to celebrate in the day, and they feel more optimistic. And when you are with them you may sense a certain equanimity, an ability to hold paradox, to be with both the sad and the happy, with the frightening and the pleasurable, and to take life in stride.

These character traits of gratitude, generosity, patience, joy, and equanimity are vital to manifesting some of the behaviors that Dr. George Vaillant, director of Harvard University's extended longitudinal study on aging, has identified as promoting aging well:

+ Being able to orient one's thinking toward the future rather than the past.
+ Maintaining a generally optimistic perspective, choosing to interpret events and choices so one sees possibilities rather than risks when given the opportunity.
+ Developing mature adaptive strategies (turning lemons into lemonade).
+ Reacting well to change, disease, and conflict.
+ Reinventing oneself.
+ Practicing forgiveness.
+ Feeling and expressing gratitude.
+ Letting go of self-importance.
+ Demonstrating for the young how not to fear death.
+ Finding a rationale for living well even in times of great loss.

Hearing such a list might prompt us to wonder whether we can really expect so much of ourselves, especially if these orientations don't come naturally to us. Can we grow and strengthen these qualities at this point in our lives? At a recent lecture in a retirement community, a man in the back row raised his hand with a question. "How is it possible to change now that we are so old?" A woman in front turned to reassure him that he was fine the way he was. Someone else asked him why he thought age ruled out the possibility of change. After all, many things were changing in his life all the time.

Change is always possible. We know from experience that it is often precipitated by dark times. The good news is that we don't have to experience crisis or severe challenges in order to make different choices in our lives. Religious traditions have always known this. Different Christians talk about this in different ways, calling this kind of change conversion, salvation, or being born again. Jews call it returning—*t'shuvah*. Often we think that this is a sudden turnabout, a momentous "seeing the light," after which everything is different; but, in fact, it is almost always a process. There may be a sudden awakening, but we still have to do the inner work to incorporate and integrate the new ways of thinking and being that we glimpsed in the moment of inspiration or decision.

With the recent work in neuroscience, we now understand a bit about how this process takes place. We know that when we cultivate new kinds of thoughts and behaviors, we are making changes in our brains that will eventually modify our habitual patterns of thought and action, yielding to new responses.

With practice we can cultivate the spiritual qualities that can help us do the work that Vaillant specifies. We can do that work using secular, spiritual, or religious practices. Buddhism, for example, has developed specific teachings for cultivating the four *brahmaviharas* (virtues): loving-kindness, compassion, empathetic joy, and equanimity. Yoga allows many people to develop both physical and spiritual flexibility and strength. Many rich and deep religious practices have been popularized in recent years, rendering them more accessible to today's seekers, many of whom define themselves as spiritual rather than religious.

Judaism provides its own example. Over centuries, Jewish teachers developed a practice called *musar* designed to foster the spiritual qualities that help us live in closer alignment with God's commandment to "be holy." These qualities, known in Hebrew as *midot* or "measures"— include gratitude, generosity, trust, humility, joy, patience, truth, and equanimity.

These traits can be identified as unique but they usually work in tandem with others. *Musar* practice is currently enjoying a resurgence of interest among secular and religious Jews, as well as some Christians.

Of the many qualities or *midot* on which *musar* focuses, we have selected five—gratitude, generosity, patience, joy, and equanimity—because we feel they enable us to do the work of wise aging well. They help us to accept the conditions of our lives and open to possibilities, to reduce fear and anxiety, to strengthen vital relationships, and to practice forgiveness more easily; they support us as we face inevitable pain and loss and as we open to a more accepting and conscious relationship with our own mortality.

As you will see, the essence of *musar* work is to open a space between our immediate experience and our decision—conscious or otherwise—of how we will be with it. When we create a space in which to consider our actions before carrying them out, we are more likely to choose positive acts rather than harmful ones. When we allow for a space between our first thoughts about a situation and the way we continue to tell ourselves the story of what is happening, we are more likely to respond with clarity than react with raw emotion. We use mindfulness to heighten and train our awareness.

We each have some measure of all of these qualities, and we want to maintain them in a proper measure—not too much and not too little. We are not given specific instructions on how to be grateful, for instance, but rather to locate ourselves in a healthy place on the spectrum of related attitudes that range from entitlement on one end (we deserve this benefit and we take it for granted), through gratitude (we see and appreciate that this benefit is a gift), to unworthiness (we do not deserve to have this benefit). At different times we will stand in any one of those places, but our practice helps us to be most often in the place of gratitude and to be aware when we are not.

Our work is to cultivate the awareness of where we stand in respect to any *midah* or trait. With regard to generosity, we seek to be in the middle of the spectrum between selfishness and self-denial. While too much impatience can turn to rage and blame, in smaller doses it can encourage us to achieve our goals. We work to recognize the patience that lies between extreme urgency and utter passivity. The internalized *midah* of joy centers us between the giddiness of pleasure, with its constant desire for more, and the despair of depression. Equanimity lies in between zealousness and indifference.

So, how do we cultivate these *midot*? Dr. Alan Morinis, author of *Everyday Holiness*, explains the connection between the spiritual practice of *musar* and paying mindful attention to what is true in each moment:

> Even in the tiniest of decisions, there is usually an option that purifies and elevates the heart, and another that works in the opposite direction. We know we don't always make the uplifting choice, and what usually keeps us from doing so are ingrained habits, conditioning, emotional scars, ignorance, appetites and other bonds that limit and restrict our free will. Those fetters cause us to make choices that keep us away from our highest destiny.
>
> The work of musar involves taking steps to liberate the heart and open it to greater freedom of choice. In practice, that primarily means cultivating our powers of attention and awareness, because awareness is the key to bolstering and restoring choice, and breaking the bonds that block the heart.

Cultivating Gratitude

Gratitude is an invaluable quality for us as we grow older. It enables us to be more open-minded and openhearted. When we feel grateful, we are more likely to feel optimism and joy. When we express gratitude, others find it more pleasant to spend time with us. When we are grateful, it is easier to be generous, and when we feel our gratitude is welcome, we are, in turn, happier. We are able to see the good in the world, and to acknowledge it, and then to find more things to appreciate.

When we experience gratitude, we have less room for fear and anxiety. We tend to focus more on what we have and less on what we don't have or what we might lose. We may experience our days as having richness in and of themselves. And as we pay more attention to the good, to the gifts we have been given, we may see more clearly that we exist in relationship to others. We are not alone. We depend on others, and they in turn rely on us. Gratitude helps us understand how intertwined our lives are with the lives of others, and can diminish the pressure we put on ourselves to remain fiercely and sometimes harmfully independent.

What is gratitude? It is a feeling that begins when we recognize the good. That good could be in another person, in a work of art, in an event, or something else. When we feel gratitude, we are experiencing the uniqueness of the moment and choosing not to take it for granted. We may even feel we have been given a gift. When we notice gratitude, we may feel its afterglow, or a heightened sense of well-being, or warmth and expansiveness. This expansive feeling may yield a sense of connection to another, or to nature, or to God. And it may move us toward acts of generosity.

We teach our children to say thank-you and encourage them to feel thankful. But sometimes we ourselves forget that lesson. When what we have becomes too familiar, we may take it for granted, flattening out the texture of life. When we want something another person has—perhaps a new car, device, or appearance—it is easy to be overcome with dissatisfaction or envy. By contemplating the possibility that we already have what we need, we can approach a state of true gratitude.

All wisdom traditions place a high value on gratitude. In Jewish and Christian traditions, gratitude is manifested as thanks and songs of praise. Texts and liturgies are abundant with psalms, prayers, blessings, and teachings about gratitude. Many people, as they grow older, find new meaning in them, whether or not they call themselves "religious."

Pastor Kathy Maclachlan, of Bremen Union Church in Maine, in teaching her congregants the importance of gratitude, tells this story:

> During the winter of 1623 the newly settled Pilgrims faced a severe shortage of food; corn became so scarce that Governor William Bradford had to ration it. Each person was given only five kernels of corn per day.
>
> Those days of fasting passed, but it became a custom at Thanksgiving in New England to place five kernels of corn at every plate as a reminder of the sacrifices and courage of those early New England settlers. The custom came to use those five kernels of corn as symbols to think about five precious blessings we have to be thankful for:
>
> The first kernel of corn stands for the beautiful bounty of nature—God's Creation.
>
> The second kernel of corn stands for the ordinary men and women of our past who have stepped forward at the right time to do extraordinary things—answering God's call.
>
> The third kernel of corn stands for the work that we have been given to do—serving God and God's people through the gifts and talents we've been given.
>
> The fourth kernel of corn stands for our friends and loved ones—those we're blessed to walk beside in our journeys of faith. As Emerson said, "Friends are not only for vacation time, but for days of shipwreck; not only to be with us on our pleasant rambles, but to be with us as we travel over the rough roads of life."
>
> The fifth kernel of corn stands for God—God's power, purpose, and presence.

Pastor Kathy discovered at some point that this story has absolutely no historical validity. But she loves to tell it anyway, because of its inspirational wisdom.

Jewish tradition also encourages looking for the good in each person, each moment, every day. Recognition of the good is one definition of gratitude. In fact, one of the first phrases in the morning prayer service is, "How good it is!"—to wake up today, to recognize goodness in some aspect of our lives, to see a world of beauty and possibility. Another prayer affirms that each day the work of Creation is renewed in goodness.

In addition to recognizing good, Jewish tradition suggests that we take the time to express appreciation of it. A simple "Wow," a quick "thank God," a prayer, a song, or a thank-you note can activate the feeling of gratitude and rewards generosity in others.

> One who crosses the sea and survives a storm thanks God. Why not thank God when there is no storm? One who survives an illness thanks God. Why not one who escapes illness altogether? (Rabbi Mordechai Yosef Leiner, the Radziner Rebbe)

A nonprayerful way of stating this idea is that when we are in the dentist's chair, we are miserable. Why aren't we grateful every day that we are not in the dentist's chair?

This prayer from the Sabbath morning service expresses boundless gratitude:

> Could song fill our mouth as water fills the sea
> And could joy flood our tongue like countless waves—
> Could our lips utter praise as limitless as the sky
> And could our eyes match the splendor of the sun—
> Could we soar with arms like an eagle's wings
> And run with gentle grace as the swiftest deer—
> Never could we fully state our gratitude
> For one ten-thousandth of the lasting love
> that is your precious blessing, dearest God,
> Granted to our ancestors and to us.

Reflection Questions

◆ When have you ever become so overcome with gratitude that you felt you couldn't express it enough?

◆ What prayers or poems of gratitude are particularly resonant for you?

Feeling Grateful Even When Life Feels Dark

Finding and expressing gratitude is more difficult when we are in an unpleasant or painful situation. That is exactly the time when we need it most. Strengthening our practice of gratitude makes it more easily available to us, and then it can help us navigate all kinds of situations. The more points of good we find in our lives, the stronger our gratitude muscle will be. We can find inspiration in stories like that of a man who lived for decades as a quadriplegic after a terrible car accident. He spent two years in utter anger and despair, then realized that although he had lost 90 percent of what he previously considered his "life," he nonetheless still had ten percent left. Finally recognizing the sparks of the good in the dark of the loss, he could resolve to live fully in the 10 percent that remained.

A counterintuitive but effective practice is suggested by Buddhist teacher Judy Lief. She teaches that "we should be especially grateful for having to deal with annoying people and difficult situations, because without them we would have nothing to work with. Without them, how could we practice patience, exertion, mindfulness, loving-kindness or compassion? It is by dealing with such challenges that we grow and develop."

Practicing Gratitude

Choose as many practices as you like but only what you can realistically fit into a daily routine.

1. Collect poems to read when you wake up. There are so many lovely ones, like this:

    ### Praise Song

    Praise the light of late November,
    the thin sunlight that goes deep in the bones.
    Praise the crows chattering in the oak trees;
    though they are clothed in night, they do not
    despair. Praise what little there's left:
    the small boats of milkweed pods, husks, hulls,
    shells, the architecture of trees. Praise the meadow
    of dried weeds: yarrow, goldenrod, chicory,
    the remains of summer. Praise the blue sky
    that hasn't cracked yet. Praise the sun slipping down
    behind the beechnuts, praise the quilt of leaves
    that covers the grass: Scarlet Oak, Sweet Gum,
    Sugar Maple. Though darkness gathers, praise our crazy
    fallen world; it's all we have, and it's never enough.
    —Barbara Crooker

2. In the morning, when you wake, sit up in bed. Before getting up, or just upon rising, say a phrase of gratitude to yourself, such as "I am grateful before You," or whatever phrase works well for you. If you feel like it, set it to a chant melody.

3. Each morning, think of and write down three things for which you are grateful. At the end of the week, review your

entries. Or, before you go to bed, think of three aspects of your day for which you feel grateful. You may want to think of this as the beginning of an ongoing gratitude journaling practice.

4. Over the course of one week:

- Choose a phrase that expresses gratitude: "I am thankful "or a verse from a psalm or a song, or simply "thank you."
- Write it on a card to put by your bed or on your kitchen counter.
- Close your eyes. Breathing in, say "I'm grateful"; breathing out, say "I have enough," breathing out any sense of deprivation.
- Say or sing your phrase out loud to yourself after waking, every day.
- During the day, notice moments in which you have felt gratitude or appreciation. See if you can notice the feelings the experience engenders in your body. Notice if you expressed gratitude.
- Notice, as well, moments when you sensed the absence of gratitude. Record your observations in your journal.
- At the end of the week, review your journal, noticing what you have learned and felt.

5. Get a gratitude buddy

Find a friend to whom you can send a daily morning e-mail describing a moment of awareness of gratitude. Ask your friend to write back with a similar message. Over time, you will build up a significant conversation, and each step will heighten awareness.

Whichever of these practices you care to adopt, we hope you will soon notice yourself feeling more appreciative and more aware of gifts you receive in the most ordinary of situations. You may feel more connected to others, even to strangers.

Cultivating Generosity

Cultivating our capacity for generosity can help us in many ways as we become older. Giving can open our hearts further to seeing others with kindness and compassion. It can help heal relationships when we let it serve as the foundation for forgiveness. Generosity can help nourish relationships, for we all like to be with others who are generous of spirit. When we give our time, our energy, our friendship, or our funds to others, we may be more able to receive from others with gratitude and appreciation, thereby strengthening our relationships and feeling less alone and frightened. Our friend Sharon speaks of her late mother-in-law as a woman who radiated generosity. Bedridden with infirmities, she nonetheless was a bright presence in the lives of family and friends. She spent time and energy making sure to call each of her children and grandchildren every week. She spoke to them of things that interested her and asked them to tell her stories of their week. She expressed no resentments or grudges and did not want her family to feel guilty that they were not with her physically. In turn, her family members welcomed her calls and made time for them. And they visited as often as they could.

Generosity—of time, energy, attention, as well as material things—grants the giver as much as it does the receiver. It matters less what we give: generosity is a way of being, of sharing kindness, respect, patience, nonjudgmental acceptance, and openheartedness. We can all grow into it more fully.

When we give consciously, we open ourselves to the pleasure of giving. Even when we give simply because it is what is obligated, we have created the possibility of a closer relationship with the recipient.

Living generously requires inner work to develop the awareness of balance. Without even realizing it, we may limit our generosity because subconsciously we feel we don't have enough—money, time, love—to go around. Like playing the game of musical chairs, we run around trying to grab the seat before somebody else does, lest we be left out. Developing our capacity for generosity can be the antidote to feeling left out or deprived.

Likewise, we need to be aware of when we are making an unhealthy sacrifice to meet the needs of others. We need to balance compassion for others with reasonable self-interest. We give, or don't give, for many reasons. We need to be discerning about our motivations. Do the gifts we are giving meet the needs of the recipient, or are they simply fulfilling some need of our own? Is our gift mostly about them, or do we give more for its self-aggrandizing rewards, such as self-promotion or a ticket onto an exclusive board? Do we give more than we can actually afford to, and risk impoverishing ourselves because we feel that is the way to please others or to justify our existence? There are no right answers, and the answers are different for each individual. The key is finding the balance between self and other.

Three Ways of Cultivating Generosity

Jewish tradition recognizes three different qualities of generosity: the first is tzedakah—disciplined sharing commanded by the core value of justice, whether or not the heart is open when giving it. The second is *t'rumah*—free-flowing, spontaneous giving from the heart. And the third is *g'milut chasadim*—acts of loving-kindness that benefit others.

Offering Because of the Commandment to Pursue Justice

Maimonides wrote of the relationship between donor and recipient. He constructed a hierarchy of giving:

1. Giving unwillingly
2. Giving willingly and with a smile, but less than you could/should have given.
3. Waiting to be asked before giving.
4. Making the gift before it was requested.
5. Giving to an unknown recipient, but knowing that the recipient will know who the donor is.
6. Giving to a known recipient anonymously.
7. Giving anonymously to an unknown recipient.
8. Giving a gift that enables the recipient to become self-sustaining.

Reflection Questions

◈ Does this hierarchy makes sense to you? What about it does, and what about it doesn't?

◈ In what way might you want to change it?

◈ When do you think there might be benefit in a face-to-face relationship between donor and recipient?

◈ Which level do you usually work from? Why do you think that is your natural level?

Offering from an Overflowing Heart

People sometimes respond to occasions with generosity that exceeds their usual levels. It may be response to a disaster, or to an inspiring leader, or an opportunity to build something they believe in. After a tsunami in South Asia, thousands of people who had never before given flooded relief organizations with donations. Families and neighbors open their pocketbooks to schoolchildren collecting pennies for the annual Penny Harvest. And after Hurricane Sandy, hundreds of volunteers descended on community service centers to cook food for displaced families or to bring food, blankets, and supplies. Some came to give legal and medical services, or to rebuild damaged structures. Just as the suffering was enormous, so was the outpouring of generosity.

The book of Exodus has a beautiful illustration of abundant, heartfelt generosity. Moses instructs the Israelites, barely released from slavery, to bring gifts in order to construct a sanctuary: "Tell the Israelite people to bring Me gifts; you shall accept gifts for Me from every person whose heart so moves him" (Exodus 25:2).

When the artisans began to build the sanctuary, they were quickly overwhelmed by the people's generosity. They said to Moses, "The people are bringing more than is needed for the tasks entailed in this work that the Lord has commanded to be done" (Exodus 36:5). Moses responded by making this proclamation throughout the camp: "'Let no man or woman make further effort toward gifts for the sanctuary!' So the people stopped bringing; their efforts had been more than enough for all the tasks to be done" (Exodus 36:6-7).

And people are often individually generous even in the worst situations. For example, Michael Belfante carried a wheelchair-bound woman down the stairs of One World Trade Center on 9/11, jeopardizing his own safety. Studies even indicate that those without financial means tend to be more generous with their charity than people who are wealthy. According to an April 2013 article in the *Atlantic*, people in the top 20 percent of income-earners gave 1.3 percent of their income to charity, while those in the bottom 20 percent gave 3.2 percent. The wealthiest gave most of their contributions to elite educational, health, and cultural institutions, while the poorest gave to local religious institutions and social service projects. Empathy developed from sharing hard conditions can move people to give generously to others in similar circumstances.

> *Light gives of itself freely, filling all available space. It does not seek anything in return; it asks not whether you are friend or foe. It gives of itself and is not thereby diminished.*
> —Rabbi Michael Strassfeld

Reflection Questions

❖ Does your body feel differently when you act generously? In what ways?

❖ What moves you to be generous?

❖ What limits your desire to be generous?

As the Sufi poet Hafiz wrote from his religious perspective:

> Even after all this time
> The sun never says to the Earth,
> "You owe me."
> Look what happens with a love like that,
> It lights up
> The whole world.

Offering as an Act of Loving-Kindness

Some acts of generosity arise simply from our desire to help our fellow human beings, rather than as a response to a commandment or to a crisis. These are known to many as acts of loving-kindness. A traditional Jewish teaching lists the following as acts of loving-kindness: honoring parents; providing hospitality; visiting the sick; helping the needy bride; attending the dead; probing the meaning of prayer; making peace between one person and another, and between man and wife.

The Random Acts of Kindness (RAK) Foundation promotes loving-kindness through yearly RAK weeks and suggests performing various acts of kindness, such as smiling at people, eating lunch with somebody new at school or work, volunteering as a sports coach, leaving a quarter in the candy machine, sending unexpected compliments to friends, measuring your carbon footprint, helping change a tire, helping somebody find a job, donating unwanted clothes, writing a thank-you note, and buying somebody's groceries for them.

Reflection Questions

◈ What do these deeds have in common?

◈ What deeds would you include as acts of loving-kindness in your life?

Love is the basic nature, the goodness of all beings, wait-
ing to manifest. Whether we offer love in silent prayer or
aloud, we are helping love to flower in all beings every-
where. This expression of our deepest nature is the loving
power of lovingkindness—as the Buddha said, "it glows,
it shines, it blazes forth."

—Tara Brach, PhD

At the core of *musar* practice and the RAK philosophy is what many know from experience: the more we practice these traits, the stronger they become within us. Just as we build our muscles with exercise, so it is with generosity—the more we give, the more generous we become. We train our hearts to open. As Shakespeare's Juliet says, "My bounty is as bound-less as the sea, my love as deep; the more I give to thee, the more I have, for both are infinite."

One stumbling block to expanding our practice of generosity is known in *musar* teachings as a "stopped-up heart." This state is often the result of self-protectiveness; we guard ourselves from the demands of others who we may fear will take advantage of us. To manifest generosity more fully we need to become aware of our resistance. Making a practice of giving directly—to an individual asking for money, or to a younger person who needs mentoring, or to a worthy cause—can help us see, feel, and under-stand our resistance points, and work on them so that we can expand our practice of generosity.

A woman we'll call Janet spoke to us of feeling hardhearted toward her new stepdaughter. After she committed herself to a generosity prac-tice of giving a quarter to every person who asked for money on the street, she reported that she felt as if something had opened her heart. She began to see the people she had called beggars as people with needs. She shifted from feeling that they were taking from her and came to see herself as giving to them. And Janet began to see her stepdaughter as a person with something to give, not just someone taking her partner

Practicing Gratitude

1. Begin several conversations and written communications with a brief but conscious word of appreciation. Rabbi Nachman of Bratslav, one of the early teachers of Chasidic Jewish spirituality, encouraged his followers to say words of encouragement to each other in order to build the other up. He recognized that people were vulnerable to such intense self-criticism that they could lose faith in their ability to better themselves. It is essential that we encourage each other and use positive self-talk to keep a healthy perspective.

2. Share something of value with someone this week and pay attention to his or her reaction in receiving it, as well as your experience in giving.

3. When you are in a community setting, look around and see yourself as a small part of a larger whole; imagine that what you are feeling is what others are feeling, and wish that only good will come to them. Note how that makes you feel. How does it affect your desire to share what you feel or have with them?

4. Loving-Kindness—A Mindfulness Perspective (adapted from a Buddhist Metta Practice)

   Prepare to sit for twenty minutes, setting a timer to ring after the time is up. Sit comfortably, with your eyes closed or gazing down at the floor. Keep your spine straight. Bring your attention to your hands resting in your lap or on your legs. Have your palms open and facing up. Let your fingers soften and relax.

   You are not in need of anything in this moment. Bring to mind a beloved teacher or mentor, or a person for whom you feel immense love. Visualize that person. Repeat these phrases, one with each in and out breath:

- May you feel safe.
- May you feel healthy.
- May you feel peaceful.
- May you live with joy.

Repeat for five minutes.

Then focus on yourself:

- May I feel safe.
- May I feel healthy.
- May I feel peaceful.
- May I live with joy.

Repeat for five minutes.

Then focus on a person you see frequently but do not know: your postal worker, grocery clerk, dental receptionist. Repeat those same phrases as you did for your mentor. Repeat with each breath, for five minutes. If you feel strong and comfortable with this meditation, you might try bringing a person to mind who is difficult for you right now, who causes you to feel tension or unhappiness. Your goal is to hold that person more softly, not necessarily to forgive—to be able to feel some compassion. If it is too uncomfortable, do not continue.

In conclusion, bring your attention back to your breath. Feel the breath leaving your body. Allow the breath to complete itself naturally. Be aware: "I have no need to hold on to this breath."

Sit for a few minutes in this posture of loving-kindness. If you notice contraction or tension in your body, or a thought of fear or judgment arise in your mind, surround it with softness. Allow whatever is presenting itself in this moment to be fine, to be good.

Open your eyes and stretch gently.

away from her. She began to pay closer attention to her stepdaughter, found kinder things to say to her, and was more receptive to her words. They did not become close, but their relationship was much easier.

Sometimes we act generously toward another and our offer is spurned. Several students in one wise aging study group described their frustration when their parents spurned offers of help. The rejection was explicit and direct: one woman's mother fired the caretaker her daughter had hired; another man's father returned the new chair his son had bought. "It is really hard to feel generous when they fight us," one man explained. He was resentful that his parents had not shown gratitude and disappointed that his plans to help had been thwarted. But through his work and insights from the other students, he came to believe that for him, as frustrating as the experience was, generosity is ultimately its own reward. It is a spirit in us that flows more freely as it gets stronger, becomes a part of us, and at its best does not demand gratitude or even acknowledgment.

> *If a person gives to another all the good gifts of the world but does so with a grumpy demeanor, the Torah regards that as if he had given nothing. But if he receives his neighbor cheerfully and kindly, the Torah regards it as if he had given him all the good gifts of the world.*
>
> —Avot de-Rabbi Natan *13:4*

Author and meditation teacher Sylvia Boorstein says the same thing but differently: "If I intend to perfect my capacity for Generosity, I need to be alert for every opportunity that presents itself in which I can share. The sharing itself, the generous act, will become the habit by means of which I can experience directly the joy of not feeling needy, the ease of a peaceful mind. When I feel I have enough, I am content."

Cultivating Patience

A season is set for everything, a time for every experience under heaven.

—Ecclesiastes 3:1

Patience is an invaluable trait for these years. We most likely have a greater capacity for it now than when we were young; we have learned that change takes time, that growth occurs slowly, and that people are who they are whether we like it or not. Patience helps us recognize what we cannot control, and to accept that it is so. When we give in to anxiety or anger, we create our own turmoil and do nothing to help ourselves respond to the situation. Learning to accept that we can't control a situation with which we must live is extremely hard. Patience allows us to keep trying.

We also need more patience now than we used to. It may take us longer to get places or to remember names. We may well have more doctors' offices to wait in and results to wait for. And if our friends or spouse are slowing down a bit too, we need to be patient with both ourselves and with them.

Or, perhaps we need patience because others look at the world differently than we do. For instance, many of us have sat in meetings—on boards or committees, perhaps—talking about some kind of action. Those who are younger may want to act fast; they may challenge us and see us as obstacles. We, who are more seasoned, may advocate learning more or being less confrontational. We may look at events with a longer time frame, without the urgency of youth. Which strategy is best? It depends on the circumstances, and there is no monopoly on wisdom. What matters is how we talk about the matters at hand, acknowledging the differences in perspective.

On the other hand, we can have too much patience. We need to be able to stand up for what is right and for what we need, to ask for service when we deserve it, to respond to injustice and discrimination (and now, in particular, to learn to sense when other people's prejudice against the elderly may be at work) when we meet it. Patience need not—should not—devolve into meekness or passivity. Patience helps us live with greater calm, and ultimately with greater strength.

We begin our practice of cultivating patience when we start to pay attention to the feelings that arise when we encounter delay or frustration—when events diverge from our plans. Perhaps we are caught in a traffic jam or our partner keeps us waiting. We may react—turning an event into a drama starring ourself as victim. Perhaps we notice sensations of heat, tension, or clenching, signs of annoyance or even anger. Perhaps we even react by seeking someone to blame. It is so easy to do, but so unhelpful. Anger may frighten people into doing our will but does not create friends or partners.

But patience is worth the work, for it offers many benefits. It allows us to step back from irritation to consider effective strategies for responding. One such strategy is to pause and think about the person who annoys us. For example perhaps our friend who is late is *not* trying to inconvenience us but has met real delays. And the people around us in the traffic jam are

It is early one morning, and I am late to teach a meditation group, stuck in a cab behind a school bus stopped to pick up children. I actually find myself cursing silently that the kids are so slow in climbing into the bus. They are making me late for my class! Then, noting this reaction, I take a breath and say to myself, "Whoa! Recalculate! This is not their fault. They are going to school! It is actually wonderful that they have a day of learning ahead of them. What would our country be if children did not go to school?" Taking that breath allows me to calm down and admit to myself that once again I had left home too late.

— Rachel

stuck too—it is not all about us. Feeling compassion for them, we may also be able to feel self-compassion and soften our annoyance.

We can gain deeper insight into the nature of patience by looking at the Hebrew word for it, *savlanut*. The word means "to bear," as in to bear a burden or bear emotional discomfort. It means being able to take on something difficult without caving under it, to work with the baggage we carry and the baggage that others carry.

The book of Numbers gives us a perfect example. In all the years that Moses leads the Israelites through the desert, his patience is often tried. One time in particular he cries out in acute frustration and grievance. The people, impatient and angry because they find the journey so hard, need a scapegoat on whom to vent their frustration. They turn on Moses. They cry to him that they long to return to the Egypt of their fantasies, where, as they remember it, they used to eat fish, cucumbers, and melons for free. Their delusion has completely erased the memories of their bitter enslavement. This burden is too much for Moses to carry another step. His forbearance is wiped out. He turns to God and says:

> "Why have you dealt ill with Your servant, and why have I not enjoyed Your favor, that You have laid the burden of all this people upon me?...Where am I to get meat to give to all this people, when they whine before me and say, 'Give us meat to eat!' I cannot carry this people by myself, for it is too much for me. If you would deal thus with me, kill me rather, I beg You, and let me see no more of my wretchedness!"
>
> Then the Lord said to Moses, "Gather for Me seventy of Israel's elders of whom you have experience as elders and officers of the people, and bring them into the Tent of Meeting....And I will draw upon them the spirit that is upon you and put it upon them; they shall share the burden of the people with you, and you shall not bear it alone." (Numbers 11:11-17)

Practicing Patience

1. Patience Meditation (developed by Rabbi Sheila Peltz Weinberg)

Take a comfortable seat.

Be sure your spine is straight.

Scan your body for places of tension and take a few deep breaths into those areas.

Prepare to sit for ten minutes without moving at all, setting a timer to ring.

Allow your attention to rest on the sensation of the in-breath entering the body and the out-breath leaving the body.

When the desire to move at all arises, remind yourself of your commitment.

Notice any unpleasant sensation or discomfort that you want to alleviate by moving.

Instead of moving to be more at ease, bring attention to the place where you are not at ease.

Become interested in the sensation, even if it is unpleasant.

What are its dimensions?

What does it feel like?

Is it changing as you observe it?

What is the quality of the attention you are bringing to your own discomfort?

Continue to soften your awareness.

Bring the same loving presence and sense of connection to the thoughts and sensations of fear.

Rest in the powerful qualities of patience and forbearance. Rest in its spacious energy.

Can you bring a soft, loving, tolerant awareness to this experience? To your desire to move? To realizing you cannot move until the bell rings?

You are practicing patience and forbearance—in this moment as you stay connected in a loving way to this unpleasant experience.

Notice any frustration, irritability, or anger, and offer those feelings or thoughts the same soft, gentle, and loving presence.

Notice any fear that arises in the body or the mind.

2. Make a list of the situations in which you often experience impatience—say waiting in a doctor's office, driving in traffic, grocery shopping, or whatever is unique to you. When next you find yourself in one of those places, bring your attention to your feelings of impatience as they rise. Do whatever you can to notice and bear the uncomfortable feelings, and to then see if you can identify with others in your situation, seeing them too as people, and let your good will flow toward others.

   Author and meditation teacher Sylvia Boorstein once made a recording called "Road Sage," in which she taught a practice of patience. Noticing her rage when stuck on the highway, she worked with that feeling by noting it, acknowledging her frustration that she was there and not in the studio she had been headed for to tape an interview. Then she breathed into it, noting that the breathing and calmer mind felt more pleasant than the rage. Gradually she came to realize that hundreds of other people were in exactly her situation, that honking their horns was not helping anybody. She tried to imagine their stories. Her heart slowly filled with compassion, and she was even able to look out the window and find some beauty in the sky, in the architecture of the bridge, and even in the softness in her heart. She was late for the interview, but she arrived calmly. *(continued on next page)*

Practicing Patience (continued)

3. Whenever you are in any moment that is trying your patience, see if you can notice the feelings of impatience rising in your body. When you learn to notice the sensations of heat, tension, or clenching that signal that your impatience is moving toward annoyance or anger, you have developed your own early-warning system. See if you can then release the tension with three breaths. Note if you feel any calm.

4. That night, write in a journal about times when you felt impatient and times when you experienced patience. Ask yourself the following:

   - What emotions were most present for me?
   - What burdens did I feel I needed to bear?
   - What did I do to maintain my patience?

Coming to understand that there is a time for (almost) everything is a reflection of the patience we develop over a lifetime. We come to see that our life has its own rhythm, its own flow of events. We do not control many of the events that pop up in our days, but we can work with them to maximize the benefits and the learning inherent in each. And that difficult work is made easier by learning simply to be with them, not trying to rush and push through.

In his rage and despair, Moses can find no way out but to quit. God offers wisdom: When the burden gets too heavy, find others to share it. Notice who God suggests that Moses invite: the elders, not the younger, physically stronger ones. Moses needs wisdom to guide him.

With patience, we can learn to respond with acceptance rather than anger. We can bear the disappointment or the frustration without flaring up. We can speak up, but in a way that does not alienate the other. We can see the way clear to better resolutions to problems.

Integrating patience into our spiritual tool kit helps us do the essential work of growing older with wisdom. Patience gives us the time and mental space to see alternatives to what we cannot change, to find the good, and to sense our gratitude. It gives us the capacity to be more loving, more forgiving, and less afraid. It makes us better friends and partners.

Reflection Questions

- How often do you enjoy the rush of impatience, the urge to move on, to make something happen already?

- When have you been able to channel your anger and make a measured and appropriate response to something that was upsetting you?

- When are you most patient? When are you least patient?

- How would having more patience improve the quality of your life?

Cultivating Joy

Joy keeps us vital as we grow older. It lifts our spirits, it helps us find pleasure in life, and it supports hope and optimism even when times are difficult. Joy is an energy that comes from within, fills us, and flows outward. Sometimes it is exuberant; sometimes it is calm and deep. Sometimes we laugh from it; at other times we weep. It is a sense of wholeness and rightness. It can flow from the gratitude we have in any moment, or it can flow from our recognition that we are woven into complex and beautiful connections with our world.

Joy can also be with us at other times. It is the spirit that lets us keep our heads up and our hearts open when we are caught in a painful situation, when we need to remember that there is hope or that things can

I remember feeling joy watching the sun set one evening when I was leading a group of teenage hikers up and over Vermont's Mount Mansfield. The peachy rose infusing the sky, and the mountain ridges extending below us like waves fading into the glowing dusk, filled me with awe and a sense of total wellbeing. We were, simply, random creatures, glowing too in the light.

I have also felt joy in the middle of services on Friday night at B'nai Jeshurun, the Manhattan synagogue to which I am fortunate to belong. I am completely caught up in the energy and lifted out of my rational mind by the music. Occasionally the pain of my husband Paul's death, buried now so deeply in my heart, jumps out, strong and pulsing, and I weep. So many of us with broken hearts, so many others rejoicing, so many stories of life—all singing together. Tears of joy flow down many cheeks.

And when I saw the tiny body of sweet little Tessa gush out of my daughter and into the arms of the midwife, I exclaimed spontaneously, "Oh look who Paul has sent us!" although I have no rational belief that our lives on earth are affected by beloved ones who have died.

— Rachel

Journaling Exercise

Write down several specific experiences of joy that you remember. Try to recall how you felt at the time, not just what circumstances caused them to arise.

change. Here, joy is a subtle presence, a spark of life that energizes us to stay strong, to feel connected to a story larger than our own.

True joy transcends and uplifts. As such, it is highly valued in many spiritual traditions. For Christians the joy of Easter, the joy that redemption has happened, is celebrated with soaring music and prayer. Yom Kippur, a solemn holiday in the Jewish tradition, closes with a joyful service of release after the purification of repentance and forgiveness.

Jewish wedding ceremonies consist of blessings and end with the breaking of a glass, symbolizing the recognition that life is also filled with brokenness. The moment the glass breaks, the music strikes up, and the guests burst out in songs of joy for the couple as they walk into their new stage of life together. The joy contains the sorrow, even as the couple, the family, and the guests move beyond it into celebration.

We each experience joy in different ways, sparked by different experiences.

It is no wonder that George Vaillant identifies a goal of aging well as living past eighty with joy. For as we grow older, we rely ever more on our inner resources to enliven our days, nourish our relationships, and spark our creativity. Joy can carry us through hard times. It can hold sorrow, grief, pain, fear, and injustice; joy can give us hope and flexibility and inner strength; it can make us laugh.

When joy is central to a spiritual occasion, song and dance rise spontaneously. Weddings, birthdays, festivals, and religious ceremonies call on people to express their feelings in their body. Many psalms praise God for turning mourning into joy—the essential work of coming through grief:

> You turned my lament into dancing,
> You undid my sackcloth and girded me with joy
> — Psalms 30:12

> Those who sow in tears shall reap with songs of joy.
> —Psalms 126:5

Rabbi Nachman of Bratslav struggled throughout his short life with deep depression. Yet his primary teachings were about joy. He believed that the greater our capacity for joy, the more we are able to hold balance and soften our sadness with compassion, letting it dissolve into a larger view of life. He wrote:

> Regarding joy, a parable. Sometimes when people are happy and dancing, they grab hold of somebody who is standing outside, being sad and melancholy, forcing him to join in the circle of dancers, making him rejoice with them.
>
> So it is with joy. When a person is happy, the melancholy and suffering are pushed off to the side. But the higher way is to struggle and pursue the sadness, to bring it into joy in such a way that melancholy itself is transformed into gladness, so that all sufferings become joy. That's the way it is when you really enter into joy; the elation is so great that you change all your worry and sadness into joy. You grab hold of that melancholy and force it into the circle. (*Likutei Moharan* II, 23)

Reflection Questions

It may seem implausible that we can force an emotion on somebody. But let's read more deeply into the text:

Bring to mind a time when you stood outside a group, resisting the invitation to join.

◈ How did you feel?

◈ If you were able to let go of the resistance and join in the fun, how did you feel then?

Hindrances to Joy

Certainly we have all experienced joy. What keeps each of us from experiencing it more fully, more often? Why can't we—why won't we—just turn on our own internal joy switch? There are many, very human, reasons.

The barriers of our own psychology are one obvious answer. If we are prone to depression and anxiety, we need to bring compassion to our suffering and acknowledge that we may need psychological counseling as well as spiritual practice to clear the clouds. Jealousy, anger, and selfishness also work to subdue joy, for they keep us locked in a view of our world that is small and that has narrow aspirations. For many of us, the work of breaking free from the burdens of these states is ongoing. Working on spiritual practices also helps to overcome these narrowing influences and open us to more expansive ways of understanding our experiences.

Paradoxically, having fun can also get in the way of joy. Fun is a good thing—it is often both pleasurable and spirit lifting. And it can cultivate happiness and life behaviors from which joy can emerge. But fun can also be used for escape, and then it is external, limiting, and ephemeral. We often entertain ourselves to distract ourselves from unpleasant truths that must be dealt with. But real joy comes with self-knowledge and self-acceptance.

Practicing Joy

1. Journaling

   Reflecting on your experience, write in your journal or
   discuss with others some of these questions:

   • Describe times that you have experienced deep joy.
     What characterized them? How did they feel in your
     body?
   • As you remember times when you were really happy,
     can you identify elements of a deeper joy in them?
   • What blocks to experiencing joy can you find in
     yourself?

2. Count Your Blessings

   Often a powerful awareness of gratitude triggers a sense
   of joy. As such moments occur, make note of them,
   identifying what triggered the gratitude. It can be small
   things, like a wonderful conversation with a friend, or
   a moment of stillness by a window, or singing in the
   shower, or doing something goofy in a group or with
   small children.

   A wonderful practice is to begin Shabbat dinner, or
   Sunday lunch, or any celebratory meal with remembering the good things that happened in the week that just
   went by.

3. Try a "Complaint Fast"

   In *The Book of Jewish Values,* Rabbi Joseph Telushkin
   recommends a "complaint fast" as a way of increasing

joy. He suggests becoming aware of complaints as you are about to make them, then choosing not to voice them. The fast can be even more effective if you share it with those who live with you. Controlling the impulse to complain before you have brought in every woe and every criticism may even help lift your mood.

You can also take on your own complaint patterns by laughing at yourself. When you do something absentmindedly in the house, like putting your cup of tea in the refrigerator rather than the milk, instead of complaining about your aging memory, make a joke of it out loud— "way to go—brilliant placement!" When somebody is coming up to you, smiling warmly, and you have no idea of his or her name, you need a lighthearted line: "I know your face, and I know your name— but the connection between the two is lost in a synapse. Can you help me connect them?" When you are calling your own misplaced cell phone for the third time in one afternoon, imagine its ring is somebody calling to tell you you've won the lottery. Or if you get clothes back from the dry cleaner and you have no memory of them, pretend somebody has given you an anonymous gift. Collect really funny cartoons about old people and put some up on your refrigerator door. Sit around with friends and tell jokes. Laughing at yourself can often help dissolve an ever-lurking fear of dementia.

It may also be helpful to set a ground-rule for the conversations about health with your peers that some call "organ recitals": "Only one organ per person."

(continued on next page)

Practicing Joy (continued)

4. Empathetic Joy

   You might try cultivating a quality the Buddhists call empathetic joy, or *mudita*. The Yiddish version would be *nachas*. It is a vicarious joy that comes from pleasure and appreciation of another's success, happiness, or good fortune. It is the opposite of feeling jealous or envious of another. Sometimes when we hear good news of others we may be tempted to wish that the news were really ours, or to compare our experience with theirs. But by openly sharing the joy or pleasure that our friends are experiencing, we can transcend this envy and connect our joy to hearing about their pleasure.

   One practical way to foster this empathetic joy is to respond to e-mails of friends on amazing vacations, while you are stuck at home or at work, by saying sincerely, "I am so happy for you." Similarly, congratulate them on an honor. Don't attempt to do this if it would feel hypocritical, but spend time with the feeling of jealousy or grudge and see if you can relax it a bit and empathize with your friend's happiness.

5. Present a Cheerful Face

   We can actually choose to smile more often—to ourselves, when we see another, or when we see something pleasing. Scientific research suggests a connection between smiling, laughter, and well-being. Laughter has been found to increase endorphins and dopamine; reduce pain and stress; reduce depression; increase creativity, well-being, friendliness, and altruism; and enhance relationships. Without any scientists telling us, we can notice that it feels good to smile. And we are more likely to be smiled at if we smile first.

As the Buddhist teacher Thich Nhat Hạnh says, "Sometimes your joy is the source of your smile, but sometimes your smile can be the source of your joy."

6. Meditate on Joy

Prepare to sit for ten minutes, setting a timer to ring after the period of time is up.

+ Find a comfortable place to sit.
+ Begin with a scan of your body, looking for places where you are holding tension or experiencing discomfort. Breathe into those places.
+ Imagine yourself in some place where you are deeply happy and peaceful.
+ Enrich the image visually and sensually.
+ Note the feeling in your body from being in that space.
+ Sit in that place, feeling it, and noticing when your mind takes you out of there.
+ Where are you going?
+ What kind of thoughts are diverting you?
+ When you realize that your mind has taken you away, check your breathing and return to the place.

Feeling *deep* joy is an experience we know; those times sparkle in our memory. These practices can help us experience the emotion more frequently. At moments when we feel deeply connected with someone else, or a group of people, or nature, our barrier of separation begins to dissolve. We recognize that we belong to larger space, larger time, and that we are part of Creation itself. Such a joyful realization liberates us from the narrow confines of the self.

Cultivating Equanimity

Between stimulus and response there is a space. In that
space is our power to choose our response. In our response
lies our growth and our freedom.
　　　　　—Viktor E. Frankl, *Man's Search for Meaning*

quanimity is a place of inner calm. It is a place where a person can
experience joy, fear, grief, delight, and other feelings, without being
thrown off balance by them. It is like the focal point of a seesaw—the
place that balances the up and the down.

Strengthening our capacity for equanimity is enormously important
for this stage of life. As we get older and feel less in control of the events
taking place in our lives, and feel more anxious about the future, having
equanimity enables us to be responsive, rather than reactive, to what is
going on in the moment. It gives us an ability to accept what is true and
then choose our response to it. The quality of equanimity, the ability to
accept and to be present with what happens—whether or not it is what
we want—is what helps us live well in the space between stimulus and
response. One might see equanimity as an internal island of calm, from
where we can clearly see all the forces that blow at us—the pleasant, the
unpleasant; the joyful, the sad; the delightful, the frightening. With the
eye of equanimity, we can see these forces change all the time—emerging
from the background into prominence and then receding, filling our heart
with pain and then leaving it relaxed. We know that no emotional condition has to define us or permanently dominate our mood.

Some might think that equanimity implies indifference. It does not.
From a place of equanimity, we have the inner space to look carefully at
our alternatives, and to choose the response that will be most effective
and constructive. From that space we can mobilize our full emotional,
rational, and spiritual resources, rather than striking back blindly from
fear and anger, or desire and grasping.

Unintended or unanticipated events, and other people's responses to us, can startle us and throw us off balance. We like to think that we have control over our lives; we take actions, we set goals, and we achieve many of them. We study, we work, and we strive. Many things turn out well; some do not. But much of importance was *never* in our control. Despite diet and exercise, we get sick. Our family members or friends make decisions we don't like. Jobs and the economy change. Nonetheless, we cling to the illusion of control, for we are terrified of vulnerability.

Equanimity allows us the strength and resilience to live with this condition. Being able to hold ourselves within the larger perspective of equanimity helps us to be aware of that urge to control and to let it relax, to let us be more open to what happens now. It helps us to seek and to find the good that is always there somewhere. We learn to balance between domination and indifference.

The Ba'al Shem Tov, the eighteenth-century rabbi and spiritual genius whose teachings were the foundations of the Chasidic movement, taught a very stark view of equanimity. "It should make no difference whether one is taken to be an ignoramus or an accomplished Torah scholar. This may be attained by continually cleaving to the Creator—for if one has [a] deep connection with God, one isn't bothered by what other people think. Rather, one should continually endeavor to attach oneself to the Holy Blessed One."

He meant that if we base our opinion of ourselves on the reactions of other people, we may become a slave of public opinion and external, rather than internal, validation. When we are motivated by transcendent values, then we balance our own need for approval and our fear of disapproval against a higher standard. When applied with some moderation, this view of equanimity can help us be more principled people. If carried to an extreme, it makes us ideologues. The practices of *musar* can help us keep the balance.

Practicing Equanimity

1. Meditation on Equanimity

   Find a comfortable position, sitting on a chair or on a cushion, with your eyes closed or looking down, your back upright but not rigid, your hands gently clasped in your lap. Check your body for places of tension and imagine breathing into those knots to relax them. Spend a few minutes finding the rhythm of your breathing, paying close attention to the sensation of air coming in, filling you up, like the tide coming in. Note the exact point where the tide changes and the breath starts to flow out. Then note the point where your lungs feel empty and the breath is drawn in to fill them up. Note the sensation. Note the calm that comes with the breathing, if it does.

   After a few minutes, as you breathe in, say phrases like these:

   • Breathing in, I calm my body.
   • Breathing out, I calm my mind.
   • May I feel balanced.
   • May I feel at peace.

   Stay with these phrases until you actually feel calmer in your body and mind. When you are feeling more balanced in mind and body, expand your awareness to a place that can acknowledge that all created things arise and pass away: joys, sorrows, pleasant and painful events, people, buildings, animals, nations, even whole civilizations. Let yourself rest in the midst of them.

Then coordinate these phrases with your breathing in and your breathing out.

2. Noticing Feelings

    Choose a fifteen-minute period during the day, one when you know that you often feel unbalanced. When you notice the feeling, do whatever you can to bear uncomfortable feelings and keep your goodness flowing toward others.

    Some people can develop awareness of the truth of an experience in the present, as it occurs, without spending long hours in sitting meditation. Dr. Ellen Langer of Harvard University says one can do this directly by not taking on tomorrow's worry today—note the worry rising and choose not to go with it. Good advice, and hard for many of us to do. Cultivating equanimity takes practice, and living with a fairly developed sense of equanimity is entirely possible.

3. Working with a Phrase

    For two or three minutes at the beginning of your day, repeat a phrase related to something meaningful to you. You might set the phrase to a melody that you know, making it a chant you can repeat. Here are a couple: "Rise above the good and the bad." "This too shall pass." "Keep your eye on the prize; march on." Or make up your own.

    Write your phrase on an index card and place it somewhere where you will see it in the morning.

Buddhists value equanimity highly and have developed extensive practices for cultivating it. Gil Fronsdal, an important Buddhist teacher, explained it this way:

> The most common Pali word translated as "equanimity" is *upekkha*, meaning "to look over." It refers to the equanimity that arises from the power of observation, the ability to see without being caught by what we see. When well-developed, such power gives rise to a great sense of peace.
>
> *Upekkha* can also refer to the ease that comes from seeing a bigger picture. Colloquially, in India the word was sometimes used to mean "to see with patience." We might understand this as "seeing with understanding." For example, when we know not to take offensive words personally, we are less likely to react to what was said. Instead, we remain at ease or equanimous. This form of equanimity is sometimes compared to grandmotherly love. The grandmother clearly loves her grandchildren but, thanks to her experience with her own children, is less likely to be caught up in the drama of her grandchildren's lives.

Having equanimity can also mean that we don't get captured by the desire for more. Just as we can suffer from lack, we can suffer from abundance. The joy of pleasure or satisfaction can be diminished by the desire to have even more, or by sadness that the pleasantness will be over soon. Our thoughts and feelings take us away from the experience. Equanimity helps us approach a situation able to enjoy it fully, knowing that it will end, that we cannot take it with us. We can see the desire to cling to the experience and let it go.

As the writer Mark Nazimova puts it:

> After practicing stilling my mind for five or ten minutes a day—basic meditation—within a few weeks I begin to have that space in my life that Frankl wrote about: the space, the moment, in which I am aware that I have a feeling, but

I am not necessarily the feeling; the space between stimulus and response; the space to choose what to do with the feeling I have. Out of such spaces can composure grow.

Reflection Questions

❖ In what circumstances do you find your equanimity most "tested"?

❖ In what ways does experiencing great good in your life challenge your equanimity?

This poem by the Sufi poet Rumi describes the challenge and the opportunity of holding yourself with equanimity:

The Guest House

This being human is a guest house.
Every morning a new arrival.

A joy, a depression, a meanness,
some momentary awareness comes
as an unexpected visitor.

Welcome and entertain them all!
Even if they're a crowd of sorrows,
who violently sweep your house
empty of its furniture,
still, treat each guest honorably.
He may be clearing you out
for some new delight.

The dark thought, the shame, the malice,
meet them at the door laughing,
and invite them in.

Be grateful for whoever comes,
because each has been sent
as a guide from beyond.

— 7 —

Living with Loss and Finding Light

There is a crack, a crack in everything,
that's how the light gets in.

—Leonard Cohen, "Anthem"

W e have been exploring the opportunities for personal growth that come with this stage of life. And there are many. Now we turn toward those opportunities that wait for us in the more difficult regions of our aging—the inevitable losses and the pain, whether physical or emotional. Most of us would forgo these opportunities if we could, sacrificing a measure of growth, a portion of wisdom for a less troubled path. But we know by now that life generally does not provide this option.

We have also learned by this stage of life that much of our growth and wisdom has been prompted by just these kinds of unwelcome opportunities. In challenging times we discover our courage and resilience; we learn that we can bear sadness; we learn that we can appreciate love and beauty in the midst of loss. Often this surprises us; we may even feel unsettled or guilty to find that we have reaped benefit from an occurrence that we judge unfair or even tragic.

Jewish tradition gives us a story by which to understand and accept the truth that greater wholeness often emerges through a shattering. It is said that the holy Ark, which the Israelites carried during their forty years in the desert, contained both sets of the tablets that Moses brought down from Mount Sinai. The fragments of the first set, shattered when Moses threw it to the ground upon seeing the Israelites dancing around the golden calf, lay next to the intact second set. Like the Ark, our wholeness always contains our brokenness. Our brokenness is part of our wholeness; it is not something from which we should flee. Rabbi Nachman of Bratslav captured a similar sentiment in his teaching: nothing is as whole as a broken heart.

Reflection Question

◈ What experiences in your own life illuminate the tale of the whole and broken tablets being treasured together or Nachman's teaching about the wholeness of a broken heart?

As we anticipate the challenges of growing older, we may want to develop our capacity to confront dark times and to grow through them, rather than being undone by them. There is a third option too, one that is highly tempting. That is holding ourselves at an emotional distance from what is truly going on in our lives, play acting at resilience, managing the situation by not allowing ourselves to experience it deeply. This denial of our brokenness actually diminishes our wholeness. So, before we look at the forms of support to which we can turn, we need to allow ourselves to look at our fears.

As we anticipate the losses and the pain of old age, our imagination is fertile. We picture the loss of body strength and capacity, the deterioration of health, as well as the dislocation from our place of residence. The prospect of the loss of the status and satisfactions of the roles we have enjoyed disheartens us. And then we dread those terrible diminishments of mental capacity—memory loss, dementia, and Alzheimer's. And finally we fear the death of friends and relatives, and most darkly, our own mortality.

But we also know that we can cultivate the spiritual practices that will help us live well through the hard places. We can nurture and strengthen important relationships, we can call on character traits or *midot* to hold us steadier, and we can cultivate new ones—like faith and mindfulness and some form of prayer, be it formal or spontaneous or poetic. We can also develop a capacity for self-forgiveness.

Loss of Status and Roles

Older people often complain of feeling invisible, or irrelevant, or insecure. Some of us report receiving fewer approving glances while walking down the street than we used to. A relief and yet a pang. At a meeting or a party people no longer ask the kinds of questions they used to, choosing instead to look past us, or perhaps smile politely, or engage in patronizing small talk, or simply move on. At the office, younger people gather around the coffee machine, not thinking to invite us into the circle. E-mail chains no longer include our names.

Fear of retirement—whether from a paid job or a volunteer position—is real for many in this stage of life. One major issue may be economic: how will we support ourselves and our family? Another may be the loss of identity. On the one hand, it is so meaningful to do work we love and/or need, and to feel that we are still making a difference. On the other hand, the fear of giving up our work identity keeps many of us working longer than we must and perhaps longer than we should. The longer we stay, the shorter time we have to explore new experiences and new learning. And, in staying on, we may be clogging the pipeline for those who come behind us, full of new ideas and different experiences.

Adjusting to new circumstances may be difficult as we search for a new sense of identity and purpose. We may feel as if we are in a strange land whose rhythms, culture, and geography are unfamiliar. This is especially true when we have not spent time during our careers—too busy or not interested—building relationships, finding community, and working on our inner lives. It takes time to learn to live with uncertainty, fluid boundaries, a more open calendar. It may feel uncomfortable not to be able to explain what we do by naming our profession. We may prematurely conclude that the best of life is over. These are all very painful feelings.

My two sisters came to visit me when I served in the Peace Corps in Guayaquil, Ecuador, in 1966. Walking in the streets of the city was often disconcerting, for men felt completely free to comment out loud on a woman's appearance or share their erotic thoughts with the public. One day Connie and Peggy and I were walking on the main street when a man whistled at us and called out "Tres flores, un jardin!" (Three flowers, a garden!).

We laughed, treating his remark as poetry rather than harassment. A year ago, now aged seventy-two, seventy, and sixty-eight, we were walking on Riverside Drive in New York. We all noticed a man eying us with approval and laughed. "Wow, tres flores," we said followed by, "This is pathetic—it feels great to be noticed! We must be desperate," we said, apologetic for taking pleasure in what we would otherwise think was an objectifying attitude.

While invisibility has the advantage of safety and anonymity, it is also lonely. In response, I have developed a practice of noticing older people—on the street, on line at the movies, in the grocery store—seeing what is beautiful in their faces, or their carriage, or their clothes; seeing their dignity in their wheelchairs; feeling the hunch as they lean over their walkers. Despite the worries about what condition I will be in when I am as old as they are, love rises in my heart. Each is an individual, and I wonder about their stories. I smile if I catch their eyes.

— Rachel

Fear may feel very palpable, but we need to move through it to discover what may be on the other side. Some who take the plunge ask themselves, "Why didn't I do this years ago?" There are so many ways to enjoy free time. There are simmering interests to cultivate and many ways to feel valuable. For example, there is a growing encore career movement that puts the skills people

> ### Reflection Questions
>
> ◈ In what ways, if any, have you felt irrelevant?
>
> ◈ More invisible?
>
> ◈ More appreciated?
>
> ◈ Does the idea of retirement frighten you and, if so, how?

used in their former employment to service in nonprofit or small business organizations. This movement is engaging thousands of people in new activity.

There are classes, social groups, and social causes. There are gardens and parks and kitchens. And there is the work we described in chapter one as the search for the authentic self—discovering what our deeper longings and passions are. Now is the time to integrate the modality of being into the familiar modality of doing. There is no shortage of opportunities.

Physical Losses

As we think about our future, our first focus is often on our bodies. Even when we do strength training or yoga, eat well, and otherwise take care of ourselves physically, we begin to feel our body aging. Perhaps we are weaker and experiencing pain in new places. Perhaps we tire more easily. We may have to give up or reduce doing some of the physical things we have loved so much, perhaps things that help us feel vital or are part of a connection to friends and our community.

In chapter three, we recalled our stories about our bodies and their influence on our lives today. Now, we invite you to take some time to reflect on your anticipated relationship with your body as your life moves forward.

Interestingly, many who work with and conduct research about the lives of older people note that in spite of the losses and challenges, they often report a surprising sense of well-being. According to author and geriatrician William Thomas, the changes in body function and life circumstances

> ...require older people to develop enterprising strategies and subtle adaptations. While it is true that muscles weaken in later life, it is also true that older people are less likely to report symptoms of depression than younger people. Hair may turn white, get thin, and fall out, but, when surveyed, older people report an enhanced sense of well-being. We grow shorter rather than taller, our toenails turn yellow, and our arches fall, and yet many older people report that their health is good or very good. These seeming paradoxes are actually the fruits of adaptation, which grows in tandem with and is nourished by the decline in physiological function....In old age, the body instructs the mind in patience and forbearance while the mind tutors the body in creativity and flexibility.

Reflection Questions

Take a few minutes with these questions, either with friends or in your journal:

◆ How do you imagine yourself ten years from now? Physically? Emotionally?

◆ What losses and challenges do you think will come as you grow older?

◆ Whom do you know who has lived well with pain and loss?

◆ How do they do so?

◆ Think of a time when you experienced a loss of physical capacity or pain. How did you get through it?

I remember a story that Sylvia Boorstein once told about going with her husband up a ski lift to eat lunch at the top. This was sometime after they'd both decided that skiing was no longer safe for them. Once they arrived at the top, Sylvia's husband turned to her and said, "Syl, what if we just take one run down?" "No," she said. "We just decided that we are too old to ski—we are not strong enough. But we'll go to the lodge, enjoy lunch, and take pleasure watching the younger people out there skiing."

I learned two lessons from that story: the difficulty of accepting change, and the power of empathetic joy to give pleasure to an observer, even when she or he can't participate.

What am I giving up now? I wonder. A lot: running is out because of my knees; hiking is hard because of newly diagnosed rheumatoid arthritis; and I've lost the energy for squeezing so many activities into a day.

On the other hand, I still can walk a lot even if I have to sit to ease foot pain, and walking is more pleasurable than running ever was. And I like the calmness that comes with doing less. I can even remember to say to myself, "I am too old to have to do that." And now I can go to bed when I am tired.

I also devised a clever (at least to me) scheme for dealing with loss. I've started a bucket list for my next life: the things I'd like to do but know I can't or won't do in the remaining years of this one. Every time I add something to this list (traveling to Mongolia, learning to play the piano beautifully, becoming fluent in a new language), I laugh at myself. But I also find a bit of comfort because I am not erasing the activity from my imagination.

— *Rachel*

Most of us would probably choose to retain our hair, height, and high arches, but if we aren't going to get a choice, perhaps we can take solace in knowing that these physical losses are helping us learn patience, forbearance, creativity, and flexibility.

Relationship Losses

When a parent, spouse, sibling, or close friend dies, a deeply meaningful and orienting part of ourselves disappears. We may feel that our hearts are broken, that we will never be whole again. And it's true—we won't ever be the same.

Earlier in our lives, losses like these were rare occurrences. But now, illness and death begin to cast a larger, darker shadow. Suddenly, it seems it has become ordinary, rather than exceptional, for friends and loved ones to fall seriously ill or die. These days we make more hospital visits and go to more funerals. Visiting and caring for loved ones more often drains energy, emotions, and time. We may even resent the burden at times, perhaps feeling guilty for having such an unworthy reaction. We wonder how we will be able to go through it over and over. And we are haunted by another concern, as a friend recently described: "It is as if we are all soldiers running across a battlefield—people are falling to either side of us. When will it be our turn? That's our life from now on. How do we get used to it?"

Somehow, we do. Those who survive the deaths of many friends and siblings develop different coping mechanisms. A woman in her mid-eighties said, "My advice to you is to make younger friends!" A great-grandmother in her nineties kept asking, "Why am I here? I have had enough." Yet she plowed on, stubbornly independent, doing the tasks of her life, adding another great-grandchild's name to her charm bracelet until she died suddenly, walking back from the grocery store. Another nonagenarian relies on her children, her grandchildren, her younger friends, the telephone, and Jane Austen for company and for living each day. She is, she tells herself, "still alive."

Roger Angell wrote on being a survivor of losses for the *New Yorker* magazine:

> We geezers carry about a building directory of dead husbands or wives, children, parents, lovers, brothers and

sisters, dentists, shrinks, office sidekicks, summer neighbors, classmates, and bosses. All once entirely familiar to us and seen as part of the safe landscape of the day. It's no surprise we're a bit bent. The surprise, for me, is that the accruing weight of these departures doesn't bury us, and that even the pain of an almost unbearable loss gives way quite quickly to something more distant but still stubbornly gleaming. The dead have departed, but gestures and glances and tones of voice of theirs, even scraps of clothing—that pale-yellow Saks scarf—reappear unexpectedly, along with accompanying touches of sweetness or irritation....My list of names is banal but astounding....Why do they sustain me so, cheer me up, remind me of life? I don't understand this. Why am I not endlessly grieving?

Other kinds of relationship changes may have profound emotional consequences as well: downsizing a beloved home, moving to assisted living or to a nursing home, putting a partner in some kind of facility because we can no longer provide adequate care, accepting a caregiver. These experiences, and the related decisions about what we are going to do, can be wrenching. Whatever we decide, there will be losses. They are losses we need to grieve.

Even more ordinary losses deserve to be acknowledged. Family members or friends move away, or we lose our community by moving to be near our children.

Florida Scott-Maxwell described her feelings when her son moved away from her—across the Atlantic.

I accept the reasonableness of the event that pains me. I see its necessity, but my heart is a storm of loss. I am part of my family as they sail down the channel only a few miles away at this moment. I am happy with them, thrilled with them, I feel the excitement of the children, the pleasure of their father as he shows them the great ship. I feel the wind blowing, I feel everyone astir with the sense of the long voyage ahead. I have all this clear in my head, but at the same time I suffer at their going. I am bereft. And I am angry that nothing can be said. It is a lie to be cheerful, and so I am left with this passion with which I can do nothing.

We might want to challenge Maxwell, however, about that "nothing." True, she cannot stop her son; nor does it seem that she would truly choose to do so if she could. What she can and does do is experience the passion, the love, the tenderness she has for this family as they depart. With her heart cracked open in this way, the intensity of her love—a dimension of her wholeness—is all the more accessible. Would we choose this? No. Can we acknowledge and own it? Yes.

Reflection Questions

◈ What aspects of your life do you recognize in Maxwell's situation? How does it feel?

◈ What do you do to address your feelings?

◈ How might you go about strengthening your community or finding one?

◈ What aspects of your life remind you of running across a battlefield with your loved ones dropping by your side? How do you cope?

Losses of Mind and Memory

Today, Alzheimer's and dementia may be the diagnoses that we most fear because they rip at our very sense of identity, and no progress on a cure has been reported. Being unable to recall a name or a place, or searching for our keys or the paper we just put down can induce a frisson of dread and an empathic nod of understanding from our partner or friends. Is this normal, or are we headed down the slippery slope? Sometimes we laugh at ourselves; other times we rush to the computer to look up early symptoms of Alzheimer's.

We fear, and embroider our fears, that we may face a long, progressive decline. There will be that awful time when we are aware that we are not who we were. Then there will be the time when the primary suffering will be transferred to those who love and care for us as they witness our further decline. We know that these illnesses place enormous emotional, financial, and physical strains on everyone. We don't want to become a burden or the guardian and caretaker of a loved one who is slipping away from whom he or she used to be.

And we wonder: Who will we be when we are no longer who we were? Once again, we are challenged by the question with which we began this book: What is the authentic self? Now, however, we are disturbed by its extension: "Might we lose that core, essential self while we are alive?" It seems especially frightening that dementia may rob us of our very personhood.

Dr. Marc Agronin, a psychiatrist for the Miami Jewish Health Systems, writes poignantly and hopefully about his work with Alzheimer's patients: "My patients have taught me two lessons. First, it is easy to miss the sparks of the person hidden under the burden of the disease….and second, we can step in to discover and even help rejuvenate the person behind the lost memories."

Rabbi Dayle Friedman, who has devoted much of her career to working with older people, offers a stunning perspective on the inner life of those with Alzheimer's. She is extremely clear about the sadness and the difficulties of facing the illness, for both the person affected and their loved ones. Nevertheless, she queries, "How do we know that a person with dementia is not on a higher spiritual level?"

Such a person, she suggests, has been stripped of the masks and public faces that most of us wear and work so hard throughout our later years to discard. As memory dissolves he or she becomes increasingly immersed in the present. So as most of us dart back and forth between thoughts of what has been and the anticipation of what might be, often struggling to live in the present moment, a person with advanced dementia lives in unboundaried time. Family members, friends, and caretakers thus have the challenge *and the opportunity* of staying in the moment as well, being in the moment with the individual, letting go of regrets and worries for the future. Even small blessings from misfortune should not be overlooked.

We may find some comfort in knowing that there are many creative ways to aid people whose memory is slipping. We know of a woman whose family made her an album of photographs and mementoes from her life. As her memory declined, she carried it with her like a portable identity that she could consult when she felt confused or that she could show to others. We know of people who become animated and lively and physically stronger for periods of time through music, as they remember the words to old songs. We hear of those who can be awakened by hearing their native language.

Another way to work with the dread of Alzheimer's is learning to calm the all-too-understandable fear and reduce the inevitable stress. We know that someday we may be put to the test. For this alone, it would be worthwhile to become practiced in mindfulness. It is important that we not let our mind run away with stories that increase our fear.

With practice, we may come to understand that fear is a temporary sensation; it is okay to have fear but important that fear not have us. As we learn through mindfulness practice to observe our fear rising up and to see that it eventually subsides, we can free ourselves—even if only for brief periods of time—from its grip. Even as we prepare to face further decline into this darkness, we can counter our tendency to catastrophize

I first began to think about such questions during the period of time that my mother lived after suffering brain stem stroke during minor surgery. She was in a state referred to as "locked in." Doctors believed that her mind remained intact, but no part of her physical body functioned under her willful control; the paralysis was complete. "Blink once if you mean yes," they would tell her; "blink twice for no." But she lacked even that simple control; she couldn't respond when the doctors asked her whether she wanted to be kept alive or not.

I couldn't help but imagine what it must be like to lie helplessly in bed listening to all the conversation about her. I could almost feel myself jumping out of my skin in a fit of frustration. But of course she couldn't even control the blinking of her eyes well enough to signal yes or no, let alone jump out of bed. I could feel the words "Shut up, all of you!" forming in my mouth, but, of course, whatever words were forming within her stayed locked in her brain, unable to take their form as sound. So I began my exploration of these existential questions with the very personal query: What if only my mind was left?

Although my father was convinced that she would never want to live this way, I was so unready to let my mother go that I sometimes imagined rolling her in to my daughter's bat mitzvah on a gurney a year hence, wanting moments to be enough to make her life worthwhile. Fortunately no one, unless it was my mother herself, had to make a conscious decision; she died suddenly one night.

But I now knew something about life—and death—that raised new questions. Would the inner work I had begun to do allow me to face such an existence with some dimension of equanimity, still able to find moments of joy at hearing the voices of grandchildren or witnessing a rose in full bloom, able to feel the accompaniment of a divine presence rather than abandonment and fear? And even harder—if I should develop Alzheimer's or dementia, what relevance would my spiritual practice have then?

— Linda

A colleague told me about her mother's descent into Alzheimer's. It was the first time I had heard any description of the disease that didn't seem utterly horrifying. She explained that her mother was past the stage of being able to recognize even her family visitors, but in a strange way, it didn't matter much. It was as though all of her mother's personality had been stripped away, and what was left was pure love. It didn't matter who you were; she greeted you with a hug and a proclamation of love. "I love you," she said to the nurses, the doctors, the housekeepers, the attendants, and the other patients, as well as to her nieces, and nephews, and daughter. Everyone in the home adored her.

I was deeply moved by the account, and it too became part of the problem with which I was wrestling. If, God forbid, I lost the self that was my cognitive mind, who would I be? I had heard of Alzheimer's patients who had become angry or violent, although they had not been so prior to their decline. Could I do enough inner work so that if, God forbid, I were stripped of my conscious intentions, it would be love that shone through? I know that others with advanced spiritual practices have not been able to manifest such love. I have no idea about myself, but the preparation in itself would be worthwhile.

I could name many longings and hopes that have kept me on the path of spiritual seeking and practice, but perhaps this desire is the foundation on which the rest stand.

— Linda

the situation—feeling as if the worst were already true—by taking a few breaths and telling ourselves that for this moment we are okay, for this moment our loved ones are okay. With this greater clarity and broader perspective, we can, perhaps, enjoy our present life more fully and feel confident that, should the occasion arise when the thing we fear now does begin to manifest, we will be able to have some degree of equanimity. Meanwhile we are doing what we can to sustain ourselves through exercise, diet, sleep, and keeping our minds and intellects active, all the

Reader Practices

Mindful Listening

A small group of members of a congregation in Brooklyn, New York, each with a parent suffering from dementia or Alzheimer's, decided to form a support group. They met over dinner for an hour and a half once a month. They set ground rules for the conversation: nobody was there to fix anybody else; they were there simply to listen to each other. No cross talk—only listening to one person at a time, without interrupting. And to notice what it felt like to not interrupt, make comments on the side, or try to intervene with a "fixing" comment.

They set the structure for their monthly meetings:

- ◈ Begin with eating and schmoozing, to create comfort with each other.
- ◈ First round: Each participant gets five minutes to say whatever she or he feels like, without interruption. After one finishes, the group sits in silence for a minute. Then the next person begins.
- ◈ Second round: Each participant has the opportunity to say what she or he needs from the group and can offer to it.
- ◈ Conclusion: a blessing practice. The participant who spoke first blesses the person who spoke second, starting with, "May you...," related to what the person had talked about during the sharing.

Reflecting on the experience, one participant said, "It was so serene and respectful and powerful, and I really, really felt safe."

things that researchers tell us might help keep our memories, our bodies, and our spirits alive.

In Genesis 1:27, God makes human beings *b'tzelem Elohim,* "in God's image." The idea that we manifest divine qualities also finds expression in the book of Leviticus 11:44 in which God proclaims, "You shall be holy for I am holy." This is often understood as a command to "Be holy." But it can just as easily be understood as a statement: "You are holy because I am holy." In this framework, we can understand the soul surviving even the ravages of dementia. In the later stages of the disease, we may get only rare glimpses of the divine sparks within. Our spiritual work may entail continuing to relate to that soul even though it now seems to be concealed from us within the body.

Loss of Life

Healing from the death of a loved one is a long, painful process that each of us goes through in our own way. We may be shocked to experience excruciating physical pain, like a knife turning in the gut or a fire encircling the heart. We may experience unexpected tearful meltdowns in random places, an acute sense of abandonment, the grayness of the day, the sudden awareness that we are in the middle of the street with traffic approaching. All of these are but examples of the myriad ways we each experience the pulsing of grief through our lives.

We find resources to help: family, friends, community, a clergy member or teacher, a bereavement group, a grief counselor. And our spiritual practices, whatever ones we have or we are spurred to develop, help us summon our resilience, our courage, and our hope. Healing generally comes slowly, and it is often an uneven process. It is not uncommon to feel that we are grieving incorrectly—taking too long; seeming to be all right too soon. It's easy to be confused and confounded by what others seem to expect of us as well as our own assumptions about mourning. At some point though we recognize that the sun does come out, that we can laugh and love, that we have work to do. We know we will be OK. We may even sense that we are different now, and that we have grown through our grief.

Studies have shown recently that most grief-stricken people find themselves less miserable and more resilient than they had imagined. They don't stop being sad, sometimes deeply so, but most of them recover a sense of their aliveness within six months or a year.

This is not to say that grief is easy. It certainly is not. But knowing that each of us has a resiliency on which to draw, and that the pain will lessen, can be a comfort to many.

Acknowledging Grief

Grief from any loss needs to be recognized. It can come from small losses or large—"I had to leave the house I've lived in for fifty years" or "My child made choices that I don't like" or "My child is suffering from mental illness, and I don't know how to help." It can come from divorce or the breakup of a valued friendship. It can come from ending a satisfying career or from the loss of a physical capacity. It most obviously comes from illness and from death of loved ones. Acknowledging the pain of these losses is important as it opens the way for us to accept them. And with acceptance, we can give up the struggle to deny or resist. We free up psychic energy and can begin to develop more clarity about the truth of the moment in which we are living. If we can see our situation more clearly, we can adjust more easily, and identify helpful resources, actions, and supporters. Perhaps we can even find new meanings in our changed circumstances.

Rumi, in his poem "Birdwings," describes the way mindfulness helps:

> Your grief for what you've lost lifts a mirror
> up to where you are bravely working.
>
> Expecting the worst, you look, and instead,
> here's the joyful face you've been wanting to see.
>
> Your hand opens and closes and opens and closes.
> If it were always a fist or always stretched open,
> you would be paralyzed.
>
> Your deepest presence is in every small contracting and expanding,
> the two as beautifully balanced and coordinated
> as birdwings.

Facing the Challenges

When we are experiencing dislocation, loss, and grief, we may feel at times that we are living in a very sad and dark place. In Jewish mystical thought, that place is called Mitzrayim, the Hebrew name for Egypt. Working with its root Hebrew letters, Mitzrayim can be read as "narrow straits," and the Jewish mystics used it to refer to our own inner places of constriction. Fear, depression, and despair are the psychological Pharaohs who oppress our hope, our imagination, and our confidence. Liberation from this narrow place comes from opening our mind to a wider, more expansive awareness, and our hearts to love and compassion.

As I write these pages I am struggling with a close friend's relapse into a life-threatening illness. I am trying my best to accept a reality that I hate. It is hard to stay calm. Fear and panic carry me off balance, knotting my stomach and making me dizzy. I am so caught in my own drama that I am not thinking clearly about how to be supportive of her. She surely does not need another anxious presence hovering around.

I am relying on the love of my family and close friends as well as wisdom from my teachers to help me live with—walk into rather than abolish—the fear and the anxiety that are crushing my spirit.

I call my friend and teacher Sylvia. She asks me, "What have you been doing to hold yourself in a place of compassion?"

I explain to her that I don't know how to feel self-compassion. I grew up as a New England Yankee, with a stiff upper lip and the stern admonition, "Don't feel sorry for yourself." I can feel my friend's pain, but I can't accept my own—it feels so petty.

"The fundamental truth," Sylvia tells me, "is that you are in pain. It is a relief just to articulate it to yourself." I begin to see that without compassion for myself, my compassion for others comes from a superficial place.

I go down to the spacious park along the banks of the Hudson River. A verse of Psalms rises in me, "From the narrow place I call out; please answer me from your wide open space." As I chant it out loud, I feel the Hudson washing some of the pain away, down its majestic tidal ebb out into the ocean. I throw a stick in, representing this narrow place; it bobs away over the ripples of the current. The pain does not go away but recedes, leaving space for me to see a larger picture of life and the situation. I know I can cope now.

— *Rachel*

Acceptance

The truth is, things happen, good and bad. When they are wonderful, we are happy to live with them. But when they are sad, frightening, or unpleasant, we resist accepting them—we simply want to make them go away. For acceptance means surrendering the illusion of control—admitting that we are not the sole architects of our lives. The prospect of sharing or losing that control can be terrifying. But it can also be liberating.

Acceptance allows us to see a situation in stark reality, for what it truly is. And from there we can decide whether and how to respond: whom we should call, what do we need, what do *they* need, what should we do? What medical, physical, emotional, and spiritual resources can we tap into? What will lift our spirits, or theirs, so that we are not dragged down by fear, or anger, or false hope? What is our support system? This is how we respond to the commandment articulated in the book of Deuteronomy: "I have set before you life and death, blessings and curses. Now choose life, so that you and your children may live." We wrest blessing from the darkness and choose the path that seems most enlivening.

In *My Grandfather's Blessings,* Dr. Rachel Naomi Remen tells of her grandfather's ability to celebrate life despite difficulties:

> My grandfather told me that l'Chaim! meant that no matter what difficulty life brings, no matter how hard or painful or unfair life is, life is holy and worthy of celebration. "Even the wine is sweet to remind us that life itself is a blessing."
>
> It has been almost fifty-five years since I last heard my grandfather's voice, but I remember the joy with which he toasted life and the twinkle in his eye as he said l'Chaim! It has always seemed remarkable to me that such a toast could be offered for generations by a people for whom life has not been easy. But perhaps it can only be said by such

---

Reflection Questions

◆ Whom do you know living a *"l'chaim"* life?

◆ What is their secret?

◆ How have you tapped into such resiliency in your life?

---

people, and only those who have lost and suffered can truly understand its power.

L'Chaim! is a way of living life. As I've grown older, it seems less and less about celebrating life and more about the wisdom of choosing life. In the many years I have been counseling people with cancer, I have seen people choose life again and again, despite loss and pain and difficulty. The same immutable joy I saw in my grandfather's eyes is there in them all.

Practices for Finding Light

Having looked at some of the darker possibilities that may come with growing older, we ask ourselves: How will we fare? What can we do to become strong enough to face such difficulties without succumbing to sadness, fear, or bitterness? How will we develop the fortitude to reap opportunities for growth and wisdom from circumstances we would never choose? How do we maintain equanimity in difficult times? Is joy really possible?

People have asked these questions throughout human history. They have faced the enormous challenge of working with these experiences—of loss, pain, and fear—and finding hope. They have developed spiritual resources to help them. People have always turned to each other in the search for comfort and strength. They have sought the support of community and the guidance of wisdom, for the task of healing ourselves is too great to do alone.

Religious traditions have arisen over thousands of years to help us do this, and new ways of working on ourselves continue to emerge.

These practices remind us that we are not the only ones to have suffered or to be suffering. They remind us that as we care for our loved ones we can open our hearts to care for ourselves and for others as well.

Visiting the Sick

Visiting the sick is a valued practice in any tradition, for it brings the compassion at the heart of religion to people in need. Visiting the sick in Jewish tradition is considered a commandment. Christians of all denominations are called to minister to the ill, bringing prayer, ritual, and comfort. The San Francisco Zen Center has developed an exquisite approach to being with the dying and is training hospice workers of all religious and secular backgrounds.

Dr. Ira Byock, a nationally recognized expert on end-of-life care, uses a powerful image of the value of companioning people with illness, as if: "we were shoulder to shoulder with a patient on a journey neither of us could choose."

Visiting seriously ill people is not so easy for many of us. Our reluctance may stem from inexperience—perhaps we don't know what to say or how we might help. Perhaps we don't want to be reminded of previous experiences with illness, or of our own vulnerability.

There are specific ways we can help one who is ill to be more comfortable and boost his or her spirits. We have the opportunity to make sure our friend or family member has all the key elements of good care: a clean room, enough to eat, things to occupy the mind. Then we can determine if our visit is even wanted. If so, when we are in the room we take a seat level with the one who is ill, not standing above. We sit close by—near the head of the bed, or in a nearby chair—in a place which tradition esteems as holy. Depending on our relationship, perhaps the person would like us to hold his hand or rub her feet. But perhaps the person wishes no physical contact.

It does not help to give unsolicited advice, to offer false cheer, or to tell the patient how to feel. We don't ask about symptoms or talk about our own or friends' experiences with the disease, unless invited to do so. The individual may be trying to retain a sense of self differentiated from the physical condition. So we sit comfortably, letting the individual direct the conversation, and listening and responding in kind. We open ourself to the patient's vulnerability—and strength—and bring our own in response. It is also quite all right to sit silently and do no more. Our physical presence is the most important thing. We should be aware of the patient's energy level, sensitive to their need to rest or to be alone. When it is time to go, we can ask if there is anything we can do, offer a blessing or a wish, and depart.

When spiritual teacher Ram Dass visited people who were ill, he would give them forty-five minutes of undivided, concentrated attention. He would conclude with a blessing. Then he would leave. At the door, he offered a silent prayer. Then he let go of their story, for he felt it helped neither the other person nor himself to carry the burden of worrying or of feeling their pain outside the room. This practice kept him strong for each visit.

Receiving Visitors

When we are the one who is suffering, it is important to allow visitors. We may feel uncomfortable because we don't look our best, or our home is not in its usual order, or we don't like to feel dependent. We may worry we don't know what to say. We can trust that a smile of welcome will put visitors at ease. We may ask visitors simply to sit with us, or ask them questions in whose answers we are actually interested. If the visit seems to be lasting too long, we can say, "I am tired now. Thank you so much for visiting." Most important: we must try not to let ourself feel alone and abandoned. A story in the Talmud relates that just as a prisoner cannot free himself, so too a patient cannot heal himself.

When patients physically can't accept visitors, many take comfort and find meaning in cards, e-mails, and very brief phone calls. Receiving them restores them to visibility and affirms that they still matter to those out there in the land of the well. The ideal phone call from a friend should be a quick check-in, unless the person wants to talk more. Patients can also ask friends to screen calls.

Dr. George Vaillant, in his longitudinal study of aging, listed one of the qualities of people who age well as being able not to feel sick even when they are sick. He did not mean false cheeriness, or denial of pain and discomfort. Rather, he meant that they found ways to identify themselves as separate from their illness.

The more we can see that we have symptoms but are not the disease, the easier it may be to lift our spirits. And of course there will be times when we can't, which is only natural. But it helps to know that these moods are not permanent—that they come and go. We experience feelings of fear, or dread, or terror. And then we experience feelings of hope, or joy, or deep love. Our feelings are not static, and we are not our feelings. With help we can free ourselves from confinement in the narrow straits of darkness.

Meditation

Meditating on difficult emotions or on uncomfortable sensations in our body helps us learn to live with discomfort. We can learn to accept the sensations as what they are, and allow them to be—without adding stories of our misery to the actual discomfort we are experiencing. People who suffer chronic pain have found that working with Mindfulness-Based Stress Reduction (MBSR) has enabled them to live more easily with it. The practice has been so effective that thousands of centers are now teaching doctors, health care professionals, and those who suffer from pain and stress to use MBSR for all kinds of stress-related issues.

Dr. Jon Kabat-Zinn, who developed the practice, explains that the meditation is not about fixing pain or making it better. It is about looking

Meditation on Turning toward Pain

Sit in your comfortable meditation position, eyes closed, spine upright but not rigid, chin slightly tucked, hands gently touching in your lap.

Find your breath and relax into it, noting breathing in, breathing out.

Bring to mind an unpleasant situation in which you have found yourself recently: feeling chronic pain, or the emotions left from an argument at home. Let your body feel these sensations. Pay attention to them and let them grow stronger. Is the pain steady or stabbing? Is it sharp or dull? Where is the discomfort located? Breathe into it and breathe out from it. If you stay with it awhile does it dissipate? Say to yourself, "It is okay to feel this. Can this feeling hurt me?"

If it becomes too uncomfortable, let the thought go and reestablish contact with your breath. You are an explorer—the more you notice, the more you will understand the impact of your emotions on your body and the transient nature of the physical sensations.

Imagine that pain is not your enemy but a sensation manifesting in your body, experienced as unpleasant. Have you spun the pain into a story that magnifies the pain, such as: *This is too hard. I can't bear it.* If it becomes unbearable, shift your body to ease the pain.

You can learn to experience even serious pain as sensation, rather than a thing that is hurting you. You can learn to separate the sensation from the story you tell yourself about it. Many people who have done MBSR training have learned to live with chronic pain they once found virtually unbearable.

deeply into the nature of pain and using our insights in ways that allow us to grow. In that growth, we can make choices that will move us toward greater wisdom, self-compassion, and freedom from suffering.

Faith

Cultivating faith helps us develop an inner steadiness. For many people religious faith provides calm support, even if they struggle to reconcile their understanding of God with the existence of pain and suffering. Sometimes these dark times trigger a shift in our understanding of God. Sometimes we simply accept our inability to understand the divine but find that we are nevertheless able to draw comfort and strength from a sense of connection with a higher power.

Faith does not necessarily mean religious faith or a belief in a divinity. It can be much broader. It can be a kind of trust and confidence in

Reader Practices

Meditation on Faith

Begin by sitting in a comfortable position.

Choose a phrase, which you can write on a piece of paper to put before you or keep by your bed. A traditional one is: "I am ever mindful of God's presence" (Psalms 16:8).

Or make up one of your own, such as: "May I see light in this moment," or "I feel peaceful," or "I hold myself with compassion."

Sit with your phrase, either with your eyes closed—to minimize distractions—or looking down at the floor.

Breathe in with the first part of your phrase; breathe out with the second. You are not trying to memorize it, but rather to imprint it in your consciousness. Repetition helps integration.

Sit in this way for five minutes or more—the longer the better.

the adequacy of our relationships, values, and practices to help us cope, and an affirmation of our steadfastness. As a leading mindfulness teacher, Sharon Salzberg writes:

> Faith does not require a belief system, and is not necessarily connected to a deity or God, though it doesn't deny one. This faith is not a commodity we either have or don't have—it is an inner quality that unfolds as we learn to trust our own deepest experience. . . . Faith is the animation of the heart that says, "I choose life, I align myself with the potential inherent in life. I give myself over to that potential." This spark of faith is ignited the moment we think, "I am going to go for it. I am going to try."

Prayer

Prayers and psalms have comforted people for thousands of years. Most traditional prayers express belief in a God who intervenes in human destiny. Today, though, many people do not believe in a God who literally answers prayers and controls the universe. If there were a God who was both just and powerful, they argue, how could a child die, a tsunami sweep whole towns away? How could slavery or genocide persist? How, they ask, can we pray to such a God for help, comfort, or hope? Others, though, find meaning in a different understanding of God—or for Christians, in Jesus or Mary—who weeps with us, who heals shattered hearts, who hears our cries, and whose presence is felt when we are alone.

Strangely enough, prayer does not require a belief in God. Prayer can be simply an exploration of ways in which words can help us reach out beyond our personal experience to connect with others, with community, or with our sense of a higher purpose or an order that we cannot even understand. Prayer can be a shout into the seeming emptiness of space. Prayer can be expressed in tears, a sigh, a wail, a melody, a chant, or silence. Prayer at times of loss and fear, even if we do not know to whom or to what it is directed, can help us articulate and understand our feeling of

When I came home after leaving Paul alone in the hospital with a diagnosis of acute myeloid leukemia, I opened the L volume of the encyclopedia only to read that his disease was inevitably fatal. Yet I knew my friend Ruth's father had recovered from it. So Paul might be cured too! I threw the book in the trash and fell on my bed, sobbing. The words that came out of my mouth were, "Save him, God. Please save him. Don't let him die."

As I was saying the words, my brain was telling me I was ridiculous, for I believed that God does not intervene in personal destiny. My mind was overwhelmed by my heart: "This is too big for me! I can't do this alone. You have to help me; I can't do it by myself." The voice of my soul was crying out my terror, my sense of utter aloneness, yet sensing that there was a force way more powerful than anything I understood that would somehow help me.

I saw that force play out over the next year in the incredible medical care Paul received; the outpouring of love, cards, home-cooked meals, visits; and in the strength Paul found in his morning prayer rituals. He found a way to be himself even in the hospital.

A year later, I was standing in synagogue during the Kol Nidrei service of Yom Kippur, holding a Torah scroll in front of the open Ark, praying again my original prayer: "Don't let him die." He died five days later.

For a while, when I went to services every morning to say Kaddish, the mourner's prayer, I felt only hurt and anger at this God—whom I always said never intervened in individual lives—for he'd betrayed us by not fixing Paul. After a month, though, I felt my hurt and anger meant there must be some notion of God that did have meaning for me. But what notion was that?

What I discovered was that the God who had been there all along was not the servant who defied my will. God was the love, the hugs, the tears, the kindness of people; the resilience and inner spirit that helped me to redirect my life on a meaningful path, and to be grateful for my children, my siblings, my friends, and my community. I knew that God from my personal experience, not from theory. And saying "God" to hold that whole cluster of emotions, strengths, gifts, and grief felt true. With that God in my heart, I could pray words of hope, anger, and love.

— *Rachel*

powerlessness, of vulnerability, of loneliness. At other times, it can be awe, gratitude, and love that burst out in our prayers.

If all that blocks our effort to call out for help or consolation, or to express sadness and anger, is nonbelief in God, we can call out to "the Universe," or "the Mystery," or "To Whom It May Concern." We can try the practice of *hitbodedut* that we described in the "Loneliness and Solitude" section of chapter four. Or we can sit in silence or walk in the woods. Many are surprised by what happens when they let go of the need to know to whom or to what they are praying; words then may come unexpectedly from within—words that we need to speak and words that we need to hear.

Psalm 23 is probably the most beloved source of strength for Jews and Christians. It is a psalm of comfort. It is a beautiful poem. It affirms that we are not alone, even when we feel we are walking in the valley of the shadow of death, even when we have no idea to whom we are speaking when we say it. It affirms that safety, calm, and abundance are available, even in the darkest times.

> God is my shepherd; I shall not want.
> God makes me lie down in green pastures and leads me beside the still waters,
> Restoring my soul, leading me in the paths of righteousness for the Name's sake.
> Yes, though I walk through the valley of the shadow of death,
> I will fear no evil; for You are with me.
> Your rod and Your staff, they comfort me.
> You prepare a table for me in the presence of my enemies.
> You anoint my head with oil—
> My cup runneth over.
> Surely goodness and mercy shall follow me all the days of my life:
> And I will dwell in the house of God forever.

Other people work with traditional prayers by adapting them to contemporary sensibilities. Rabbi Sharon Brous, spiritual leader of a

Working with Prayer and Psalms

Whether we are believers in the power of prayer, or we are looking for ways to express our feelings, we can find much of relevance in prayers and psalms. We can use them to call out, to comfort, to reassure, or to protest. We can say, sing, or chant them in our place of religious community, out in nature, or to ourselves quietly.

At some point in our lives, when we are in trouble that we don't know how to get out of, when we feel lonely, lost, or scared like a child, many of us will find ourselves praying spontaneously. We make bargains—"If I get out of this alive, I promise I will do X." We sing to give ourselves courage. Or we may just cry out an impromptu plea. A wave of relief comes over us when we get out of a tight situation, and we say "Thank God!" Or we make love and say, "Oh God, that was amazing!" In all these ways, we are expressing our deep need for strength from outside to bolster our inner spirit. Or we are expressing our sense of awe.

For many people, the steady confidence expressed by liturgical prayers is strengthening. Muslims recite their prayers five times a day. Catholics recite prayers with rosary beads. Buddhists have chants for particular practices. Participants in twelve-step programs end their meetings with the Serenity Prayer, by Reinhold Niebuhr:

> God grant me the serenity
> to accept the things
> I cannot change,
>
> Courage to change the
> things I can, and the
> wisdom to know the difference.

Reflection Questions

Choose the ones that seem most helpful to you:

◆ What associations, if any, do you have with this psalm?

◆ What comfort, if any, do these particular words offer you? What images speak to you? Where does it fall short?

◆ What verse(s) might be helpful for you to remember?

◆ What might it feel like, or does it feel like, to have faith that there is a benign presence in the universe, in your life, that exists completely apart from your control?

◆ What image of safety and protection would give you great strength at a difficult time?

◆ Have you found comfort/consolation/strength in prayer? If so, when?

◆ What are your most important resources for spiritual comfort?

Try writing your own prayer that would be helpful to you in recovering from a loss or in finding your balance. Try saying it in the morning and before you go to bed.

synagogue called Ikar in Los Angeles, teaches us to work with prayer as protest. We have adapted her teaching.

Begin with reading or chanting words from Psalm 118 to yourself:

> From out of the depths
> I called to You.
> You answered me,
> from a place of great expansiveness.

Then move into "a place where it is safe to take your anger, your fear, your longing, your sense of injustice, your disgust." Rabbi Brous tells us, "You may not think of prayer as an act of protest, but in the Jewish tradition that's precisely what it often is....Take your beef to God. Say it out loud—even in a whisper. Call out from your narrowest place—and you might just find expansive possibility."

What we find is that when we work with prayers or psalms in a personal way, we experience a twofold connection: to our current life story, and to the story of our tradition or humanity at large. We see this in the way that Jonathan Spear, a young father, has appropriated the Sh'ma as a practice that can touch many aspects of his life. He wrote about it on the thirteenth anniversary of 9/11:

Thirteen

years ago,
I could not just fall asleep—
exhausted, anxious, worried, sad, angry, confused,
and with fighter jets flying circuits overhead.

So I said the Shema,
as a form of Kaddish,
and positive affirmation,
and because the falling darkness demanded that the end of that terrible day be recognized.

For the following two weeks, I said the Shema each night,
as I lay down, looked out the window, and saw the smoke still rising over the debris.

Then baby Jacob was born,
and I said Shema every night as I sung him to sleep.
Often he would cry if I stopped singing, so I'd sing it over and over again.

And a few years and many repetitions later,
Tessa was born. And I've continued singing the Shema almost every night.
Sometimes with closed eyes in hushed tones,

Sometimes looking out the same window at the different scene,
A couple of times, connected by phone, when I was in Denver or
Orlando or somewhere else they were not.

Tonight I sing Shema again,
with a particular memory for the pain of that day
and a deep appreciation of all that I've been so fortunate to
enjoy since.

Reader Practices

Journaling Exercise

Look through the prayers and the psalms above and
write down verses or phrases that speak to you. Choose
and memorize at least one verse that might provide you
with comfort when you are feeling sad, or frightened, or
alone. Add your own poems to these prayers and psalms,
creating in your journal a book of comfort, inspiration,
and compassion.

The words of Leonard Cohen opened this chapter with the image of
light coming through the cracks. By this time of life, we know that most
of what we once thought solid now shows cracks. Which turns out to be
good for us—at least spiritually. Cracks release what is hiding inside: our
private pain, our shame and regret, as well as our delight and joy. Cracks
make us vulnerable, and once we admit our vulnerability, we can see that
others too are hurting. We can see them and ourselves more honestly
and compassionately. We can open to gratitude for the small blessings in
our life, for the good that is around us everywhere. As love and gratitude
grow stronger, our inner light shines out through eyes that see beauty in
the other, through touch that caresses, through ears that hear the other's
whisper, through a cracked heart that is open, vulnerable, and loving. We
are stronger than we ever were before.

—8—

Conscious Dying

Life's ultimate meaning remains obscure unless it is
reflected upon in the face of death.

—Abraham Joshua Heschel

E ven our deaths are part of our legacy. Although we will be
discussing legacy in the next chapter, the issues surrounding
dying and death are related to the inheritance of what we leave
behind. How we die is part of what we bequeath to our loved ones, our
friends, our colleagues, and our caretakers.

Toward the end of one's life it is common to think back to the deaths
of one's parents. They are often the closest models we have of what the
dying process is like. It may be a frightening model or a peaceful one. We
too will inevitably become models for others. Knowing this, we may find
additional motivation for doing our own work around death—accepting
its inevitability; facing our fears; and making arrangements with doctors, lawyers, and above all with our children or loved ones. Among the
challenges we will face is how to open this frightening territory to conversation. We will need to figure out how we let our children know that while
we feel profoundly sad at the thought of leaving them, we feel good about
our lives and trust that they will carry on, continuing to grow and find the
particular way they have been called to contribute to the world. We will
need to think about how we respond to young grandchildren when they
innocently ask, "When are you going to die, Grandma?" Or, "When you
die, where do you go?"

As his sister-in-law prepared to die, Henri Nouwen, Catholic priest, professor, and author, reflected: "Having taught all her life, she now teaches through her preparation for death. It strikes me that her successes and accomplishments [as a painter and poet] will probably soon be forgotten, but the fruits of the dying may well last a long time....She has shown me, in a whole new way, what it means to become the parent of future generations."

One of the men in George Vaillant's study of aging articulates a similar idea: "I think it enormously important to the next generation that we be happy into old age—and confident—not necessarily that we are right but that it is wonderful to persist in our search for meaning and rectitude. Ultimately, that is our most valuable legacy—the conviction that life is and has been worthwhile right up to the limit."

Do We Really Want to Talk about This?

Death is all around us. We learn about it from newspapers, television, social media, books, and movies. As we age, it increasingly is a part of our lives as it takes friends and family from us.

But seldom are the times when we can think seriously about death. Our emotions resist it, and our culture encourages only trivial discussion, diverting us from serious conversation. All manner of social conventions and norms discourage the discussion of our fears, questions, and concerns. In his book *Wrestling with the Angel*, Rabbi Jack Riemer reports a controversy in Vail, Colorado, over a proposal to alter zoning laws and establish a cemetery. The cofounder of the local newspaper protested by writing, "A cemetery in Vail is against what Vail is all about....People come here in order to have a good time and ski and enjoy the atmosphere. It would be bad for business if we did anything that would depress them."

Wendy R. Uhlmann, genetic counselor and coordinator of the Medical Genetics Clinic at the University of Michigan, remembers the awkwardness she felt after her father died. Well-intentioned friends, colleagues, and neighbors would ask, "How are you?" fully expecting the usual response of "fine" or "OK." "But," she writes, "I wasn't fine. My father had just died of leukemia. I was with him throughout the dying process and his actual death. Part of me had just died, too, no longer able to converse with my dad or see him again." Uhlmann discovered that few people knew how to offer even simple words of condolence: "my condolences"; "I'm sorry about your loss."

Most of us grew up at a time when people were even more averse to conversations about death than today. The word *cancer* was uttered in a whisper, if at all. Children were left at home for funerals, even those of grandparents.

The publication of Elizabeth Kübler-Ross's *On Death & Dying* in 1969 stirred conversation first in the medical field, then more broadly, by focusing attention on the emotions associated with dying and grief. The hospice movement, starting in the mid-1970s, provided motivation for asking ourselves questions about how we would want to die. Because AIDS was an epidemic, and initially a puzzling one, death itself moved further out of the closet and into greater public view. Because most who were dying were young and middle-aged, their prolonged decline and deaths seemed much more jarring than those of the elderly or even those of cancer patients.

Now, with the aging of the self-reflective baby-boom generation, we are seeing increased interest in preparation for death reflected in books, media, film, and lectures. Memoirs that tell the story of a parent, spouse, or partner's illness and death are proliferating. Some authors record their own journeys toward death after receiving a terminal diagnosis. A few doctors and caretakers are beginning to write about what patients and their loved ones should know in order to negotiate the medical system and make decisions about end-of-life care.

Mindful of the recent advances in medicine that often extend life, many of us ask ourselves when and how we want to die. More than previous generations, we are aware that we may have some control and choice about the way we conclude our lives. Under what circumstances do we want our health proxies to approve or forbid "heroic measures"? Do we want to be treated with antibiotics in the last few months of our life if our illness is terminal? The older we get, the more we understand that the answers are not altogether straightforward and in fact direct us to more profound questions. When is life worth clinging to? When do we surrender to death's inevitability? How do we prepare ourselves? How do we prepare those who will accompany us to death's threshold?

We open the newspaper, we attend a funeral, we drive past a cemetery, our physician's office calls and says they want to do another test. We wake up from a frightening dream, we sit with a dying friend, we recite memorial prayers and suddenly think, "Someday my daughter will be saying this for me."

We cannot avoid death. Yet few of us face it squarely.

Denial: When Does It Serve; How Does It Hinder?

Despite death's ubiquity, few of us approach this subject with equanimity. Many of us divert our attention from the issue of death, focusing instead on hopes and expectations that science and medicine will soon be able to extend our lives even further. When we do speak death's name, we often cloak our references in dark humor. As Woody Allen said, "I'm not afraid of dying. I just don't want to be there when it happens."

Although our culture may be more death avoidant than many, the lore of traditional societies assures us that our fears, our resistance, and our denial are part of the more general human condition. In the *Mahabharata*, the Hindu epic, we read about an instance where the virtuous King Yudhisthira is asked, "What is the most wondrous thing in the world?" He replies, "That all around us people can be dying and we don't believe it can happen to us."

Rabbi Nachman appeared to Rava in a dream. Rava asked him, "Was death painful?" Rabbi Nachman replied, "It was like a hair being drawn from milk. But if the Holy One were to say to me, 'Go to that world and be as you were before,' I would not want that. Fear of death is so great."
—Talmud, *Mo'ed Katan* 28a

Yosef was desperately poor, and his aging body hurt every time he bent down to pick up another twig or scrap of wood. In fact his body hurt all the time, but bending, lifting, and carrying were his only means of livelihood. "Oh God," he moaned, "I can't do this any longer. What kind of life is this? Take me, I'm ready!"

One day, as he was loading a larger than usual piece of wood into his sack, the sack ripped, and all that he had gathered lay scattered on the ground. "God!" he shouted,

— 251 —

"I told you I've had enough of this wretched life. Take me away from this pointless life. Let me die!"

Suddenly the Angel of Death appeared before him. "You called for me?"

"Yes," said Yosef in a quivering voice. There was a long pause before he spoke again. "I was wondering whether you could help me pick up all these sticks?"

—from *Consolation*, by Maurice Lamm

When Moses realizes that the decree of death has been sealed against him, he utters more than fifteen hundred prayers. He draws a circle around himself, stands at the center, and proclaims, "I will not move from this spot until the judgment against me is suspended." God promptly orders every gate in heaven locked, lest Moses's prayers find an opening.

The prayers are fruitless in the end, and when Moses sees this, he begs heaven and earth, the sun and the moon, the stars and the planets, the mountains and the rivers, and finally the sea itself to intercede for him, to no avail.

God asks, "Why are you so aggrieved at your impending death?" And Moses answers, "I am afraid of the sword of the Angel of Death—the pain of death itself." God replies, "If that is the reason, then don't worry, I won't deliver you to the Angel of Death." But Moses still clings desperately to life. A few hours before his death, God says to him, "How long will you endeavor in vain to avert your death? You have only three hours to live. Better make use of them." But Moses bargains on furiously, "Let me live on the wrong side of the Jordan," he begs. "Let me live someplace different altogether. Let me live on as a beast of the field or a bird in the sky." "Now you have only one hour," says God. "Now you have only a few minutes."

—from *This Is Real and You Are Completely Unprepared*, by Alan Lew

We were particularly intrigued to read Stephen Levine's personal account of resistance in his book, *A Year to Die*. Levine, who has spent his lifetime counseling the dying, decided to take on a radical challenge: to spend a year living as if it were his last, even though he faced no explicit terminal diagnosis. About that experiment, he wrote:

> Let's see now, before it's too late, how I may be magi-think-ing my way toward death, what I have secretly kept swept under the rug, how I delude myself that I "know death."
>
> [Six months into the year my] mind realized with a start that it was more than halfway through the "last year of life," that more time had elapsed than remained. And it began to bargain for an extension. It threatened to sue. It insisted that "last year" had not begun until six weeks after New Year's, when the process got up to full steam and the writing had begun. It argued that it had until next Valentine's Day to live and did not have to let go before then. I gave the mind a cookie and a warm glass of milk and told it to soften its body and prepare to die. It grumbled for a moment, then it burst into laughter. It was learning to trust the process.

Cultural anthropologist Ernest Becker has suggested that much of human behavior, on both the individual and societal level, is motivated by our anxiety about death. The forces of denial and repression are so strong that we only rarely get a glimpse of our underlying fears. But, he argued, they can be detected in everything from our shopping, drinking, and drugging to our projects of heroism, creativity, and service.

How could addictive shopping *and* heroic attempts to better the world be similarly rooted in our awareness of mortality? We, Becker explains, are "split in two." On the one hand, we are aware of our "splendid uniqueness" and believe that we tower over nature. At the same time, we are aware that ultimately we are "food for worms."

It is a terrifying dilemma, and our response to this tragic destiny, according to Becker, is to embark on or join an "immortality project," something that will allow us to see ourselves as heroic and eternal, worthy of being remembered, part of something that will last forever. From Becker's perspective, religion, philosophy, charity, and science are all immortality projects. When a society fails to provide adequate options for immortality projects, society instead contrives to help us forget, offering distractions from the mystery and terror of death with entertainments, consumption, and addiction.

At times, denial may serve us well. We recently heard of a woman whose last words at the end of a long battle with cancer were, "I'm not dying." Perhaps her ongoing denial allowed her to battle her disease with a spirit that doctors tell us sometimes seems to prolong life. Or maybe it allowed her to have hope and granted her quality time she might not have had if she had accepted the prognosis that her cancer was terminal.

Most of us however are unable or do not want to deny so completely. Growing comfortable with the idea of our death takes work. But if we avoid facing it until it is staring us down, we are forced to begin the work in a weakened state and a hurried fashion. Instead, if we begin now, we increase the likelihood of a more dignified, meaningful, and peaceful death. Moreover, there are reasons to suspect that avoiding contemplation of our mortality limits our ability to live as fully realized human beings.

When we look underneath all our denials, we find a myriad of concerns: How much time do I have? Will I suffer? Who will be with me? How can I make it easier for my loved ones? How will I be remembered? These are questions that are worthy of our contemplation now. Working with them allows us to prepare ourselves and our loved ones. Difficult as they may be, these preparations can foster our growth.

Beyond the questions we need to discuss to ease our anxiety and fear, many of us want to confront the existential questions that death raises. We, like the naïve child, experience a death and ask in wonder, "But where did she go?" "Where did he, who a moment ago was so very much here, disappear to?" "What exactly is it that seems to have slipped right out of the body, leaving it lifeless and cold?"

Reflection Questions

- What ways have you been aware of resistance or denial in your own confrontations with death?

- How do you feel when you are in conversation with someone facing a terminal disease or someone who has just lost a loved one?

- What is the most difficult part of visiting someone in the hospital or at a house of mourning? What feelings and emotions do you experience?

- Have you had an experience around death that you'd like to discuss with someone but feel that the right opportunity has not arisen? Whom would you choose as a conversation partner? How might you initiate such a conversation?

- Are there other conversations related to death that you are aware of avoiding? Perhaps making a will? Discussing where and how you want to be buried? Arranging for the care and establishing the guidelines for life-sustaining interventions that you will want at the end of your life?

We simply do not know.

The mystery confounds us. And in our discomfort we may cut off our questions and fears about death, refusing to acknowledge them as part of the way we need to learn about life. It's more comfortable that way, but when we resist thoughts about death, we lose the insights that can come from confronting them.

An interesting phenomenon has arisen in response to the Western reluctance to talk about death: death cafes. According to their originator, Bernard Crettaz, death is cloaked in "tyrannical secrecy." Death cafes are informal gatherings of people who feel the need to speak openly about death and are generally held in pleasant neighborhood cafes, where people feel comfortable revealing their questions, concerns, and recent experiences. Begun about ten years ago in Switzerland and France, death cafes have more recently been held in cities in the United States. Some death cafes meet regularly; others are one-time events.

If such an idea appeals to you, you could invite a small group of trusted friends to engage in a comparable gathering. Use this chapter to lend structure and depth to the conversation.

Accepting Death Enriches Life

In his essay "Death as Homecoming," Rabbi Abraham Joshua Heschel contends that "the fact of dying must be a major factor in our understanding of living." We can imagine many ways that acknowledging mortality can influence the way we live. In a commencement speech at Stanford University, Steve Jobs, cofounder of Apple Inc., spoke of the way it worked for him.

> When I was 17, I read a quote that went something like: "If you live each day as if it was your last, someday you'll most certainly be right." It made an impression on me, and since then, for the past 33 years, I have looked in the mirror every morning and asked myself: "If today were the last day of my life, would I want to do what I am about to do today?" And whenever the answer has been "No" for too many days in a row, I know I need to change something. Remembering that I'll be dead soon is the most important tool I've ever encountered to help me make the big choices in life. Because almost everything—all external expectations, all pride, all fear of embarrassment or failure—these things just fall away in the face of death, leaving only what

is truly important. Remembering that you are going to die is the best way I know to avoid the trap of thinking you have something to lose. You are already naked. There is no reason not to follow your heart.

Although he acknowledges that death is "grim, harsh, cruel, a source of infinite grief," Heschel asserts that it takes on a redemptive cast when it is perceived as congruent with life rather than opposed to it. If we experience life as a mystery, a surprise, a wonder, a gift, then the incomprehensibility of death can be seen as an extension, a magnification, of life.

Indeed when we accompany someone through his or her final breath, we can be struck dumb by the subtlety of the difference between last breath and no breath. What we witness is deeply mysterious. We are escorted into the realm of no speech; we have entered the silent domain of fearsome awe. Theologian and scholar of comparative religion, Rudolf Otto, described it as the *mysterium tremendum,* a feeling that is outside the self, an intense response to something whose nature is concealed and esoteric, beyond our conception and understanding, extraordinary and unfamiliar. This feeling compels and fascinates; it generates fear and trembling. Some consider this the domain of the holy; for others it is wholly other.

Perhaps it sounds like theology or philosophy to assert that our understanding of life's fragility and preciousness will be enhanced by embracing both life and death as related dimensions of our mysterious existence. But our most convincing teachers are those who have discovered this truth through their lived experience, those whose backs are up against the wall of death's finality.

Philip Gould, a British political consultant, was told he had three months to live. A few weeks before he died, in a piece entitled, "I'm Enjoying My Death. It's the Most Fulfilling Time of My Life," he wrote:

> [I] can go for a walk in the park and have a moment of ecstasy....I go to the exhibition tent and I sit there and have a coffee and I feel ecstasy after ecstasy after ecstasy.

This is built upon this feeling of certainty, of knowledge of death. There is ecstasy because I am not dead yet.

Only then [with the prognosis of a very short time to live] do you become aware of death, and suddenly life screams at you with its intensity. I have entered the Death Zone. My death has become my life. And my life has gained a kind of intensity and power that it had never had before....I am defining myself now through death. I am giving meaning to myself through death....I feel at one with the world.

One More Fear: Not Having Lived

Another reason for our denial of death may be the awareness or fear of not having fully lived, of having left things undone or failed to remedy something we still wish to fix. How can we gracefully surrender our life if we feel that we have lived it incompletely? If we feel we are not yet done?

The film *The Bucket List* explored the notion that we might want to make a list of things to do in the remaining years of our life. Reviewing bucket lists on the internet reveals that many people focus attention on travel—desiring to see more of the world. Many also expressed a desire to try something new and untested: bungee jumping, riding an untamed bronco, flying upside down in a plane, shaking hands with a president, learning a foreign language, learning how to paint, publishing a book, dyeing one's hair orange, participating in a mud fight. And a few had philanthropic wishes, like paying for a child's cleft-palate surgery.

Reading these lists, one can only wonder about what lies under the surface. What does each achievement mean to the person wishing it?

When we read "dyeing my hair orange" it made us think of our friend Jordana, who often says, "I'm really unconventional—I've just never had the chance to act it out." Does a list of daredevil experiences signal a desire to feel more fully alive? What pain or need or longing are the philanthropic desires meant to address? Stephen Levine suggests that we resist facing our mortality because we have not yet fully lived.

> So much of ourselves postponed. So little have we investigated what has caused us to retreat in pain from our lives. So often our inquiries into who we are have been "called on account of rain" because it was too painful to go deeper....It is as if we had never fully touched the ground of being. Never placed our two feet squarely in the present. Always juggling and toe tapping, waiting for the next moment to arrive.

Reflection Questions

- Do any of us really know what parts of ourselves are inadequately lived?
- How fully do you feel you have lived?
- What parts of yourself would you like to unmask and explore?
- What's on your bucket list? What fills in the blank when you say, "Someday I hope I can...." If you look beneath the surface of your bucket list, are there any hints about what parts of yourself are longing to be expressed?

Letting Death Touch Us

Most traditional societies create collective ways of helping people face death. The Catholic Church celebrates All Saints' Day (November 1) and All Souls' Day (November 2) as the time to remember saints, martyrs, and then all the faithful departed. Halloween, with its ghosts and demons running wild, is another form of confronting and laughing in the face of death. The Mexican holiday of *Dia de los Muertos* (Day of the Dead) has become a national Mexican holiday. Friends and family gather to remember those who have died, honoring the deceased by placing skulls made of sugar, marigolds, and the favorite foods and beverages of the departed on small *ofrendas* (alters) in the home or at the cemetery.

Poet and essayist Octavio Paz observes:

> To the inhabitants of New York, Paris, or London, death
> is a word that is never uttered because it burns the lips.
> The Mexican, on the other hand, frequents it, mocks it,
> caresses it, sleeps with it, entertains it; it is one of his
> favorite playthings and his most enduring love.

Buddhist meditations on death involve very deliberate confrontation and preparation. Common forms involve contemplating the certainty and imminence of death. We have included a set of these meditations toward the end of this chapter. In another form of Buddhist meditation, the practitioner rehearses and simulates the actual death process as it is described in the *Tibetan Book of the Dead*, with the intention of diminishing fearfulness through familiarity and preparing to encounter each stage of dying when the time comes.

During the Easter season, Christians journey beside Jesus as he approaches death and then resurrection. In some churches, the journey is reenacted by physically moving through the "Stations of the Cross" located around the circumference of the church. Some report that they are most strikingly brought to awareness of their personal mortality through the ritual of Ash Wednesday. Eleanor Harrison Bregman writes:

> As the priest puts the ashes on my forehead, [saying] "Remember that you are dust, and to dust you shall return," I remember putting the ashes of my mother's remains into the earth a little over two years ago. This is real. Death will happen, someday....As I approached the priest this morning and those memories surfaced, I wept, and I thought, "Oh my God, it really is all going to end. It ended for my mother, it will end for me, someday, too.... Yet immediately upon the heels of that fear—almost terror—of dying, something else even more powerful welled up. I felt deep, deep thanksgiving for life. It is when you walk right up to your own mortality, or the mortality of those you love, that you know what and for whom you live and love. If you are lucky, you feel the grace of God so deeply that you know that even when it seems like it is all over, it isn't, because we are all resting in the palm of God's hand, now and forever.

Judaism includes a special memorial service (known as Yizkor) on major holidays, but the most dramatic Jewish mode of practicing for both conscious living and conscious dying is the rituals of the Day of Atonement, Yom Kippur, itself. The entire day is structured like a death and rebirth. Traditionally, Jews dress in white (the color of the shrouds for burial) and refrain from all the things that support physical lives, such as eating, washing, having sex, shaving, and wearing makeup. Having used the previous month of Elul to make amends for misdeeds and reconcile relationships, Jews confess and ask for forgiveness. Perhaps the best-known piece of Yom Kippur liturgy, the Un'taneh Tokef, speaks of how fragile life really is, how little we know about whether we will survive the year, how many ways we might die, "like withering grass...a dissipating cloud...a fleeting dream..."

By midafternoon, weakened by hunger from the fast and lulled into contemplation by the repetitive liturgy, worshippers begin an upward movement, a kind of resurrection. The pace picks up in anticipation of the day's finale, with its most beautiful liturgical poems and melodies. At sunset, as the day ends, congregants are fully alive, one with the community, standing and calling out "Sh'ma Yisrael!"—the very same words that will be recited on their deathbeds. Gathering in homes to break the fast, and resurrected to full strength, Jews make ready to greet the holiday of Sukkot, known as the "Time of Our Rejoicing."

What Could Conscious Dying Look Like?

Like conscious living, conscious dying will take on a different cast for each of us. For some, the focus will primarily be on anticipating and taking care of practical matters so that our loved ones will not be unduly burdened. Some of us will place the emphasis on the actual transition into death, wanting to remain conscious and viewing it as a ritual passage. Some of us will work to be sufficiently in touch with our mortality so that we are motivated to live our remaining days with fuller presence.

Dignity in death is more than avoiding being hooked up to tubes and machinery. It is also taking responsibility for setting our affairs in order, preparing the next generation, saying good-bye, receiving farewells, offering and receiving forgiveness, bestowing blessing, and modeling how to die without fear. Those are the tasks of a mature spirit.

The art of conscious dying is not new. The eighth-century *Tibetan Book of the Dead* is studied as a guide through the states of consciousness one encounters from death to rebirth. In some instances Tibetan lamas aimed to control the timing of their deaths, turning around three times, sitting down to meditate, and consciously stopping their hearts and breath. Until the late eighteenth century the *Art of Dying*, or *Ars moriendi*, a body of Medieval Christian literature, provided guidance for the dying and for those attending them. A contemporary conscious dying movement has begun to grow out of the hospice movement under the tutelage of such teachers as Ram Dass, Stephen Levine, Joan Halifax, and others.

Ram Dass teaches that what worries us today is going to worry us on our deathbed, suggesting that what we have resolved in life will no longer be a source of worry in our dying. If we have developed some comfort with the idea that death is an integral part of life, we will approach death with greater equanimity. Reconciling our relationships will allow us to die with fewer regrets and less self-judgment. Acknowledging how little we really are in control of our lives, we may be less surprised by our death. If we feel that we have fully experienced our aliveness, it may be easier to let it go. Knowing that our lives have been meaningful and that something of us lives on, we are more likely to face death with grace.

In his collection of Chasidic tales, Martin Buber notes that it was customary for pious Chasidim to calmly wash their hands before dying, thus treating death as a final religious ritual. He tells a more dramatic tale about a disciple of the Kotzker Rebbe. Surrounded on his deathbed by grieving family, "he opened his eyes and asked for some spirits to drink *l'chayim,* a toast 'to life!'" They thought he had taken leave of his senses, but he explained to them that whenever a Chasid performs God's will, he does so with joy at the opportunity to do a mitzvah. "If God has willed my death," he said, "I am now performing His will. And it is proper to do so in a joyous spirit."

Facing death with joy may be more than most of us can imagine; we'd happily settle for some degree of equanimity. For such an example, we turn once again to Rabbi Heschel. The following story is told by Rabbi Samuel Dresner, one of his students.

> Several years before Abraham Heschel's death in 1972, he suffered a near fatal heart attack from which he never fully recovered. I traveled to his apartment in New York to see him. He had gotten out of bed for the first time to greet me and was sitting in the living room when I arrived, looking weak and pale. He spoke slowly and with some effort, almost in a whisper. I strained to hear his words.
>
> "Sam," he said, "when I regained consciousness, my first feelings were not of despair or anger. I felt only gratitude to God for my life, for every moment I had lived. I was ready to depart. 'Take me, O Lord,' I thought, 'I have seen so many miracles in my lifetime.'"
>
> Exhausted by the effort, he paused for a moment, then added: "That is what I meant when I wrote…'I did not ask for success; I asked for wonder. And You gave it to me.'"

Dresner later reflected: "I understood then what I had experienced: the lesson that how a man meets death is a sign of how he has met life."

Completing Earthly Business, Both Spiritual and Practical

Conscious dying involves both practical and spiritual preparation. Oddly enough, the practical and the spiritual dimensions are not so easily differentiated. The great nineteenth-century *musar* teacher, Rabbi Israel Salanter, when asked how he tended to his own spiritual needs, replied that the physical needs of others constitute a primary obligation of his spiritual life. We engage in this preparatory work for ourselves, but also for our friends and family, and for others who will care, and may be required to make decisions, for us as we approach death.

Making Decisions about Treatment and Dying

Few of us approach this work with ease because it requires imagining ourselves facing illness and death. Our minds resist. Not only do many of us want to avoid such imagining, we furthermore find the terrain nearly unfathomable. Nevertheless, if we consider it our spiritual obligation to ease our loved ones' practical obligations, we can gently move ourselves forward.

Letting one's wishes be known should not wait until death or old age is near, though it's not always easy to engage our family or even our physicians in the conversations we need to have. If we have managed to overcome our own resistance, we still may encounter a child or a doctor who says, "Oh, you don't have to worry about that now." "You still have plenty of time to think about such things." "Why you're looking so much better now!" "Lots of people live for a long time with this disease."

For several years after my husband raised the issue, I avoided the duty of deciding where I wanted to be buried. I no longer felt rooted in a particular place but, undoubtedly, there was also a dimension of denial. What helped break through my resistance was believing that I had an obligation not to burden my daughters with this decision in their time of sadness. I was surprised to discover that once I began to consider this as an obligation to my children, I could make the arrangements rather lightheartedly—picking a location near a paved walkway, so that if my daughters chose to visit in high heels, their shoes wouldn't sink in the grass. I can't say that I meditate on being "food for worms," but I do experience a sense of contentment at the thought of spending eternity beside a rosebush, my mother's favorite flower.

— Linda

Generally it is helpful to arrange for such a conversation to take place intentionally rather than to raise the topic without warning, catching our family or friends off guard. Giving notice and setting up a mutually convenient time conveys our seriousness and gives our loved ones time to think about their own questions and concerns.

It may take thoughtful planning to move these conversations forward, but the stakes are high. Without talking with our family and friends, we could end up with treatments that we do not want or leave our loved ones with weighty decisions that they feel ill at ease making. There is a good deal of literature indicating that our reluctance to clearly specify our desires in advance leaves families with the heavy and sometimes contentious task of deciding for us.

Reflection Questions

◆ Which areas of decision making around your death are settled for you? Is your family informed about your desires? Which areas are unsettled?

◆ Which of the unsettled areas will be hardest for you to address? What makes them difficult? Where could you find the information, the support, or the guidance you would need to begin working on these tough areas?

Unfinished Business

Beyond issues such as the formal business of wills, trusts, and charitable gifts that we want made by our estate or in our memory, there are other personal and spiritual loose ends of our lives that need to be tied up. Primary among them is finishing the business of our relationships. Although perhaps we now wish we had tended to them earlier in life, it is never too late. A friend who had done everything she could think of to reestablish a relationship with an alienated daughter finally succeeded when, terminally ill, she was able to let go of her hurt, let go of her need to know what had alienated her daughter, and let go of her desire to explain herself. In lieu of these things, she reached out in unconditional love. In the end, all that was important to her was that a healing take place so that her daughter would know that she had never stopped loving her, and so that her daughter would not carry a burden of guilt after her mother had died. The purity of that desire broke through when nothing else had been successful.

Even relationships with people long dead can be resolved so that we are released from the weight of anger, resentment, and guilt. Sometimes this happens in the midst of inquisitive reflection, alone or with another. Recalling her resentment at her father's unwillingness to pay for her college education, a student of ours suddenly paused and said, "I always thought he just assumed that I wouldn't amount to much, that he couldn't acknowledge that I was bright and curious. Now, I'm just thinking…he had recently divorced. Maybe he couldn't afford sending me to school. Maybe it was shame and not lack of caring." Sometimes just the thought that it might have been other than we have always believed is enough to help us release our resentment or disappointment.

Sometimes we have to work harder to free ourselves of the issues that have tugged at our souls. Writing a letter to a deceased parent, spouse, sibling, or friend can help us let go of our feelings of guilt or resentment. Sometimes a more dramatic ritual is required: a woman we know wrote a letter to her deceased mother and, accompanied by two friends, read it aloud at her mother's grave—she then ceremonially burned the letter.

We should also ask ourselves whether we have missed opportunities to express gratitude to those who have embraced us or helped us grow. We can use these final years to tell our loved ones just how much we cherish them. The Talmud says that we should repent or realign ourselves the day before we die, and then the rabbis note that because we do not know when this will be, we should do so daily. Perhaps that is the practice we should adopt when it comes to expressing our love.

Rabbi Zalman Schachter-Shalomi was deliberate about what he called his "December Project." By this point in his life, he had already thanked his teachers and made his amends, but in his weakened state he could not be sure that he would see all his students one more time. Within hours after his death, many of his students, scattered around the world, received a phone call not only informing them of his death, but conveying his personal blessing. Schachter-Shalomi had organized a cohort of friends to make these calls and to deliver his individualized messages and blessings to many of those whom he had mentored, ordained, and counseled.

Practicing toward Death

Many of the practical forms of preparation we have suggested can become forms of spiritual preparation when we do them with intent. For example, if you are discussing burial preferences and buying a cemetery plot, spend time contemplating that your body really will end up there. When you give or assign possessions to your heirs, take time to reflect on their lives continuing beyond yours, on your utter absence.

We offer the practices below in the belief that facing our mortality does free us to live our lives more fully. Many traditions have such practices, ranging from the subtle to the extreme. When we were in grammar school, the following children's bedtime prayer, first published in the *New England Primer* in the late 1600s, was still circulating in popular culture:

> Now I lay me down to sleep,
> I pray the Lord my soul to keep;
> If I shall die before I wake,
> I pray the Lord my soul to take. Amen.

At the other end of the spectrum are the instructions to Buddhist monks to meditate in the presence of decaying bodies with the phrase, "Verily, also my own body is of the same nature; such it will become and will not escape it."

One day this antique wicker rocking chair will pass on to my grand-daughter. I want her to know that its meaning is far greater than its material value. Purchased in anticipation of her mother's birth, it symbolized both the unarticulated hopes I had and the mystery I perceived in bringing new life into the world. I have written down for my grand-daughter the memories it holds for me, especially those that involve my own mother, for whom she is named but whom she never met. Perhaps I will live to see it welcome yet another generation, but it provokes both sadness and comfort to acknowledge that this is unlikely. I can't yet imagine letting go of my desire to know and hold and nurture the children yet to come, but these reflections allow me to see myself as part of a chain that reaches back through the maternal grandmother I did not know to the generations that will be born when I am no longer here. In that I find comfort.

— Linda

The Sh'ma is Judaism's central prayer and assertion of God's unity, which many people recite at bedtime as well as in the morning and evening liturgy. It is also meant to be a last utterance before death. Consequently, reciting it as we close our eyes and let ourselves relax into sleep functions as both a spiritual practice and preparation for death.

The Sh'ma is generally the first prayer a Jewish child learns, but it is hardly a child's prayer. Composed of only five words, one of which is repeated, it is nearly impossible to translate with any real clarity. Jewish discourse offers layers of interpretation, and most Jews simply recite it as an affirmation—of belief, of identity, of peoplehood.

The mystical interpretation of the Sh'ma is the proclamation that all existence is one or unified. But it is not necessary to sort out its multiple interpretations to adopt reciting the Sh'ma as a bedtime practice that expresses well-being, trust, and acknowledgment of our mortality. The words are relatively easy to say:

Sh'ma Yisrael Adonai Eloheinu Adonai Echad

A standard translation is "Hear O Israel, Adonai our God, Adonai is One."

The full bedtime Sh'ma ritual follows a pattern very similar to the Jewish ritual observed at the time of death, and the Talmud suggests that sleep is a mini-death. Developing a practice of saying the Sh'ma at bedtime may help us prepare to ultimately let go of life with trust. The full bedtime ritual concludes with these words:

> I place my spirit in God's care....
> When I sleep, as when I wake,
> God is with me; I have no fear.

Reflection Questions

- ◈ What do you think—and how do you feel—about the equation of sleep with death?
- ◈ Beyond the permanence of death, in what ways are death and sleep similar, and in what ways are they different?
- ◈ Both living and dying, according to Heschel, are related to the mystery of preexistence. Dying is returning to the source, "a supreme spiritual act, turning oneself over to eternity." That is, Heschel believes that the soul or some dimension of consciousness exits both before and after its embodied existence. When are you most likely to experience yourself as part of a larger whole? Has this changed as you've grown older? Does it ease your sense of the future, of your death?

Reader Practices

Phrases for Contemplation

The following contemplations are based on the writings of Atisha, an eleventh-century Buddhist scholar. Choose whichever one speaks to you most powerfully.

Find a comfortable but alert position, relax, and let your mind and body calm down and settle in. Bring attention to your breath. Then silently repeat the contemplation you have chosen. Stay with it for as long as it seems interesting to you. Notice the different meanings the statement can take on. Notice any resistance you feel. Notice moments in which the statement comforts you. Notice whether it seems to be growing more vividly true to you, or perhaps less so.

◈ All of us will die sooner or later. Death is inevitable; no one is exempt. Holding this thought in mind I abide in the breath.

◈ My body is fragile and vulnerable; my life hangs by a breath. Holding this thought in mind, I attend as I inhale and exhale.

◈ My material resources will be of no use to me. Holding this thought in mind, I invest wholeheartedly in practice.

◈ My loved ones cannot save me. Our loved ones cannot keep us from death; there is no delaying its advent. Holding this thought in mind, I exercise nongrasping.

◈ My own body cannot help me when death comes; it too will be lost at that moment. Holding this thought in mind, I learn to let go.

Jewish tradition has a form of deathbed confession called the Viddui. In it, the dying person asks to be forgiven for having missed the mark, requests protection for his or her family, and places him- or herself in God's care. It can be used to help us enter into death in a state of heightened awareness and acceptance. Rabbi Yosef Caro, author of the

Reflection Questions

Sit down for at least twenty uninterrupted minutes, more if you would like. Start at the top of this list of questions and work your way down. Write your answers in your journal.

◈ If I knew that I had ten years to live, how would I want to use them?

◈ If I knew that I had five years to live, how would I want to use them?

◈ If I knew that I had one year to live, how would I want to live it?

◈ If I knew that I had one month to live....

◈ If I knew that I had one week to live....

◈ If I knew that I had one day to live....

◈ If I knew that I had one hour to live....

◈ If I knew that I had one minute to live....

Now go back to the bucket list you created earlier in this chapter, and see what insights come from comparing that with your answers to the questions above. As you've done the work of this unit, what have you learned about your values and about how they are or are not adequately manifest in your life?

Reader Practices

Working with a Poem

Try using the following steps with a poem that speaks to you of mortality, death, or dying (you can try it out with Jane Kenyon's poem "Otherwise," found in chapter 3).

◆ Sit quietly and let yourself settle before beginning. Then silently read the poem once.

◆ Read the poem a second time, this time aloud.

◆ Then return to reading it in silence, this time slowly, pausing at the phrases that focus your attention on your mortality.

◆ Ask yourself what image arose for you as you read or contemplated the poem. How might it look if you painted it?

◆ Ask yourself what feeling or feelings the poem leaves you with. How did your feelings shift as you read and reread the different lines?

◆ If you were to write a line or two of this poem differently, what would you write?

Shulchan Aruch, the most widely consulted code of Jewish law, reassures a person who believes him- or herself to be near death that "many have said the Viddui and not died," suggesting that it is all right to err on the side of reciting it prematurely. For those unable to speak, it may be recited for them or it may be recited in one's heart.

This contemporary version of the Viddui was written by Rabbi Vicki Hollander:

> My God and God of my ancestors.
> Accept my prayers.
>
> Forgive the wrongdoings I've committed in my lifetime.
> I beg Your pardon.
>
> Cleanse me of my misdeeds.
> Shield me. Send healing to me.
> My life depends upon You.
>
> And if You have decreed my death.
> Be with me, and shelter me in the shadow of Your wings.
> Make a place for me in the world to come.
>
> Guardian of the vulnerable.
> Please, I pray,
> protect those whom I love.
> Those with whom my soul is bound.
> Tend them and walk with them.
>
> I now place myself into Your hands.
>
> Shema Yisrael Adonai Eloheinu Adonai Echad.
> Adonai Hu Ha-Elohim.
> Adonai Hu Ha-Elohim.
>
> Hear O Israel, Adonai our God Adonai is one
>
> Adonai is God

Is Death the End of Us?

Responding to his student's query about what happens after one dies, a Zen master said, "I don't know." "But you are a Zen Master!" complained his disciple. "Yes," said the teacher, "but I am not a dead Zen master."

We may understand that no one really knows what happens after death, but the human mind still inquires. We wonder where our loved one, so recently full of life, has disappeared. We wonder whether we will still "be" in any meaningful way, even after our body is committed to the earth.

Wondering what will happen to us and to our loved ones is part of being human. Every culture has its stories and its answers. Some provide comfort, some promise to redress the injustices we witnessed in life, others promise that we may have another chance—or many chances—to live again. Some console us with the assurance that death is not final; others insist that death is our absolute end.

The range of religious beliefs is impressive: reunion with family and loved ones, resurrection of the body at the end of days, reincarnation, eternal reward and punishment, blissful existence in the presence of God and angels, eternality of the soul, or absolute nothingness.

◆ What ideas and feelings do you have about the possibility and nature of some form of existence beyond death?

◆ What influences have helped to shape these ideas? Religious teachings? Parents, family, friends, teachers? Philosophy? Science? Popular ideas in the culture? Experiences you or people close to you have had?

◆ How much thought have you given to this subject in the past? Is it of interest to you currently?

Many of us find ourselves holding a mix of conflicting beliefs and images. Judaism itself does this: all of the possibilities named above are included in Jewish discourse about what happens after we die. Whenever the ancient rabbis were faced with the dilemma of choosing between equally probable propositions, they would proclaim: "Both these and these are the words of the living God," meaning, even two different and conflicting ideas can simultaneously be correct, if both contain wisdom within them. So we urge you to muse on the question of afterlife without feeling constrained by the expectation that your thoughts will have internal consistency.

Rabbi Richard Rubenstein offers a wonderful example of our ability to live with conflicting viewpoints. He writes:

> I am convinced that I have arisen out of nothingness and am destined to return to nothingness. All human beings are locked in the same fatality. In the final analysis, omnipotent nothingness was the lord of all creation. Nothing in the bleak, cold, unfeeling universe is remotely concerned with human aspiration and longing....Only death perfects life and ends its problems, and God can only redeem by

slaying. We have nothing to hope for beyond what we are capable of creating in the time allotted to us.

Nevertheless, in spite of his belief in an empty nothingness, Rubenstein also reports that when his youngest son Aaron was dying of a brain tumor, his daughter-in-law called him, concerned that her husband was fighting to hold on to life for her sake. Rubenstein asked his daughter-in-law to hold the phone to Aaron's ear:

> "Aaron," I asked, "can you hear me?" Carol told me that he nodded affirmatively.
>
> "Aaron," I continued, "God calls us into life. When our time comes, He calls us back to Himself. It's all right to go."
>
> Aaron died the next day.
>
> I had given my son permission to die and he had taken it. In spite of the fact that neither he nor Carol, whose background is Southern Baptist, had ever joined a religious community, such permission could only meaningfully be given in the language of religion. In any other language, I might have seemed harsh and perhaps unfeeling. By telling him that God was calling him back, I was relating his dying to the cosmic order of things.

Reflection Questions

❖ How do you understand Rabbi Rubenstein's use of an idea that he seems not to believe in? Do your own musings on the possibility of an afterlife sometimes include contradictory thoughts?

❖ Do you find the idea that death is an absolute end to be comforting or unsettling? Does it seem true to you, or do you feel that some element of a person continues beyond death, even if you are not quite sure what that element is?

Like Rabbi Rubenstein, we may find that certain beliefs that we resist taking literally will work for us as metaphor. Rabbi Zalman Schachter-Shalomi does this with the religious idea of resurrection of the dead. Acknowledging that he recites the phrase "Blessed are You, who revives the dead" three times each day (as part of the daily Amidah prayer), he explains:

> I do not believe that the crypts will open up in cemeteries and corpses will crawl out of them. [But] do I believe that at some time at the end of days the individual cells of my remains will be reconstituted?...I believe resurrection of the dead is the resurrection of matter. In the past we used to think of matter dead and unconscious. Today...we speak of atoms, molecules, and cells as strings of information. Resurrection...can then mean the coming to total awareness of the planet as a living organism with which we are connected.

The metaphor works for Schachter-Shalomi at least in part because it directs his awareness in a way that fosters his unfolding perception of the interconnectedness of all being; it supports the spiritual growth that he wants to foster in himself.

Similarly, without explicitly considering her traditional beliefs as metaphor, well-known writer and Jewish leader Blu Greenberg suggests that what is important to her is less the literal truth of her beliefs about the afterlife than the impact those beliefs have on her behavior. Greenberg confesses that she is "surprised to find how powerfully I hold a view of the afterlife and how deeply and profoundly it influences so many of my decisions and actions." This in spite of the fact that she "rarely thinks about afterlife in any coherent or systematic way."

Greenberg notes that when she introduces couples who go on to marry, she not only rejoices in the couple's happiness but also "instinctively notes" that those who make successful matches among people desiring to get married are rewarded with a place in the world to come. Greenberg muses

❖ In what ways might ideas about some form of existence (or nonexistence) after death shape your decisions and actions? Your beliefs may be contradictory or barely acknowledged, but they may still have an impact on your behavior.

❖ How comfortable or uncomfortable are you with the not-knowing stance of the Zen master cited at the beginning of this section? What are the benefits and the drawbacks of this not-knowing in your own life?

❖ Are there ideas that you don't literally believe but that work for you metaphorically? There might be a religious idea that you find meaningful but more as myth than as fact; there might be an idea or ideal about your country, city, family or organization that is only partially true but that captures your desires and hopes and informs your behavior. How comfortable are you holding such ideas?

that her tacit belief in an afterlife serves to inhibit her baser instincts and pushes her to higher levels of integrity, such as returning overpayments, speaking up in situations that might feel awkward, deciding not to eavesdrop when tempted, or repressing the desire for revenge when hurt.

This parable, retold by Morrie Schwartz, presents another way of viewing the mystery of what might follow death:

> There's this little wave, a he-wave who's bobbing up and down in the ocean off the shore, having a great time. All of a sudden, he realizes he's going to crash into the shore. In this big wide ocean, he's now moving toward the shore, and he'll be annihilated. "My God, what's going to happen to me?" he says, a sour and despairing look on his face. Along

comes a female wave, bobbing up and down, having a great time. And the female wave says to the male wave, "Why are you so depressed?" The male says, "You don't understand. You're going to crash into that shore and you'll be nothing." She says, "You don't understand. You're not a wave; you're part of the ocean."

Reflection Questions

◈ When are you most likely to experience yourself as part of a larger whole?

◈ Has this changed as you've grown older?

◈ Does it ease your sense of the future, of your death?

◈ Heschel spoke of dying as "returning to the source." Is this a helpful way of perceiving death for you?

Some of us cannot help but ponder the mystery that lies beyond death, and others of us feel it nothing but foolishness to do so. What seems true for most of us, however, is that if we can do the difficult work of contemplating our mortality with acceptance and equanimity, our actual experience of living is enriched.

> Doesn't everything die at last, and too soon?
> Tell me, what is it you plan to do
> with your one wild and precious life?
> —Mary Oliver, "The Summer Day"

—9—

Legacy and Stewardship

*Every person born into this world
represents something new, something that never
existed before, something original and unique....
[T]here has never been someone like him in the
world, for if there had been...there would be
no need for him to be in the world. Every single
person is a new thing in the world and is called
upon to fulfill his particularity.*

—Martin Buber

These were the words—with the modification of gender—that I, Linda, read at the eighth-day covenantal naming ceremonies of my daughters, thirty-nine and thirty-four years ago. We recited them again as we celebrated the births of my grandsons. These words have always moved me deeply as I contemplate the infinite worth and mysterious potential of a new soul being born into the world.

Now, standing so much closer to the end than the beginning of my own life, I am struck by the different resonance they have as I read them glancing backward rather than forward into the future. What was the need for which I came into the world? What is left for me to do? What can still be reshaped or refined in the time left to me? Will I have the strength, the wisdom, the will to fulfill my particularity? These are about legacy.

When we begin to think about legacy, we notice that the story of our lives extends backward before we were born into the world, just as it will continue forward beyond our lifetime. Our legacies include what we have inherited from the past and how that has influenced the shape of our lives. Accordingly, we need to look in both directions. We ask, what have we done with that inheritance, and in what ways does our life ripple outward from it, beyond ourselves?

Reflection Questions

◆ In what ways has your life been influenced by family legacies? What parts of your family legacy would you like to pass on? What parts would you like to shed?

◆ What did your parents leave to others through their work, their accomplishments, their character, their values, and their commitments? Are there any aspects of their legacy that are negative?

◆ When you think about your own legacy, what comes to mind?

Legacy

Some people find it difficult to think about the subject of legacy at all. They may compare their lives with the lives of famous people and feel insignificant. Others may feel daunted by the prospect of articulating their legacy because they really do not know what it is they have contributed to the world. Understanding our legacies is a dynamic process, unfolding as we grow older, and we urge you to think about legacy as expansively as possible. Our legacies are grounded in all the ways in which we have conducted our lives. As we suggested at the beginning of the last chapter, even our death is part of the legacy we leave.

Some people leave public legacies that can be tallied in dollars, books, films, music, paintings, or scientific discoveries. All of us engrave our legacies in the hearts and minds of those with whom we have had direct contact: family, friends, colleagues, neighbors, students, and teachers. Many times we never even know the full impact of our legacies. We may teach a lesson through behavior or example, or change a life, even though our contact was fleeting. We may be the nameless stranger who did or said something that made a difference far beyond anything we could imagine. And, those whom we touch will touch the lives of others, including those yet unborn.

If we have already taken the opportunity to conduct a life review, or to keep journals, or simply to reflect on the sweep of our life, we may be developing a clearer sense of what is important to us. Taking time to think about legacy encourages us to develop even greater clarity about our enduring values as we ask ourselves: What has mattered most to us, and in what ways have we mattered to others? What have we done that we are proud of and what do we regret? Whom have we been to others and to ourselves? How have we been in the world, and what have we modeled?

We do not have to imagine ourselves at death's door to begin thinking about our legacies. At this stage of life, it is appropriate to acknowledge the parts of ourselves about which we can feel proud. As we reflect on the enduring impact of our lives, we can also see the things that we would like to change in order to move forward in greater alliance with our deepest values. With a better understanding of our unique place in the world, we discover an agenda that can help shape the remaining years of our life. Looking backward is a way of projecting ourselves forward to inhabit our lives even more fully.

Understanding Your Legacy

Here are some basic questions to help you start thinking about legacy. What are the values that have come to be most important to you? How are they manifest in your life? Expect that you will not be able to answer these questions easily. Carry them around in your mind for a while; it could take some time for the things that are most significant to surface.

- Based on your work and your relationship as a family member, a friend, a colleague, or a mentor, what achievements and accomplishments do you feel most proud of or deeply satisfied by?
- What practical skills, traditions, interests, and traits of character have you passed down?
- What recipes, songs, and poems have you taught? What stories have you told?
- If your friends or family members were asked what values were most important to you, what might they answer?
- As you think about people you have known and those whom you have influenced, consider what values they might have received from you. How do you think you mattered to them? What skills and spiritual qualities have you modeled in the way you live? What might be the unique role that you were born to fulfill in each of their lives?

How Shall We Hold the Regrets?

The integrity and wisdom that we want to be developing at this stage of life involves being able to claim our lives as a whole, saying "yes" to all that has been, including the painful. We've worked on transforming some of our regrets through granting and seeking forgiveness. We've engaged in assessing our character strengths and flaws, working on character traits that will further refine our souls. We've begun to let go of the protective

About twenty years ago I was asked to write a short essay about the roots of my work as a Jewish educator. The immediate source of that work was clear: more than ten years of study with Rabbi Jonathan Omer-Man, one of the teachers to whom this book is dedicated. But I was also aware that the study with Jonathan had reopened doors to my childhood memories. Searching for the older sources of my spiritual connections, small family scenes, usually around the celebration of holidays, would knock on the doors of my mind.

While it was my mother who cooked the holiday foods, stitched together Purim costumes, and decorated for Hanukkah so that we wouldn't feel bereft when all of our friends were celebrating Christmas, it was my father who kept coming to mind: standing beside him as a tiny girl in synagogue, gathered close to light the menorah, inspecting dark corners with a candle in search of crumbs that needed to be discarded before Passover. My father was a rather quiet man; he didn't explain a lot, but somehow I understood in those moments of ritual that he was transmitting the legacy of his own beloved father, who had died before I was born.

The memories themselves have an ethereal quality. Unlike my mother, he knew the Hebrew incantations, and he recited them in a whisper, as if he were sharing a precious secret. I could feel something tugging me backward in time, back to the old country, then back to Jerusalem, then back to Creation. And he sang. He never sang, except in those ritual spaces.

By the time I wrote the essay, my father had become nonobservant, and he was stunned to read that I attributed not only my career but my spiritual longings to his influence. And while he protested, I have always been glad that there was an opportunity to tell him how much his quiet deeds had shaped me and how successfully he had extended his father's legacy to another generation.

— Linda

Your Journal—Exit Interview

Some of us are wary of taking credit for the goodness of our lives. Whenever we think of something good we have done, a "but…" may arise. Author Anna Quindlen notes that "the thing that is really hard, and really amazing, is giving up on being perfect and beginning the work of becoming yourself." This exercise is designed to help you stay on the positive path as you reflect on what you have done and whom you have been. There will be time to look at the "buts" later. Let us imagine an exit interview, just as we are leaving life. We are seeing God as a sweet and kindly social worker who is interested in helping us articulate only the good parts of our lives. There is no test, no passing or failing, just a summing up of life's positive dimensions. Start with silence and at least five minutes of meditation. Sit comfortably, and relax your body and your mind. Place yourself in the kind of physical environment that puts you at ease. You could be lying on the grass beside a stream, resting on the

masks that keep us at a distance from our most authentic selves. All of that work will continue.

For those of us who carry burdensome stories long after we have integrated the lessons learned from them, this is a good time to let go of the regrets and the "buts" that arose as we focused on the positive elements of our legacies.

What does that look like? We turn to Diana Athill, literary editor and author. In her memoir, even as she acknowledges her "own lacks and lazinesses, omissions, oversights, [and] the innumerable ways in which one falls slope of a hill, or sitting in your favorite chair. It's your special time with this sweet and kindly God, so you get to choose.

Write down all the positive things—large and small—you have done, or created, or touched in your life, tangible and intangible. Think about the family or friendship circles you have been part of, the interactions you have had over so many years with workmates, clients, students, neighbors, acquaintances, youngsters, strangers. Don't be shy; let the kindly Social Worker sitting beside you add some of the things you might not remember: "What about _____?"

If a qualifying "but" arises in your mind, dismiss it. "There will be time for all that later," says the Social Worker.

Stay with the assignment for at least twenty minutes. You will need that much time to recall some of the less obvious things on your list.

When you are finished, reflect for a few moments on how you feel, what you learned, and anything that might have surprised you.

short of one's own ideals," she finds herself surprised by her lack of regrets. When she digs a little deeper, she finds two areas that disturb her, what she calls "that nub of coldness at [her] center"—shutting her eyes to the problems of a cousin raising small children and "never having had the guts to escape the narrowness of my life": "So there are two major regrets, after all. But I can't claim they torment me, or even that I think about them. And at those two I shall stop, because to turn up something even worse would be a great bore. I am not sure that digging out past guilts is a useful occupation for the very old given that one can do so little about them."

◆ What regrets do you have? Can you still do healing work around them?

◆ What regrets is it time to carry more gently or let go of?

◆ Do you agree or disagree that it is not useful to dig out past regrets? When does this seem true to you and when does it not?

◆ Turn back to the practices for self-forgiveness on page 157. Use or construct your own version of this statement: "I have taken responsibility for my actions and done what I could to rectify the difficulty I caused. I forgive myself for _____ and _____. I will no longer dwell on the bad feelings that surround this incident."

It's Never Too Late

We may sometimes shy away from thinking about legacy, feeling that it's too late. But it's not. True, we know we cannot turn around and retrace the steps of our journey, choosing a different route. Confronting a serious shortcoming can be painful. Ruminating excessively on our character flaws or habitual patterns can result in a sense of emptiness, hopelessness, or even despair. But it needn't. Because it's not too late. Awakening to dissatisfaction with the lives we have lived so far is the first step toward finding a new path to our more authentic selves.

Among the most uplifting stories we hear are those of personal transformation that occurs late in life. In his book, *Mindsight*, University of California at Los Angeles professor of psychiatry Daniel J. Siegel describes a ninety-three-year-old man named Stuart who had lived his entire life alienated from his emotions. On hearing that his law partner had been diagnosed with lymphoma, he confessed, "I felt nothing. People get sick, they die. That's it." He knew that he *should* feel something, but he was completely cut off from the world of feelings. Initially he couldn't imagine changing at the age of ninety-three, especially since he didn't understand what it was that he was supposed to change. However, wanting to be a better partner to his wife of sixty years, he agreed to work on discovering first the felt sense of his body and then of his emotions. The work involved exercises similar to the one adapted from Schachter-Shalomi's *First Steps to a New Jewish Spirit* that we introduced in chapter 3, reflection and

After months of mourning Paul's death, I began to agonize about what we should do to memorialize his life. I wanted to create something concrete and appropriately grand to perpetuate his memory. Our synagogue organized an annual memorial lecture on topics that were important to him, but I still felt guilty that I hadn't done enough to keep his name alive.

Gradually I came to realize that he had already created his own public legacy through his books and articles. Thirty-four years after he wrote An Orphan in History, people still come up to me and to my children to tell us how the book changed their Jewish identity and helped them turn more deeply into exploring Jewish meaning in their lives.

Only later did I become acquainted with an entirely different dimension of Paul's legacy, when two doctors told me stories about Paul's impact on them while they were medical students. When they came into his room during rounds, Paul would be sitting up in bed, wearing comfortable clothes instead of the hospital gown. He greeted them cheerfully with, "Welcome to Leukemia 101. What can I tell you?" They were each so drawn to him that they would go visit him after they got off their shifts. And each now teaches their students how to see a patient as a person and not a disease.

Now I see our son and daughter quite deliberately teaching their children what they learned from their father. Paul did not need help from me; his legacy is still rippling out into the world.

— Rachel

journaling, and work with imagery. Over time Stuart learned to assess emotional states within himself and then in others, to respond to both himself and others with empathy and compassion. Nine months after beginning this work, his wife called Siegel and asked whether he had given Stuart a brain transplant. As Stuart approached his ninety-fourth birthday, he wrote Siegel a thank-you note claiming, "Life has new meaning now."

Stuart's case was extreme: ninety-three years of disconnection from his emotional life required the help of an expert who understands the neurological foundations and interconnections of emotional responsiveness. Few of us have such a difficult starting point. We retell Stuart's story to illustrate that it's never too late to change and because the kind of exercises we recommend—body awareness, reflection questions, journaling, and imagery—can help us do the work of change.

It is not uncommon to hear of people who are dramatically changed in the last few years or months—or even days—of their lives by their confrontation with mortality. We may react to their stories with sadness at the limited amount of time they had to live from their deeper, more authentic selves. At the same time, however, we think of the remarkable legacy that they have left for those who have witnessed their transformation. These family members, friends, colleagues, and caretakers now know, in the most undeniable way, that change is always possible, that it is never too late to change one's life. Far better than dwelling on regrets, we can always choose to grow more fully into our authentic selves, and those who witness that growth will inherit a worthy legacy.

Rabbi Nachman of Bratslav addressed himself to the double-sided difficulty of reorienting parts of our lives. On the one hand, he aimed to assure his disciples that change is absolutely possible; on the other, he felt obliged to acknowledge how difficult this can seem.

According to Rabbi Nachman, it is an encouraging sign when we realize that we are far from God or far from living authentically. Up until this new awareness, we have been too far from the goal to even know of its existence. Thus, the desire to change is itself a major leap forward. But then we become aware of the obstacles we face. The surprising part of this teaching is that Rabbi Nachman believes that if we look carefully enough, "God Himself" is hiding in the obstacle. The obstacle is actually placed there to increase our desire, our motivation to change, because only those whose desire is great enough will find a way to turn in a new direction. And, says Rabbi Nachman, we can be assured that finding the obstacles to be very large indicates the greatness and desirability of our goal. When the strength of our desire matches the strength of the obstacle, change is then a genuine possibility.

Reflection Questions

◈ What have you learned about conscious, personal change from your own experience?

◈ Rabbi Nachman teaches that the path to change is through rather than around the obstacles. How does this teaching resonate with your experience?

◈ As you continue to fashion your legacy by the way you live, what might you want to do differently? How strong is your motivation? What obstacles are you aware of? How might you use the obstacles to move toward your goal?

It Stops Here!

We generally think of a legacy as something that is handed down from one generation to another, but we have also witnessed a form of legacy that we've come to call legacy *via negativa*—defined by what is not handed down. In spiritual counseling, people often speak of their conscious effort not to pass certain parts of their inheritance on to the next generation: a woman who comes from a family in which no one hugged or said "I love you"; a man whose family measured worth in terms of the university one attended; the son of a slum landlord; the daughter of a compulsive shopper.

For some of us, it is a struggle to shed judgments, behaviors, and thought patterns we grew up with—or, in some cases, the defenses we built up in order to protect ourselves from them. When we are able to reject the part of our inheritance that has been unhealthy or damaging, and work mindfully to avoid passing it on, we deserve to count this as part of what we have contributed to the world. We believe that a legacy *via negativa* deserves as much recognition as those elements that we are more accustomed to recognizing. If you've left it out of your exit interview, be sure to add it in.

Sharing Our Legacy through an Ethical Will

Once we have a sense of our legacy, we may wonder, Is there something we can do in order to leave it in a more tangible form for our family, friends, and descendants?

The ethical will, a Jewish tradition that dates back to the Middle Ages, is a parent's letter to his or her children, offering hope, guidance, and wisdom for life in the years ahead. We may think that, after living with and observing us all these years, our children are well acquainted with our values and our sense of what is important. Yet sometimes people are surprised to read what their parents have written to them as their ethical will. Even when not surprised, the recipients are usually moved and grateful for this gift. Rabbi Elana Zaiman, author of a book on ethical wills, writes:

> I was a teenager when my father handed me a copy of his ethical will. As I read his words, I cried. I was in awe of his ability to admit his weaknesses, to state his beliefs and values, to acknowledge his hopes and prayers for us, his children. I still cry when I read his ethical will. And I read it often. I read it when I'm annoyed with him, when I feel far away from him in distance, or in spirit. And always, I feel his love.

According to Zaiman, many report that ethical wills or letters are among the most meaningful possessions left to them by loved ones. Decades or even centuries later, ethical wills often become treasured family heirlooms.

As with material possessions, some people choose to give their ethical wills to their loved ones before their deaths. Others leave them to be read once they are gone. A woman with whom we have worked rewrites hers every five years. It is a practice she considers part of her own spiritual work, and she intends to have the document read by her survivors after her death.

We've been fascinated to learn that a number of law firms have begun to encourage clients to write a supplementary ethical will in order to mitigate the cold legalese of standard wills. They encourage clients to explain how the family money was made and restate the values they hope will be promoted by its use in future generations. They believe that this kind of message by the patriarch or matriarch can help avert family conflict.

Getting Started

Some people prefer simply to start with a blank piece of paper and plunge in, writing from the heart and seeing what develops. Knowing that this is just a first, ragged draft, they trust that organization and refinement will happen later.

Others prefer to begin with a structure, even if it must change as their writing develops.

For your ethical will, you can use the list of possible topics below to give yourself a starting point.

- Important events in my life.
- Experiences that have shaped me.
- Life's hard lessons and what I have learned from them. Mistakes I have made that I hope you will not repeat.
- Things I am grateful for—loves and passions.
- Values (beliefs and opinions), including what success or a good life means to me.
- Wisdom that has guided my life.
- Reminders of how much my loved ones mean to me, how great my love is for them, and how grateful I am that they have been the ones with

whom I have shared my life. Statements about particular things I am grateful to them for.

+ Stories about my childhood, adolescence, and adulthood; what I know about parents' and grandparents' lives. Descriptions of "how life was back then."
+ Things I learned from parents, grandparents, siblings, spouse or part-ner, friends, teachers, children, grandchildren—the people who have shaped me.
+ Hopes and concerns for the future—for my family, community, the world.
+ Blessings for loved ones.
+ Family history, genealogy, and location of graves.
+ Apologies and requests for forgiveness; the offering of forgiveness.
+ The personal meanings of possessions I am leaving to my heirs: this is why they are important to me; this is why I want my heirs to have them.
+ Hopes that my loved ones will care for and remain close (or heal relation-ships) with a surviving parent, siblings, aunts and uncles.
+ Desires that my survivors will continue to support causes that are important to me.

It Doesn't Need to Be Comprehensive

An ethical will does not need to be long or all-inclusive. Here is an example of a brief, contemporary ethical will that conveys great and enduring love. The author's requests are so simple, yet life affirming, that this woman's heirs are likely to feel that remembering and honoring her is something they can do with ease, gratitude, and reciprocal love.

> I fully expect that I will live for a very long time, to see you well into adulthood and to share your future with you. There is much to look forward to, and I am planning on being part of all the adventures and all the challenges and all the joys. But if for some reason I am not, the most important thing you need to know is how much my love for you created the person that you will remember as me. I

made you, quite literally in my womb, but you made me, too. I am so proud of you and so grateful to you. When the time comes, and none of us can answer the question of when that will be, you need to know that without a doubt, I was fulfilled in my life. I have had a wonderful life and I don't want you to mourn me—maybe a little, but not too long! Carry me forward by recreating the net that I was for you and be it for others. Carry me forward in your kitchen with our favorite coffee cake, muffins and pie, warm from the oven and made for your own delectable pleasure, or for those you care about. Carry me forward with an optimistic outlook and tenacious devotion to what you know is best. Carry me forward and I will be with you always.—Mom

Thinking about How It Will Be Received

Writing an ethical will presents challenges that our ancestors were less likely to face. Few generations have been as aware as we are now of how rapidly the circumstances and perspectives of our lives are changing. It is important that we approach such writing with both humility and trust, desiring to teach, inform, and comfort, but relinquishing whatever remnants of control we still may be holding on to. An ethical will should not be an instrument of rebuke, lament, or self-pity. Nor should we voice expectations in it that will induce guilt in heirs who cannot live up to them.

Unlike memoirs, which are usually written for a larger audience, an ethical will is very pointedly written for our loved ones. Several generations from now it might be read as an interesting historical document that reveals the tenor of times past, but in the main, it is written and read as a gift from one generation to the next. That should be our guideline for deciding what to include and especially what not to include. This is not the place to reveal family secrets or to recount the misdeeds of others, or to boast about success. It is possible to express our values, articulate our concerns, and explain why our opinions and commitments seem wise to us without creating feelings of guilt in those who follow us. The document we hand on to the next generations should be written with love and respect—love for those we leave and respect for our descendants' freedom to find their own way.

Memoirs and Videos

A few of us will be motivated to write about our lives in detail. We may feel that our lives have been so compelling that our descendants will genuinely be interested. We may feel that we have lived through particularly noteworthy times and want to give our descendants a more personal sense of history than what they will learn in school.

Activist Louise Diamond, after learning that her cancer was terminal, was aware that she did not have sufficient time to write a life story that included four degrees, eleven careers, and peacebuilding activities in twenty-three countries. Instead she told her story in a series of videotaped interviews:

> What is emerging from all this is a view of the whole—an integrated, colorful, sometimes whimsical tapestry of a life well-lived, on purpose, and astoundingly coherent. At the very least it is a telling for my grandchildren—when they reach that point of wondering—of their own heritage and lineage.
>
> But clearly it has been valuable to me, as I complete the journey of this incarnation, to follow the threads and celebrate the intricate design that they've created over the years.

Video and multimedia ethical wills are gaining popularity. Some, as in Diamond's case, are quite elaborate, with hours of interviews and complex editing. Other ethical wills are recorded much more simply on smartphones. Some people add photographs, music, or short segments of videos taken earlier in life.

Committing to writing or recording at all is a matter of choice; the most important thing is to do the work for ourselves. Reflecting on the legacy we will leave, whether we write, video, or merely contemplate, provides opportunities for summing up, making meaning of our experience, and shaping the next chapters of our life.

Stewardship

Are we being good ancestors?
—Jonas Salk

Our generation's collective legacy is the world we leave for the next generations. Age does not exempt us from contributing what we can. In *From Age-ing to Sage-ing*, Rabbi Zalman Schachter-Shalomi reminds us that "[Elders] are wisdom keepers who have an ongoing responsibility for maintaining society's well-being and safeguarding the health of our ailing planet Earth."

Chapter 4 discusses the legendary Choni Hame'agel, who slept for seventy years. Choni's lengthy nap was precipitated by the difficulty he had imagining the benefit of investing in a future he would not live to see.

> One day Choni was going on the road, and he saw a certain man planting a carob tree. Choni said to him: "How many years does it take for this carob tree to bear fruit?" He said to Choni: "Seventy years." Choni said to him, "Is it clear to you that you will live another seventy years?" He replied to Choni: "This man found a world containing carob trees. Just as my ancestors planted for me, so too, I plant for my children."
>
> Choni sat down and ate bread; drowsiness overcame him, and he fell asleep. An outcropping of rock arose around him as he slept. He became hidden from sight and slept for seventy years. When he arose, he saw what looked like that same man picking some of the fruit from that carob tree he had planted! Choni said to him: "Are you indeed the man who planted this tree?" He replied: "I am his grandson." (Talmud, *Ta'anit* 23a)

What are we planting for our grandchildren and their children? For children throughout the world and for their descendants? In what ways

---

Reflection Questions

- ❖ What have you planted in your life for future generations, the fruits of which you are unlikely to see yourself?

- ❖ Can you articulate your decision to work for a future you will not see?

---

will we now bring ourselves to the task of making a difference in the world they will inherit from us?

This is our time to invest in the future of our society, through vehicles such as a second career, volunteer opportunities, political work, or neighborhood projects. We can join groups that are reshaping the social, political, and economic contours of our communities, our country, and the planet. Some of us will take on expansive projects; some of us will focus our skills and commitment in a limited domain in order to intensify their impact. And we must lovingly acknowledge that our energy level may not be what it used to be and give ourselves permission to act accordingly.

When we think about the kind of world we would like to leave to future generations, it is easy to feel overwhelmed by all that needs fixing and to become paralyzed by the enormity of the task. When that happens, we can call on the guidance of our Talmudic ancestor, Rabbi Tarfon, who taught, "It is not incumbent upon you to complete the job, but neither may you desist from it" (*Pirkei Avot* 2:21).

Before we commit to anything, we need to decide what we care most about, and what roles we have the resources and desire to take on. We might pay attention to the wisdom of theologian Frederick Buechner, who wrote, "The place God calls you to is the place where your deep gladness and the world's deep hunger meet."

Being and Doing

In a paper he prepared for the President's Council on Bioethics, "After the Life Cycle: The Moral Challenges of Later Life," historian and professor of medical humanities Thomas Cole invoked Rabbi Hillel's Talmudic teaching: "If I am not for myself, who will be for me? If I am only for myself, what am I? If not now, when?" (*Pirkei Avot* 1:14). As children and adolescents, he notes, we tend to see the world as our oyster. In midlife adulthood, our maturation is largely gained through taking responsibility to attend to the needs of others. In later life, he suggests, "we must learn to balance our own needs with the needs of future generations."

For some of us, it will be the manifestations of our inner, contemplative work more than external activism that proves to be our unique particularity, the need, as Buber wrote, for our having been born into the world. The compassion, generosity, gratitude, and loving-kindness that we enact and model may not be splashy or hailed, but it may be an important contribution to the repair of the world.

Norman Fischer, poet, Jewish teacher, and renowned Zen master, tells us that our legacies may more easily be understood by looking at who we have become than by examining our curriculum vitae:

> We admire people who are wealthy, famous, or skillful in some way, but it is not too hard to be like that. If you are born with some talent, and a little luck, and know the right people, you can do that. Many people do that. But much more difficult and much more wonderful is to be a *bodhisattva* [one whose life is devoted to uplifting the lives of others]. Not someone that many people know about and talk about but someone who has the almost magical power of spreading happiness and confidence wherever he goes. What a vision for your life, for your family, to be a light for those around you. To think of everything you do, every action, every social role, every task, as being just

a cover for, an excuse for, your real aspiration, to spread goodness wherever you go. This requires no luck (even if everything goes wrong in your life, you can do it), no special skills, no need to meet special people and get special breaks. We can all do this.

As we look for balance and purpose in our lives, we also can be teaching future generations what it means to grow into wisdom, that it is possible both to remain connected to the needs of the world and to take time to appreciate its richness. In this respect, legacy extends beyond the personal. We also are contributing to a collective legacy, teaching the next generation how to grow old. By becoming models of dignity and purpose, and by continuing to grow and seek meaning until the final moments of life, we can help those who come after us to regard aging as an opportunity as well as a challenge.

Letting Go Yet Again

In the novel *From Here To Eternity*, the character Malloy smiles and says, "The little bit you and me might change the world, it wouldn't show up until a hundred years after we were dead. We'd never see it." His pal responds, "But it'd be there."

So here is yet another of those paradoxes we seem called upon to embrace as we grow in wisdom. On the one hand, thinking about our legacies can be important. Knowing that we have made some contribution to the world and that our years will leave their mark is a source of comfort. Wondering about the legacy we are leaving can guide our choices about how we will spend our time and to what we will devote our passion over the coming years. On the other hand, our legacy should not be yet another object or identity to which we become attached. Our spiritual growth is not served by efforts to control or fully understand our legacy. As with all that we will eventually leave behind, it is for future generations to carry our legacy forward in ways that we might not even be able to imagine.

We live in a world more multifaceted and mysterious than we can perceive. Our lives look different when seen from different perspectives. Our legacies will as well.

In the 1940s my father created a business devoted to helping working-class families pay off their debts without taking on further loans or entering bankruptcy. He negotiated with their creditors, convincing them to forgive portions of the debt owed and to accept small but steady payments extended over time. Meanwhile, he counseled and cajoled his clients into living in line with the severe budgets on which he placed them.

Aware of how easily people in debt could be taken advantage of by predatory tactics, he spent several years commuting long distances, lobbying for legislation to regulate this type of business. During that time it seemed like he was away more than he was home.

Legacy #1 I imagined him as something of a modern knight in shining armor riding off to do good in the world, modeling righteousness, justice, and helping others. Although our domains of interest are demonstrably different, I sense that my work in spiritual counseling and nurturing personal transformation can be traced back to what I observed in my father's actions.

Legacy #2 Not long ago I shared these memories with one of my sisters. "Really?" she said. "I never saw Dad that way as a kid. I was always angry that he was away from home so much." Interestingly, she is the daughter who ended up taking over my father's business! Her style is radically different, but her focus is on nurturing her clients, just as his was.

Legacy #3 One day in the late 1960s, when my father was stopped for speeding, the policeman looked at his driver's license and said, "I can't give you a ticket. You saved my father's life by getting us out of debt." How many other families are thriving today because of my father's actions? His life continues to ripple out.

— Linda

In the end, we give over not only our lives, but the stories of our lives, to the future.

How fortunate we are to be alive in a new era that affords many of us more years of good health to enjoy the opportunity we have to grow older with rich experience, emotional maturity, and mindfulness. In the chapters of this book we have explored spiritual practices to enhance these years. We have seen how ageism—our own and others'—can inhibit us, how the paradigm of decline can frighten us, and how the paradigm of possibility can inspire us. We have sought integrity and wholeheartedness in reviewing the flow of our lives—identifying our strengths in hard times and our passions in good times. We have worked to accept our bodies as they are, and to care for them and enhance them as we choose. Relationships are key to our well-being, and now, we are reminded, we have time to nurture them, to heal and to forgive. Through mindfully bringing the qualities of patience, gratitude, generosity, trust, and compassion more fully into our lives, we find balance and openheartedness.

All of this work softens the pain and loss that are inevitable. With courage and dignity we can face, and perhaps even welcome, the prospect of conscious dying so that our last days are lived with the presence, gratitude, and joy that have distinguished our active lives. We create our legacies as we go—in the ways we live, the ways we love, they ways we teach and build and create. We find our own way to leave a better world to the next generations.

The teachings are quite simple: learn to accept whatever life brings with compassion. Stop, breathe, and feel. Open your heart to the awesome nature of the world, and experience yourself as part of something so much bigger than you are. Find the prayers, melodies, poetry, silence, and rituals that express your awe, your pain, your gratitude, and your love. Find a spiritual friend to hear you and hold you. Build a community of people that meets its members' needs and reaches out to serve the world.

The righteous shall flourish like the palm tree;
they shall thrive like a cedar in Lebanon....
They shall bear fruit even in old age;
they shall ever be fresh and fragrant....
(Psalms 92:13-15)

May we live like the palm and the cedar, bearing the fruit of wisdom, fresh with the aliveness of being present to each moment. May we each discover a path that can help shape our remaining years with wisdom, resilience, and spirit.

Acknowledgments

The work of creating this book was inspired, informed, and nourished by many people. We gratefully acknowledge our thought partners: Rabbi Laura Geller, Rabbi Marion Lev-Cohen, Rabbi Rachel Timoner, Ruth Abram, Sylvia Boorstein, Bonnie Fatio, and Marvin Israelow; and Rabbis David Jaffe, Lisa Goldstein, Nancy Flam, Marc Margolius, Sheila Peltz Weinberg, and Jonathan Slater of the Institute for Jewish Spirituality. We also would like to thank Sherry Israel, Harriet Rosen, Karen Frank, Ruth Rosenblum, and Rabbi Shmuel Birnham, who read and commented on one or more chapters. We are deeply grateful to the members of the original Wise Aging group, who have been continuously exploring the terrain of this stage of life with us for the past nine years, to the members of the Wise Aging group at Central Synagogue in New York City, and to the members of the Growing into Wisdom group at Leo Baeck Temple in Los Angeles: we have endeavored to share your wisdom and experiences, which have helped to shape our thinking.

And praises to Beth Lieberman for her skillful and dedicated thinking, editing, and shepherding; to David Behrman, who recognized the full potential of this work even before we did; to Ann Koffsky, who, along with David, provided the kind of collaborative editing that no writers get these days; and, again, to Lisa Goldstein, for her belief in the importance of bringing spiritual practice to a generation considerably older than hers and for the support she provided to make it possible.

We have been blessed with funders who supported the Wise Aging work as it grew from one pilot group into many groups scattered across the country, and from a small curriculum into this book: the Righteous Persons Foundation; the Harold Grinspoon Foundation; the Covenant Foundation; and to Nancy Belsky and the Rita J. and Stanley H. Kaplan Family Foundation.

The Bedtime Sh'ma

(Sh'ma al Hamitah)

The Sh'ma is the central prayer and assertion of Judaism, which many people recite at bedtime as well as in the morning and evening liturgy. It is also meant to be a last utterance before death. Consequently, reciting it as we close our eyes and let ourselves relax into sleep functions as both a spiritual practice and preparation for death.

Part 1: Forgiveness Prayer

I now forgive all who have hurt me, all who have done me wrong, whether deliberately or by accident, whether by word, by deed, or by thought, whether against my pride, my person, or my property, in this incarnation or in any other. May no one be punished on my account.

May it be Thy Will, Eternal One, my God and the God of my fathers and mothers, that I be no more bound by the wrongs which I have committed, that I be free from patterns which cause pain to me and to others, that I no longer do that which is evil in Thy sight.

May my past failings be wiped away in Your great Mercy, Eternal One, and may they no longer manifest through pain and suffering.

Let my words, my thoughts, my meditations, and my acts flow from the fullness of Your Being, Eternal One, Source of my being and my Redeemer.

Part 2: Who Closes My Eyes (Hamapil)

Praised are You,
Adonai, our God,
Ruler of the universe,
who closes my eyes in sleep,
my eyelids in slumber.

May it be Your will,
Adonai,
My God and the God of my ancestors,
to lie me down in peace
and then to raise me up in peace.

Let no disturbing thoughts upset me,
no evil dreams nor troubling fantasies.

May my bed be complete and whole
in Your sight.

Grant me light
so that I do not sleep the sleep of death,
for it is You who illumines and enlightens.

Praised are You,
Adonai,
whose majesty gives light to the universe.

Part 3: The Shema Itself

Hear, O Israel, Adonai, our God, Adonai, is One. (Deuteronomy 6:4)

Forming a
Wise Aging Group

One way to take the journey further after you have read this book is to form a wise aging group. A Wise Aging group is a small, trusted circle of peers—perhaps friends, close family, colleagues, or community members—in which you will be guided to do the reflective work that enables you to come to new understandings about your life, your inner self, and your deepest values. With this new perspective you will be able to make decisions that enhance your well-being as you move through the active aging phase of your life and as you prepare for later old age.

Creating a group framework of safety, honest communication, gentle humor, and intimacy makes it all more productive and more comfortable. When you set out to create a group, think of people who have an ability to listen, to be aware of not taking up too much airtime themselves, and to be reflective. The group is not a traditional support group, so people who are bringing intense pain or anger would find more constructive help in a grief or anger-management group.

We suggest beginning your exploration together with the earlier of the book's nine chapters. You may choose to spend more time on those chapters that are richest for you, or you may narrow your focus to one dimension of a chapter. Any topic could take several sessions on its own, depending on your interests. Each chapter in *Wise Aging* contains texts, poems, and readings from Jewish and non-Jewish sources; instructions for experiential exercises; directions for leading meditations; as well as other spiritual practices. The person who facilitates each meeting might guide the discussion and study that takes place within the group; you might choose to have one facilitator or, instead, opt to take turns leading.

Each chapter contains a variety of texts, poems, essays, and stories that touch on the chapter's theme, written by people who are able to articulate what has not yet become "speech ripe," perhaps not even "thought ripe," for the rest of us. These texts are meant to stimulate "aha moments" of recognition and insight. Some texts appeal primarily to the intellect; others to the heart and soul. It is more conducive to personal growth to link them to personal experience, rather than simply analyzing them intellectually.

You will enhance your experience and the group's by taking seriously the invitation to engage in active meditation, cultivation of qualities (*midot*), spiritual practices, gentle movement, contemplative listening, and journaling. We offer further explanations of their benefits below.

1) Mindfulness Meditation

We believe that cultivating skills of mindful awareness through meditation helps us to grasp the truth of what is happening in the present moment. With greater awareness of what is going on in our bodies, our feelings, and our thoughts, we can see that we have choices about how to respond wisely to any given situation, rather than simply reacting to it. For general background in meditation, we recommend: *Mindfulness: An Eight-Week Plan for Finding Peace in a Frantic World* by Mark Williams and Danny Penman (Rodale Press).

2) Cultivation of Spiritual Qualities: Tikun Midot

Judaism contains a powerful practice called *musar*, which is designed to help us to reach our highest spiritual and ethical potential. In the book we link the *musar* practice with mindfulness practice to help us be more aware of the influences that shape our actions. *Musar* can increase our ability to pay attention to the ways we act—intentionally and unconsciously—in our daily lives. For background reading in *musar*, we recommend *Everyday Holiness* by Alan Morinis (Trumpeter).

3) Spiritual Practices

An important part of the spiritual work of aging can be finding some deeper meaning and relevance in religious practices. Prayer can offer comfort, provide an opportunity for self-expression, or help one acknowledge the blessings in one's life. While many of us struggle with prayer and traditional notions of God, we also feel a deep yearning for "something more"—something older, wiser, and truer than oneself. Prayer, study, and meditation can help connect one's particular experience with that spacious sense of time, continuity, and possibility. If traditional forms don't appeal to you, find poems, readings, music, art, and/or experiences in nature that lift you out of your focus on yourself.

4) Gentle Movement

We suggest that you make time in your group for exercise—restorative yoga, qigong, or stretching. Movement is important in order to:

- Keep the body flexible, increase circulation, strengthen muscle, enhance memory, and maintain balance.
- Develop awareness of the inner workings of the body—where energy is blocked, where tension is held, where changing posture can make a difference, and how attention to breathing can relax and open up the flow of blood and energy.
- Help us accept the body as it is.

5) Contemplative Listening

The core idea of contemplative listening is paying close attention to the speaker, without commenting, interrupting, judging, or critiquing. The gift of listening is a generous offering to another to feel heard—a rare experience. Listening carefully is an important social and health-related skill. It is, though, often difficult to do. Listening is too often disrupted by thinking about what one will say next and looking for the chance to jump into the conversation. We are so used to fixing, suggesting, commenting, agreeing, or disagreeing that we don't realize how often we actually stifle speakers' thinking by causing them to react to us, rather than to listen more deeply to their own thoughts and feelings. Contemplative listening is a skill that is developed through practice. We therefore ask you to process your experience of contemplative listening by viewing it not simply as a way of conducting a class but rather as an important skill for the personal work of aging.

6) Journaling

Bringing a journal to each session, taking notes on what you have learned and/or an insight you have gained, and spending some time in reflective journaling during each session will help you to integrate what you have understood, and add new insights to what you have already written. Your journal exists only for you. You do not have to share it with anyone.

We hope that these new skills, which can be cultivated within the safe space of a wise aging group, will support you as you learn to live with more optimism, generosity, and gratitude. Our wish for you is that you become an older adult who looks on your past and your present as full of blessings, and who feels that in doing so, you are becoming your truest self.

About the Institute for Jewish Spirituality

The Institute for Jewish Spirituality seeks to revitalize Jewish life by teaching spiritual practices that cultivate mindfulness on the individual and the communal level, so that we can act with enriched wisdom, clarity, and compassion.

The Institute teaches Jewish leaders the core practices of Torah study, prayer, mindfulness meditation, *tikun midot* (the development of ethical character traits), yoga, and singing as embodied practices. These practices provide participants with valuable skills for effective leadership while creating opportunities for them to deepen their inner lives and connect meaningfully with the Divine.

The Institute utilizes traditional and contemporary forms of authentic Jewish practice to enrich everyday life with Jewish wisdom, link the search for inner wholeness with *tikun olam* (repair of the world), and create a vibrant, enduring Judaism now and for generations to come.

Visit the Institute for Jewish Spirituality at www.jewishspirituality.org.

About the Authors

Rabbi Rachel Cowan was named by *Newsweek* magazine in 2007 and 2010 as one of the fifty leading rabbis in the United States, and by the *Jewish Daily Forward* in 2010 as one of the fifty leading women rabbis. She was featured in the PBS series *The Jewish Americans*. She received her ordination from Hebrew Union College-Jewish Institute of Religion in 1989. From 1990 to 2003 she was program director for Jewish life and values at the Nathan Cummings Foundation. From 2004 to 2011 she served as executive director of the Institute for Jewish Spirituality and then became a senior fellow there to develop the Wise Aging program. She is currently a consultant to the Institute's Wise Aging program. Her work has appeared in *Moment* magazine and *Sh'ma*, as well as in anthologies, including *Illness and Health in the Jewish Tradition: Writings from the Bible to Today* and *The Torah: A Women's Commentary*. She is the author, with her late husband Paul Cowan, of *Mixed Blessings: Untangling the Knots in an Interfaith Marriage*. She lives in New York City, near her two children Lisa and Matt, and four grandchildren—Jacob, Tessa, Dante, and Miles Moses.

Dr. Linda Thal, after establishing her career in children's and family education, pioneered some of the early work in synagogue transformation, guiding congregations through a process of re-envisioning and revitalizing their programming. For the past twenty years her work has focused on adult spiritual development. Dr. Thal was the founding codirector of the Yedidya Center for Jewish Spiritual Direction, an institute that trains rabbis, cantors, therapists, and others in providing spiritual guidance. She has a private practice in spiritual direction and serves on the faculty of the Center for Mindfulness at the Jewish Community Center in Manhattan.

Linda is a recipient of the Covenant Award for Excellence in Jewish Education. Her work has appeared in *Reform Judaism* magazine and in books such as *What We Know about Jewish Education, A Congregation of Learners, Jewish Spiritual Direction: An Innovative Guide from Traditional and Contemporary Sources,* and *Every Ending Has A Beginning: Clergy Retirement* (forthcoming). She is primary author of *Vetaher Libeynu: The Institute for Jewish Spirituality Curriculum for Nurturing Adult Spiritual Development.*

In addition to teaching in both the United States and Israel, she has conducted classes and workshops in Canada, Brazil, Argentina, South Africa, China, Singapore, and Hong Kong. She lives in New York City with her husband, Lennard, and travels to California frequently to teach and to see her daughters, Alona and Ariella, and grandchildren, Mo, Zeke, Noa, and Zev.

Permissions, Notes, and Credits

All Bible excerpts, unless otherwise noted, are reprinted from the TANAKH: The Holy Scriptures by permission of the University of Nebraska Press. Copyright 1985 by The Jewish Publication Society, Philadelphia.

All liturgical excerpts, unless otherwise noted, are excerpted from *Siddur Sim Shalom for Shabbat and Festivals* (1998) and *Mahzor Lev Shalem* (2010) with the permission of The Rabbinical Assembly).

Introduction

Stanley Kunitz, "Reflections," in *Collected Poems* (New York: W. W. Norton and Company, 2002).

Abraham Joshua Heschel, "To Grow in Wisdom," in *The Insecurity of Freedom: Essays on Human Existence* (Philadelphia: Jewish Publication Society of America, 1966), 76.

Art Green, *Restoring the Aleph* (Council for Initiatives in Jewish Education, 1996), 7.

The Center for Contemplative Mind in Society, "What Are Contemplative Practices," www.contemplativemind.org/practices. © 2000-2014 The Center for Contemplative Mind in Society. Used with permission.

Chapter 1

Rabbi Laura Geller, "The Torah of Our Lives: On Writing the Next Chapter" *Jewish Journal* (May 23, 2012).

Robert N. Butler, *Why Survive? Being Old in America* (Baltimore: Johns Hopkins University Press, 2002), 12.

Frida Kerner Furman, *Facing the Mirror: Older Women and Beauty Shop Culture* (New York: Routledge, 1997), 94.

Carlo Strenger and Arie Ruttenberg, "The Existential Necessity of Midlife Change," *Harvard Business Review* (February 2008).

Caroline Stoessinger, *A Century of Wisdom: Lessons from the Life of Alice Herz-Sommer, the World's Oldest Living Holocaust Survivor* (New York: Random House, 2012).

Carl Jung, *Modern Man in Search of a Soul* (New York: Harcourt, 1933), 109.

Adin Steinsaltz, *The Thirteen Petalled Rose: A Discourse on the Essence of Jewish Existence and Belief* (Northvale, New Jersey: Jason Aronson, 1992), 140-2.

Heschel, "To Grow in Wisdom," in *The Insecurity of Freedom,* 81.

Jon Kabat-Zinn, *Wherever You Go There You Are: Mindfulness Meditation in Everday Life* (New York: Hyperion, 1994), 4.

Sara Lawrence–Lightfoot, *The Third Chapter: Passion, Risk, and Adventure in the 25 Years after 50* (New York: Farrar, Straus and Giroux, 2009).

"Love after Love" from *The Poetry of Derek Walcott 1948-2013* by Derek Walcott, selected by Glyn Maxwell. Copyright © 2014 by Derek Walcott. Reprinted by permission of Farrar, Straus and Giroux, LLC. and Faber and Faber Ltd.

Chapter 2

Virginia Woolf, *Mrs. Dalloway* (New York: Harcourt Brace; 1925, 1953, 1981).

Zalman Schachter-Shalomi and Ronald S. Miller, *From Age-ing to Sage-ing: A Profound New Vision of Growing Older* (New York: Warner Books, 1995).

Harold Berman, *Interpreting the Aging Self: Personal Journals of Later Life* (New York: Springer, 1994), 180.

William Stafford, "The Way It Is" from *Ask Me: 100 Essential Poems.* Copyright © 1998 by the Estate of William Stafford. Reprinted with the permission of The Permissions Company, Inc. on behalf of Graywolf Press, Minneapolis, Minnesota, www.graywolfpress.org.

Chapter 3

From "Toward Myself" by Lea Goldberg (1911–1970), translation by Rachel Tzvia Black in *Selected Poetry and Drama*, Toby Press, 2005, translated by Rachel Tzvia Black and prose by T. Carmi. Used with permission.

William F. May, "The Virtues and Vices of the Elderly," in *What Does It Mean to Grow Old? Reflections from the Humanities,* eds. Thomas R. Cole and Sally A. Gadow (Durham, North Carolina: Duke University Press, 1986), 44-61.

Vivian Diller, *Face It: What Women Really Feel as Their Looks Change and What to Do about It* (Hay House, 2011), 31.

Rhoda P. Curtis, "There Are So Many Good Things about Getting Older," blog post, June 10, 2010.

Florida Scott-Maxwell, *The Measure of My Days* (New York: Penguin Books, 1968), 13-14.

William L. Randall, "The Importance of Being Ironic: Narrative Openness and Personal Resilience in Later Life," *Gerontologist* 53, no. 1 (2013), 9-16.

Sarah Lyall, "With Willing Spirit, a Reprise for Ailey Dancers," *New York Times*, December 24, 2013.

Mary Chase Morrison, *Let Evening Come: Reflections on Aging.* (New York: Doubleday, 1998), 2.

Talmud, *Berachos* 60b. Reprinted with permission from the Schottenstein Edition of the Talmud (New York: Artscroll Mesorah Publications, 1997).

Mitch Albom, *Tuesdays with Morrie: An Old Man, a Young Man, and Life's Greatest Lesson* (New York: Doubleday, 1997), 49.

Jane Kenyon, "Otherwise" from *Collected Poems of Jane Kenyon.* Copyright © 2005 by the Estate of Jane Kenyon. Reprinted with the permission of The Permissions Company, Inc. on behalf of Graywolf Press, Minneapolis, Minnesota, www.graywolfpress.org.

Susan Moon, *This Is Getting Old: Zen Thoughts on Aging with Humor and Dignity* (Boston: Shambhala, 2010), 41-42.

Linda Weltner, *No Place Like Home: Rooms and Reflections from One Family's Life* (Quill, 1990).

Zalman Schachter-Shalomi, *First Steps to a New Jewish Spirit* © 2003 by Zalman M. Schachter-Shalomi (Woodstock, VT: Jewish Lights Publishing). Permission granted by Jewish Lights Publishing, P.O. Box 237, Woodstock, VT 05091, www.jewishlights.com.

Ronald Rolheiser, *The Holy Longing: The Search for a Christian Spirituality* (New York: Doubleday, 1999), 197.

Cynthia Ramnarace, "Till Dementia Do Us Part? As a Spouse Is Stricken with Alzheimer's Disease, More Caregivers Seek Out a New Love," *AARP Bulletin*, September 13, 2010.

Joyce Wadler, "My Body Changed. So Did Intimacy," *New York Times*, October 18, 2013.

Elkhoanon Goldberg, *The Wisdom Paradox* (New York: Gotham Books, 2005), 220-34.

Louis Cozolino, *The Healthy Aging Brain: Sustaining Attachment, Attaining Wisdom* (New York: W.W. Norton, 2008), 72.

Roger Angell, "This Old Man," *New Yorker* (February 17, 2014).

Bonnie Lee Black, "Youth and Beauty," *Persimmon Tree*, persimmontree. org. Bonnie Lee Black is a writer, editor, and teacher in Taos, NM. bonnieleeblack.com. Used with permission of the author.

Ram Dass, *Still Here: Embracing Aging, Changing, and Dying* (New York: Riverhead Books, 2002).

Ari Seth Cohen, *Advanced Style* (New York: PowerHouse Books, 2012).

"'We Need a Theoretical Base': Cynthia Rich, Women's Studies, and Ageism," interview by Valerie Barnes Lipscomb, *NWSA Journal* (January, 2006).

Talmud, *Ta'anit* 7a. Original translation by Rabbi Avraham Greenstein and Beth Lieberman.

Berachot 58b from the *Koren Talmud Bavli* and prayers from *The Koren Siddur*, Koren Publishers, Jerusalem, 1962, 2009, pages 1002-3. Text and translation © Copyright Koren Publishers Jerusalem Ltd. Used with Permission.

Leviticus Rabbah 34:3. Original translation by Rabbi Avraham Greenstein and Beth Lieberman.

Daniel C. Matt, "Bringing Forth Sparks," *The Essential Kabbalah* (New York: HarperCollins, 1995), 149. Reprinted by permission of HarperCollins Publishers.

Chapter 4

Joan Chittister, *The Gift of Years: Growing Older Gracefully* (New York: Bluebridge, 2008).

Debra Rapoport, "Ageless Fashionistas Prove There's No Expiration Date on Style," *Huffington Post*, September 26, 2014, http://www.huffing-tonpost.com/debra-rapoport/advanced-style-film_b_5884352.html.

Andrew Sullivan, *Love Undetectable: Notes on Friendship, Sex, and Survival* (New York: Vintage, 1999), 209.

Three Levels of Friendship from Maimonides, Commentary on *Avot* 1:10.

Heschel, "To Grow In Wisdom," in *The Insecurity of Freedom*, 83.

Lee Kravitz, *Unfinished Business: One Man's Extraordinary Year of Trying to Do the Right Things* (New York: Bloomsbury, 2010).

Robert Frost, "The Death of the Hired Man," in *Poetry of Robert Frost: The Collected Poems* (New York: Holt, Rinehart and Winston, 1979).

May Sarton, *Journal of Solitude* (New York: Norton, 1973).

May Sarton, *The House by the Sea* (New York: Norton, 1977).

May Sarton, *After the Stroke* (New York: Norton, 1988).

Albert Einstein, "The World As I See It" in *The World As I See It* (New York: Crown, 1954).

Sara Ruddick, "Virtues and Age," in *Mother Time: Women, Aging, and Ethics,* ed. Margaret Urban Walker (Lanham, Maryland: Rowman and Littlefield, 1999), 45-59.

Sheila Solomon Klass, "A Very Ungrateful Old Lady," *The New Old Age* (blog), *New York Times*, November 8, 2013, http://newoldage.blogs. nytimes.com/2013/11/08/.

Perri Klass, MD, "She Wasn't So Ungrateful After All," *The New Old Age* (blog), *New York Times*, May 27, 2014, http://newoldage.blogs. nytimes.com/2014/05/27/.

Chapter 5

Dale Carnegie, *How to Win Friends & Influence People* (New York: Simon and Schuster, 1936, 1964, 1981)

Solomon Schimmel, "How Can I Forgive?," *Reform Judaism* (Fall 2004). Also see Dr. Schimmel's *Wounds Healed by Time: The Power of Forgiveness* (Oxford: Oxford University Press, 2002).

`Abdu'l-Bahá, The Promulgation of Universal Peace, p. 92. *The Promulgation of Universal Peace* is a collection of 140 talks given by `Abdu'l-Bahá—the son and appointed successor of Bahá'u'lláh, the prophet and founder of the Baha'i faith—during his extensive tour of North America in 1912.

"A Mindfulness Practice for Forgiveness" is based on a meditation from the Fetzer Institute, http://fetzer.org/.

Harold Kushner, *Living a Life That Matters: Resolving the Conflict Between Conscience and Success* (New York: Anchor, 2002).

Frederic Luskin, "What Is Forgiveness?" Greater Good Science Center, University of California, Berkeley, August 19, 2010, http://greatergood.berkeley.edu/article/item/what_is_forgiveness.

Schachter-Shalomi and Miller, *From Age-ing to Sage-ing*. Reb Zalman said that this exercise was inspired by the verse in Psalm 23, which begins, "You have set a table before me in the presence of my enemies...."

Matthue Roth, "Repentance Poem #4," www.zeek.net/poetry_0210.htm. Used with permission.

Gerald G. Jampolsky, *Goodbye to Guilt: Releasing Fear through Forgiveness* (New York: Bantam Books, 1985).

Rabbi Nachman of Bratzlav, *AZAMRA (Likkutei Moharan* I:*282).*

David R. Blumenthal, "Repentance and Forgiveness," *CrossCurrents,* www.crosscurrents.org/ blumenthal.htm.

Albert Einstein, "Human Rights" (acceptance speech upon receiving an award from the Chicago Decalogue Society of Lawyers, February 20, 1954), *New York Times,* February 21, 1954.

Wendy Lustbader, *Counting on Kindness: The Dilemmas of Dependency* (New York: Free Press, 1991).

Genesis Rabbah 54:3. Original translation by Rabbi Lisa Goldstein.

Phyllis Korkki, "The Science of Older and Wiser," *New York Times,* March 12, 2014.

Chapter 6

George Vaillant, *Aging Well* (Boston: Little Brown), 161.

Alan Morinis, *On Mussar,* monograph for IJS.

Five Kernels of Corn: Story told by Pastor Kathy Maclachlan of Bremen, Maine.

"Train Your Mind: Be Grateful to Everyone," a web exclusive from *Tricycle* magazine, in which Acharya Judy Lief, a teacher in the Shambhala tradition of Chogyam Trungpa Rinpoche, comments on one of Atisha's fifty-nine mind-training slogans, http://www.tricycle.com/web-exclusive/train-your-mind-be-grateful-everyone.

"Praise Song" by Barbara Crooker, from *Radiance,* p. 82. Word Press, 2005. Used with permission.

Hafiz, "The Sun Never Says," *The Gift,* trans. Daniel Ladinsky. From the Penguin Random House publication *The Gift: Poems by Hafiz,* by Daniel Ladinsky. Copyright © 1999 Daniel Ladinsky and used with his permission.

Tara Brach, *Radical Acceptance: Embracing Your Life with the Heart of a Buddha* (New York: Bantam Books, 2003).

Lovingkindness—Patience Meditation created by Rabbi Sheila Peltz Weinberg. Used with permission.

Sylvia Boorstein, *Pay Attention, for Goodness' Sake: The Buddhist Path of Kindness*, (New York: Random House, 2007).

Menuchat HaNefesh based on the curriculum for the Tikkun Middot Project of the Institute for Jewish Spirituality. Used with permission.

Nachman of Bratslav, *Likutei Moharan* 2:23.

Viktor E. Frankl, *Man's Search for Meaning*, trans. Ilse Lasch (New York: Washington Square Press, 1963).

Ba'al Shem Tov, *Tzava'at HaRivash*, trans. Rabbi Rachel Barenblat, *The Velveteen Rabbi* (blog), August 30, 2012, http://velveteenrabbi.blogs.com/blog/2012/08/cultivating-equanimity.html.

"Meditation on Equanimity" adapted from Jack Kornfield, *A Wise Heart: A Guide to the Universal Teachings of Buddhist Psychology* (New York: Bantam, 2009).

"Working with a Phrase" based on the Mindfulness & Tikkun Middot Project for Jewish Organizations of the Institute for Jewish Spirituality.

Gil Fronsdal, Buddhist teaching on equanimity (lecture, May 29, 2004).

Rumi, "The Guest House" from *The Essential Rumi*, translated by Coleman Barks with John Moyne, A J Arberry and Reynold Nicholson (Penguin Books, 1999). Copyright © Coleman Barks, 1995. Reprinted with permission.

Chapter 7

Leonard Cohen, lyrics from "Anthem."

William H. Thomas, MD, *What Are Old People For? How Elders Will Save the World* (St. Louis: VanderWyk and Burnham, 2004).

Roger Angell, "This Old Man," *New Yorker* (February 17, 2014).

Florida Scott-Maxwell, *The Measure of My Days* (New York: Penguin, 1979).

Adapted from The Truth about Grief, by Ruth Davis Konigsberg. (New York: Simon and Schuster Inc., 2011).

Rumi, "Birdwings," from *The Essential Rumi*, translated by Coleman Barks with John Moyne, A J Arberry and Reynold Nicholson

(Penguin Books, 1999). Copyright © Coleman Barks, 1995. Used with permission.

Rachel Naomi Remen, *My Grandfather's Blessings* (New York: Riverhead Books, 2000), 78.

Dr. Ira Byock quote from a November 9 article in Reuters on a Buddhist Contemplative Care Symposium at the Garrison Institute.

"At Home in Our Bodies: An Interview with Jon Kabat-Zinn," by Joan Duncan Oliver, *Tricycle*, September 2002.

Sharon Salzberg, *Faith: Trusting Your Own Deepest Experience* (New York: Penguin, 2003).

Miriyam Glazer, *Psalms of the Jewish Liturgy* (New York: Aviv Press, 2009), 201.

Rabbi Sharon Brous, "Pray Like You Mean It" (www.ikar-la.org). Used with permission.

Reinhold Niebuhr, "The Serenity Prayer."

Jonathan Spear, "Thirteen." Reprinted with permission of the author.

Chapter 8

George Vaillant, *Aging Well* (Boston: Little Brown), 161.

Ella Knox, a cofounder of the weekly *Vail Trail* in Vail, Colorado, as quoted in Robert Weller, "Vail Tries to Bury Plan to Build a Cemetery, but It Just Won't Die," *Los Angeles Times*, September 11, 1994.

Wendy R. Uhlmann, "The Ultimate Homework Assignment," *Newsweek*, October 2, 2008.

Talmud *Mo'ed Katan* 28a. Original translation by Rabbi Avraham Greenstein and Beth Lieberman.

"Yosef and the Angel of Death" is a précis of a story recounted in Maurice Lamm's *Consolation* (Philadelphia: Jewish Publication Society, 2004).

Alan Lew, *This Is Real and You Are Completely Unprepared* (Boston: Little, Brown, 2003).

Stephen Levine and Ondrea Levine, *Who Dies? An Investigation of Conscious Living and Conscious Dying*, (New York: Anchor Books, 1989), 9.

Philip Gould, "I'm Enjoying My Death. It's the Most Fulfilling Time of My Life, *Daily Mail*, May 2, 2012, http://www.dailymail.co.uk/femail/article-2138631/Philip-Gould-Im-enjoying-death-Its-fulfilling-time-life.html.

Octavio Paz, *The Labyrinth of Solitude and Other Writings* (New York: Grove Press, 1994).

Reverend Eleanor Harrison Bregman, "Ashes to Ashes, Dust to Dust," Huff Post Religion (blog), February 22, 2012, http://www.huffingtonpost.com/rev-eleanor-harrison-bregman/ashes-to-ashes-dust-to-du_b_1293629.html.

Samuel Dresner, introduction to *I Asked for Wonder: A Spiritual Anthology*, by Abraham Joshua Heschel (New York: Crossroad, 1983).

Abraham Joshua Heschel, "Death as Homecoming," in *Moral Grandeur and Spiritual Audacity* (New York: Noonday Press, 1996), 371.

Joan Halifax, *Being with Dying: Cultivating Compassion and Fearlessness in the Presence of Death* (Boston: Shambhala, 2009).

Richard Rubenstein is particularly known for trying to find a theology that made sense "after Auschwitz," which was the name of his first book. He has revised some of his thinking in the light of his study of Kabbalah. Richard L. Rubenstein, "The Making of a Rabbi," in *Varieties of Jewish Belief*, ed. Ira Eisenstein (New York: Reconstructionist Press, 1996), 179, 194-5.

Richard L. Rubenstein, "There Is Nothing Final about the Death of God, *New English Review*, April 2010, http://www.newenglishreview.org/Richard_L._Rubenstein/There_is_Nothing_Final_About_the_Death_of_God/.

Zalman Schacter Shalomi in *Wrestling with the Angel*. (ed.) Jack Riemer, NY: Schocken, 1995 p. 348. Also Introduction to Simcha Raphael's *Jewish Views of the Afterlife*.

Blu Greenberg, "Is There Life After Death?" in *Wrestling with the Angel*, ed. Jack Riemer (New York: Schocken Books, 1995), 319.

Morris Schwartz, *Morrie: In His Own Words* (New York, Bloomsbury, 2009), 126-7.

Mary Oliver, "The Summer Day," *New and Selected Poems,* vol. 1 (Boston: Beacon Press, 1992).

Chapter 9

Jonas Salk, "Are We Being Good Ancestors?" (speech in New Delhi, India, January 10, 1977).

Martin Buber, *The Way of Man* (Woodstock, Vermont: Jewish Lights, 2012), 16-17.

Anna Quindlen, as quoted in *A Guide To: "Loving Myself and Beyond,"* by M.C. Wilden (Hamburg:Tredition, 2010).

Diana Athill, *Somewhere Towards the End: A Memoir* (New York: W.W. Norton, 2008), 168.

Daniel J. Siegel, *Mindsight: The New Science of Personal Transformation* (New York: Bantam, 2010), 103, 119.

Rabbi Nachman of Bratslav, *Likutei Moharan* II, 68; *Likutei Moharan* I, 115; *Likutei Moharan* I, 66.

Rabbi Elana Zaiman, "Write an Ethical Will," ElanaZaiman.com. This article first appeared in *JTNews.* Used with permission. Rabbi Elana Zaiman is currently completing a book on ethical wills.

Susan Turnbull, "Contemporary Ethical Will," from Personal Legacy Advisors, www.personallegacyadvisors.com. Used with permission.

Louise Diamond's blog is called "Are We Having Fun Yet? Approaching Death with a Joyful Heart," http://blog.louisediamond.com.

Schachter-Shalomi and Miller, *From Age-ing to Sage-ing.*

Talmud, *Ta'anit* 23a, Reprinted with permission from the Schottenstein Edition of the Talmud (New York: Artscroll Mesorah Publications, 1991).

Frederick Buechner, *Wishful Thinking: A Theological ABC* (New York: Harper and Row, 1973).

Thomas Cole, "After the Life Cycle: The Moral Challenges of Later Life," in *Midrash and Medicine: Healing Body and Soul in the Jewish Interpretive Tradition*, ed. Rabbi William Cutter (Woodstock, Vermont: Jewish Lights, 2011).

Norman Fischer, *Training in Compassion: Zen Teaching on the Practice of Lojong* (Boston: Shambhala, 2013), 76.

James Jones, *From Here to Eternity* (New York: Random House, 1951, 1991).

The Bedtime Sh'ma

Ted Falcon, "Forgiveness Prayer." Prayer is reprinted in *Getting to the Heart of Interfaith: The Eye-Opening, Hope-Filled Friendship of a Pastor, a Rabbi & a Sheikh* © 2009 by Pastor Don Mackenzie, Rabbi Ted Falcon and Sheikh Jamal Rahman (Woodstock, VT: SkyLight Paths Publishing). Permission granted by SkyLight Paths Publishing, P.O. Box 237, Woodstock, VT 05091, www.skylightpaths.com.

"Who Closes My Eyes: A Blessing at Bedtime" from the Winter 1992-93 *The Outstretched Arm* by Rabbi Simkha Y. Weintraub, CSW © 1992. Published by National Center for Jewish Healing. Also in *Healing at Bedtime: The Traditional Kriat Sh'ma*, Jewish Board of Family and Children's Services. Used with permission. For more information/ materials, go to www.jbfcs.org/ncjh.